Queens County Sentinel

QUEENS COUNTY, NEW YORK

Index of Birth, Marriage, and Death Announcements

1858–1878

Compiled by
Anthony Hood

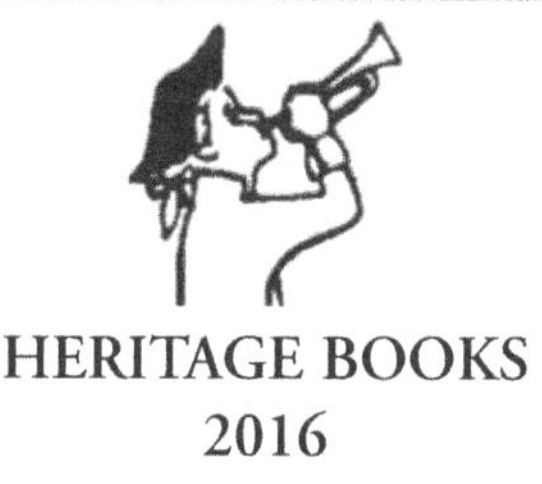

HERITAGE BOOKS
2016

HERITAGE BOOKS
AN IMPRINT OF HERITAGE BOOKS, INC.

Books, CDs, and more—Worldwide

For our listing of thousands of titles see our website
at
www.HeritageBooks.com

Published 2016 by
HERITAGE BOOKS, INC.
Publishing Division
5810 Ruatan Street
Berwyn Heights, Md. 20740

International Standard Book Numbers
Paperbound: 978-1-55613-496-8
Clothbound: 978-0-7884-6326-6

INTRODUCTION

The Queens County Sentinel began publication as a weekly newspaper in June
1858, with offices in Hempstead, NY. When Queens County was incorporated into
Greater New York in January 1898, part of the county separated. On January 1,
1899, the separated portion was renamed Nassau County. At some time after that
date the paper changed its name to the Hempstead Sentinel. The last edition of
the Queens County Sentinel available on microfilm is dated May 26, 1898; the
first available issue of the Hempstead Sentinel is dated June 1, 1899. There
is no record of what happened to the paper between those dates. The last issue
was published on January 27, 1949, at which time the paper ceased publication
because of changing conditions and rising costs. The paper had been in
existence for 90 years under four generations of the same family. At the time
it closed the paper was under the control of Kenneth B. Van De Water, Editor
and Publisher, and Stephen E. Campbell, Jr., Managing Editor.

The events listed in this index are found mostly in a separate column,
although some of the announcements, particularly deaths, are found in the news
items. The announcements usually contain additional information, such as name
of parents or spouse, place of birth, location of event, residence or an
obituary. Deaths of famous people, that can be found in other sources, are not
included in this publication. The Nassau Genealogy Workshop will be pleased to
send a copy, or an abstract, of an announcement to anybody interested. Please
send a contribution of $5 and a self-addressed, stamped envelope, to: Nassau
Genealogy Workshop, c/o Port Washington Library, 245 Main Street, Port
Washington, NY 11050.

Some dates are given, as they were written in the newspaper, in the form
"ult." or "inst.". Ult. means "in the previous month"; inst. means "in the
present month", although this expression is sometimes used at the beginning of
a month to refer to the previous month. The abbreviation "ca." means "about."

Names beginning with M' or Mc are indexed as if they were spelled Mac.
Names with a separate prefix, such as De Mott or Van De Water, are indexed as
if they were spelled without a space.

Acknowledgements

Appreciation is given first to the late Eugene Gibney, under whose
direction and enthusiasm this project was initiated.

Thanks also go to those members who contributed their time and efforts in
compiling this information: Martha Blais, Sister Mary Caritas, Jerry McGee,
Mary Montoux, Harriet Stempel, Dick Strong, and Bea Thomas.

Lastly, none of this would have been possible without the cooperation,
work, leadership, and tenacity of Anthony Hood, the Director of this project.

Libraries with microfilms of
Queens County Sentinel

Brooklyn Historical Society
128 Pierrepont Street
Brooklyn, NY 11201
(718) 624-0890

Hempstead Public Library
115 Nichols Court
Hempstead, NY 11550
(516) 481-6990

Hofstra University
Hempstead Turnpike
Hempstead, NY 11550
(516) 463-5967

Long Island Studies Institute
Nassau County Division of
  Museum Services
Hofstra University
Hempstead Turnpike
Hempstead, NY 11550
(516) 463-5097

New-York Historical Society
70 Central Park West
New York, NY 10024
(212) 873-3400

Queensborough Public Library
89-11 Merrick Boulevard
Jamaica, NY 11432
(718) 990-0770

SUNY at Stony Brook
Stony Brook, NY 11794
(516) 246-5977

    The workshop members who extracted these announcements worked at Hempstead
library and Hofstra University library. Both of these libraries have
extensive, though incomplete, holdings. Phone the library you plan to use for
information on hours and availability of records.

Last Name	Parent's Names	Date of Birth	Date of Newspaper
		Unidentified	
ZELL	(triplets) Henry & --?-- Zell	Thursday	Jul 22, 1875
		Female	
AKLEY	John A. & --?-- Akley	13 Feb 1875	Feb 25, 1875
BURT	Alfred & --?-- Burt	21 Dec 1863	Dec 31, 1863
CURTIS	Joseph & Sarah E. Curtis	18 Mar 1863	Mar 26, 1863
GRAY	Hamilton & Catherine Gray	6 Mar 1864	Apr 7, 1864
HENDERSON	Thomas & --?-- Henderson	21 Jul 1863	Aug 6, 1863
HORTON	D.P. & Caroline Horton	1 Mar 1863	Mar 19, 1863
LEVEL	Joseph & Catherine Level	5 Dec 1863	Jan 7, 1864
PINE	Ludlow & Annie Pine	14 Mar 1863	Mar 19, 1863
POWELL	Charles A. & Martha W. Powell	15 Feb 1864	Feb 18, 1864
RUSHMORE	Merwin & --?-- Rushmore	24 Mar 1863	Apr 2, 1863
STEAD	Geo. A. & --?-- Stead	28 Jan 1875	Feb 4, 1875
VAN DE WATER	Lott & --?-- Van de Water	13 Apr 1870	Apr 21, 1870
WILLIAMSON	Stephen & Rebecca A. Williamson	13th inst	May 14, 1863
		Male	
AGNEW	Hamilton & Sarah H. Agnew	11 Aug 1863	Aug 13, 1863
ALLEN	George D. & --?-- Allen	20 Dec 1871	Dec 28, 1871
BALDWIN	Henry A. T. & Mary Ann Baldwin	12 Oct 1863	Oct 22, 1863
CARPENTER	James & Letty Carpenter	16 Feb 1863	Mar 19, 1863
DONOHUE	(triplets)--?-- Donohue	last week	Nov 3, 1870
GILDERSLEEVE	Jonathon & Louisa Gildersleeve	31 Aug 1863	Sep 10, 1863
GILDERSLEEVE	Malbone J. & --?-- Gildersleeve	4 Dec 1863	Dec 31, 1863
HAMLETT	John & Catharine Hamlett	31 Aug 1863	Sep 17, 1863
HOLLAND	William & --?-- Holland	Tuesday	Jul 23, 1874
IRISH	Henry & --?-- Irish	19 Dec 1863	Dec 31, 1863
KARST	Valentine & --?-- Karst	2 Feb 1877	Feb 8, 1877
LOSEE	Alonzo & Amelia Losee	11 Mar 1863	Mar 19, 1863
LOSEE	Richard & Hannah Losee	8 Feb 1864	Feb 18, 1864
LUSH	James & Margaret Lush	1 Mar 1863	Mar 19, 1863
MCCOUN	Willet & --?-- McCoun	11 Dec 1863	Dec 31, 1863
MALONEY	John & --?-- Maloney	10 Aug 1875	Aug 12, 1875
MERRILL	George & Emma FitzRandolph Merrill	1 Aug 1863	Aug 6, 1863
NIX	John & --?-- Nix	11 Mar 1863	Mar 19, 1863
PINKHAM	Joseph & --?-- Pinkham, Jr.	30 Jan 1877	Feb 1, 1877
POWELL	James & Cornelia Powell	14 Mar 1863	Mar 19, 1863
PRAY	Elias L. & --?-- Pray	21 Feb 1875	Feb 25, 1875
RALPHS	Clarence R. & Mary Elizabeth Ralphs	29 Jun 1863	Jul 9, 1863
RAYNOR	William & Elizabeth Raynor	20th inst	Apr 23, 1863
SEABURY	Albert H. & Elizabeth Seabury	27 Aug 1864	Sep 1, 1864
SNEDEKER	Wilson B. & Sarah M. Snedeker	9 Mar 1863	Mar 19, 1863
TAYLOR	George Lansing & --?-- Taylor	no date	Aug 1, 1872
TERRY	J. Spencer & Emily Terry	5 May 1864	May 12, 1864
VANDEWATER	Edgar H. & Agnes Vandewater	21 Mar 1864	Apr 7, 1864
VANDEWATER	Lott & Caroline Augusta Vandewater	22 Oct 1863	Oct 29, 1863
WILLIAMSON	Stephen & Rebecca A. Williamson	13th inst	May 14, 1863
WOODBRIDGE	James S. & Lucretia Woodbridge	1 Aug 1863	Aug 6, 1863

Groom's Name	Bride's Name	Date of marriage	Date of newspaper
ABBOTT, Benjamin H.	Sarah Elizabeth Farnham	19 Jun 1867	Jun 27, 1867
ABRAHAMS, Augusta Ferdinand	Hannah Catherine Essens	25 Nov 1858	Dec 9, 1858
ABRAHAMS, Smith	Susan M. Combs	15 Oct 1864	Oct 27, 1864
ABRAMS, Abram J.	Ellen Highfield	3 Jun 1861	Jul 25, 1861
ABRAMS, Alanson	Amelia S. Pearsall	13 Dec 1865	Dec 21, 1865
ABRAMS, Albert H.	Ida A. Langdon	4 Jul 1878	Jul 11, 1878
ABRAMS, Arender	Georgianna Simonson	22 Nov 1871	Nov 30, 1871
ABRAMS, Arnet	Phebe Eliza Abrams	22 Mar 1873	Mar 27, 1873
ABRAMS, Charles R.	Phebe A. Sprague	no date	Jun 15, 1865
ABRAMS, Charles V.	Mary Lester Rhodes	8 Dec 1871	Dec 14, 1871
ABRAMS, Coles	Charlotte Bedell	3 Feb 1869	Mar 11, 1869
ABRAMS, Cornelius	Agnes Cornwell	24 Jan 1861	Jan 31, 1861
ABRAMS, Daniel	Elizabeth Brower, (Mrs)	4 Nov 1863	Dec 10, 1863
ABRAMS, Dewitt C.	Sarah Francis	16 Sep 1860	Oct 11, 1860
ABRAMS, Ezekiel	Susan A. Cornwell	21 Jul 1861	Jul 25, 1861
ABRAMS, Frank	Annie A. Bedell	ca. 4y ago	Mar 15, 1877
ABRAMS, Hegamen	Mary Ann Abrams	20 Nov 1858	Nov 25, 1858
ABRAMS, Henry B.	Alice Ann Demott	24 Nov 1869	Dec 2, 1869
ABRAMS, Hewlett	Elockey Wright	6 Oct 1861	Nov 7, 1861
ABRAMS, Jacob	Sarah L. Combs	28 Oct 1869	Nov 4, 1869
ABRAMS, Jacob H.	Adalade L'Hommedieu	15 Sep 1877	Nov 29, 1877
ABRAMS, John A.	Ann A. Abrams	22 Jul 1869	Jul 29, 1869
ABRAMS, Langdon	Armenia Southard	26 Nov 1865	Nov 30, 1865
ABRAMS, Samuel	Josephine Carman	10 Jan 1869	Jan 21, 1869
ABRAMS, Samuel	Sarah Amelia Jackson	29 Jan 1869	Mar 11, 1869
ABRAMS, Samuel D.	Eleanor Craft	14 Oct 1874	Oct 22, 1874
ABRAMS, William Henry	Martha A. Pearsall	29 Apr 1859	May 5, 1859
ACKERLY, George M.	Annie D. Corwin	25 Dec 1867	Jan 2, 1868
ADAMS, Floyd	Mary Bedell	no date	Jan 19, 1865
ADAMS, Frank J.	--?-- Deems	17 Oct 1878	Oct 17, 1878
ADAMS, George	Anna Remsen	26 Dec 1867	Dec 26, 1867
ALBRO, John	Antoinette R. Stone	15 Jul 1865	Jul 20, 1865
ALDEN, John H.	Sarah M. Bennett	12 Apr 1864	Apr 21, 1864
ALEXANDER, James	Eusolie M. Lawrence	26 Aug 1858	Sep 9, 1858
ALEXANDER, William	Emily Johnson	25 Feb 1859	Mar 17, 1859
ALLEN, Frank A.	Josephine Cornell	no date	Apr 9, 1863
ALLEN, George D.	Mary N. Overton	13 Oct 1869	Oct 21, 1869
ALLEN, John E.	Priscilla J. Smith	1 Jan 1878	Jan 24, 1878
ALLEN, Julien E.	Bessie B. Brady	25 Dec 1863	Jan 7, 1864
ALLEN, William A.	Kate M. Tilley	9 Oct 1878	Oct 24, 1878
ALLEN, William S.	Jennie F. Jagger	28 Dec 1875	Dec 30, 1875
ALLIGER, Richard D.	Anna A. Kissam	19 Jul 1865	Jul 27, 1865
ALTHAUSE, William H.	Sarah A. Smith	13 Jan 1870	Jan 27, 1870
AMES, Frederic W.	Mary A. Daniels, (Mrs)	28 Dec 1867	Jan 2, 1868
ARMSTRONG, Goodale	Lucia E. Peck	26 Aug 1860	Nov 15, 1860
ASHDOWN, William	Catherine Hingle	15 May 1872	May 23, 1872
AULD, John	Fanny Murray, (Mrs)	7 Nov 1863	Dec 10, 1863
AUSTIN, Joel	Mary Ann Berry	18 Jan 1859	Jan 20, 1859
AYRES, Charles H.	Serena T. Martin	22 Jun 1858	Jun 24, 1858
BAILEY, Charles A.	Mary E. Burt	27 Dec 1876	Feb 1, 1877
BAKER, Charles I.	Emma Augusta Taylor	17 Apr 1859	Apr 21, 1859
BALDWIN, Albert	Henrietta Abrams	9 May 1865	May 11, 1865
BALDWIN, Charles	Elizabeth Ann DeMott	22nd inst	Aug 2, 1860
BALDWIN, Edwin W.	Catherine Weekes	14 Mar 1859	Mar 17, 1859
BALDWIN, James	Eliza Jane Denton	10 Feb 1877	Feb 22, 1877
BALDWIN, Smith S.	Emma L. Maginnis	13 Nov 1878	Nov 21, 1878

MARRIAGES - GROOMS

Groom's Name	Bride's Name	Date of marriage	Date of newspaper
BALDWIN, Townsend	Ann Amelia Post	2 Oct 1864	Oct 6, 1864
BALDWIN, William S.	Clarissa Noon	25 Dec 1869	Feb 10, 1870
BALFOUR,	Carrie Spooner	no date	Oct 14, 1858
BALLOU, Samuel B.	Charlotte Haviland	3 Jun 1858	Jun 10, 1858
BANKS, George B.	Sarah McDougall	14th inst	Mar 22, 1860
BARTEAU, Frank	C. Jennie Dunbar	15 Nov 1869	Nov 18, 1869
BARTO, Obadiah	Lyvancha Conklin	8 Sep 1869	Oct 28, 1869
BARTON, Henry H.	Josephine Baeder	no date	Aug 26, 1858
BAUKNEY, John	Catherine Jane Amberman	22 Oct 1865	Oct 26, 1865
BAXTER, Charles W.	Jane Armstrong	20th ult	Sep 14, 1865
BAYLIS, Frank P.	Evelyn G. Miller	10 Nov 1875	Nov 25, 1875
BAYLIS, Isaac W.	Celia Remsen	6 Oct 1863	Oct 15, 1863
BAYLIS, Jacob	Sarah A. Hendrickson	10th inst	Nov 17, 1864
BAYLIS, John C.	Elizabeth J. Cornelius	30 Oct 1861	Nov 7, 1861
BAYLIS, Mortimer	Josephine B. Jayne	25 Oct 1868	Nov 5, 1868
BAYLIS, Oliver	Josie Bassett	27th inst	Jan 30, 1868
BEACH, Hoffman	Kate Van de Water	8 Oct 1874	Oct 22, 1874
BEARE, Henry	Arabella Smith	2 Oct 1877	Nov 8, 1877
BEATTY, John F.	Mary Tilford	27 Sep 1876	Oct 26, 1876
BEDELL, Abran	Susan E. Mott, (Mrs)	10 Feb 1868	Feb 13, 1868
BEDELL, Alanson	Alfretta Ryerson	7 Jul 1878	Jul 11, 1878
BEDELL, Charles	Harriet A. Brown	30 Apr 1874	May 7, 1874
BEDELL, Charles L.	Eliza J. Orr	25 Jan 1871	Feb 9, 1871
BEDELL, Edward A.	Josephine Monfort	24 Dec 1861	Jan 2, 1862
BEDELL, Elisha	Frost, (Mrs)	24 Aug 1859	Sep 1, 1859
BEDELL, Eugene F.	Annie B. Powell	14 Jan 1869	Jan 21, 1869
BEDELL, Frank D.	Fannie Pitt	23 Nov 1870	Dec 1, 1870
BEDELL, George	Lucinda Thomas	11th inst	Apr 19, 1860
BEDELL, George H.	Mary E. Lush	4 Jun 1876	Jun 8, 1876
BEDELL, Henry T.	Elizabeth E. Sprague	7th inst	Jun 14, 1860
BEDELL, Jahn R.	Sarah Elizabeth Soper	31 Aug 1859	Sep 8, 1859
BEDELL, John	Amelia Ann Abrams	12 Sep 1858	Sep 16, 1858
BEDELL, John H.	Mary E. DeMott	21 Jul 1865	Jul 27, 1865
BEDELL, John H.	Phebe E. Frost	7 Apr 1870	Apr 14, 1870
BEDELL, John Henry	Esther A. Stringham	31 Jan 1865	Feb 9, 1865
BEDELL, John W.	Mary E. Rider	28 Feb 1864	Apr 21, 1864
BEDELL, Nehamiah C.	Amanda Brower	26 Mar 1865	Mar 30, 1865
BEDELL, Richard	Eliza Ann Moore	17 Feb 1869	Mar 11, 1869
BEDELL, Stephen	Phebe Louisa James	17th inst	Oct 19, 1865
BEDELL, William	Sarah Rhodes	1 Dec 1869	Dec 23, 1869
BEDELL, William H.	Josie Smith	16 Aug 1870	Nov 3, 1870
BEEKWITH, Jerry	Frances Selissa Shearman	no date	Nov 4, 1858
BELCHER, Thomas J.	Rachel Maria Spader	14 Feb 1864	Feb 18, 1864
BELL, Isaac, Jr.	Jeanette Bennett	last Thurs	Sep 26, 1878
BELL, John Van	Adelaide Gilfillan	3 Feb 1874	Jul 23, 1874
BELLAMY, Charles L.	Hattie L. Thompson	14 May 1869	Jun 17, 1869
BELLOWS, Theodore	Susan A. Pine	7th inst	May 10, 1860
BELLOWS, William H.	Cherrilla J. Griswold	24 Aug 1862	Aug 28, 1862
BENEDICT, Cromeline	Henrietta Pinckney	21 Jul 1858	Jul 29, 1858
BENJAMIN, George O.	Esther L. Robinson	4 Aug 1858	Aug 19, 1858
BENJAMIN, Horace H.	Sallie R. Edwards	no date	Aug 5, 1858
BENNETT, George A.	Emily E. Ketcham	24 Dec 1867	Jan 2, 1868
BENNETT, George M.	Lydia Conger	24 Jun 1863	Jul 2, 1863
BENNETT, Melancthon C.	Francis Snedeker	16 Dec 1872	Dec 19, 1872
BERGEN, Cornelius	Mary Alice Phraner	15 Jan 1874	Jan 22, 1874
BERGEN, Leonard M.	Hannah C. Willets	24 Apr 1861	Oct 31, 1861
BEVETLAND, Henry	Sarah Scott	no date	Sep 30, 1858
BIRDSALL, Edwin	Drusilla Moore	15 Mar 1868	Mar 19, 1868
BIRDSALL, William	Antoinette Ryerson	26 Aug 1865	Aug 31, 1865

Groom's Name	Bride's Name	Date of marriage	Date of newspaper
BIRDWALL, Mott	Susan J. Pettit	14 Jan 1869	Jan 21, 1869
BISHOP, Edward	Annie Maria McCabe	28 Jul 1872	Aug 1, 1872
BISHOP, George Henry	Mary Mott	16 Jan 1873	Jan 30, 1873
BISHOP, William H.	Katie L. Dunbar	15 Oct 1872	Nov 7, 1872
BISLAND, Thomas L.	M. C. Brownson	24 Jun 1858	Jul 1, 1858
BOARDMAN, J. L.	Carrie Fairweather	24th ult	Feb 2, 1860
BORST, Abner H.	Sarah Ann Verity	22 Nov 1865	Dec 21, 1865
BOUKER, DeWitt C.	Sarah G. Drake	28th ult	Jan 12, 1865
BOWDEN, M. Luther	Stella Sutphin	14 May 1878	May 23, 1878
BOWDITCH, George C.	Margaret Dix	29 Jun 1858	Jul 15, 1858
BOWER, John	Catherine Jetter	no date	Jul 22, 1858
BOWERS, Peter	Phoebe Maria Cornelius	18 Aug 1861	Aug 29, 1861
BOX, Francis	Phebe Ann DeMott	14 Oct 1865	Oct 26, 1865
BOX, John	Mary Flemming	1 Oct 1878	Oct 3, 1878
BOYDEN, George	Susie Patterson	recently	Sep 6, 1877
BRACKEN, William	Josephine W. Rogers	18 Apr 1859	Apr 28, 1859
BREAR, Mark	Mary Ellen Marshall	no date	Nov 11, 1858
BRENTON, Benjamin J.	Orvetta Hall	4 Sep 1861	Sep 12, 1861
BREWER, Richard	Phebe Ann Cornwell	13 Mar 1859	Mar 31, 1859
BRINCKERHOFF, James B.	Sarah Jane Parsons	5 Jun 1876	Jun 8, 1876
BROMFIELD, Percy B.	Emma Rushmore	6 Sep 1876	Sep 7, 1876
BROOKS, Alvah	Caroline M. Berry	21 May 1876	Jun 1, 1876
BROWER, Alexander	Katie E. Rhodes	13 Sep 1876	Sep 14, 1876
BROWER, Alfred	Amanda Pettit	19 Dec 1861	Jan 9, 1862
BROWER, Cornwell	Sarah Bond	7 Sep 1865	Sep 21, 1865
BROWER, Elijah	Mary E. Miller	10 Sep 1878	Oct 24, 1878
BROWER, Furman	Mary Ellen Rider	8th inst	Nov 29, 1860
BROWER, Joseph	Mary E. Bedell	9 Jan 1861	Jan 17, 1861
BROWER, Singleton	Nancy Brower	12 Jan 1861	Jan 24, 1861
BROWER, Stephen R.	Hannah J. Seaman, (Mrs)	28 Nov 1869	Dec 2, 1869
BROWER, Thomas W.	Sarah Elizabeth Doxsey	16 Jan 1861	Jan 17, 1861
BROWN, Edward M.	Addie F. Mayher	22nd inst	Nov 29, 1860
BROWN, George	Fanny Taylor	27 Nov 1873	Dec 4, 1873
BROWN, Richard S.	Sarah A. Seaman	13 Jun 1865	Jun 15, 1865
BRUSH, Benjamin W.	Sarah W. Robbins	7 Feb 1869	Feb 11, 1869
BRUSH, Henry F.	Sarah E. Robbins, (Mrs)	6 Jan 1870	Feb 10, 1870
BRUSH, Thomas	Addie F. Carman	28 Apr 1869	Apr 29, 1869
BRUSH, Thomas	Ardelissa Terril	14 Dec 1863	Dec 24, 1863
BRYANT, William H.	Emma A. Whitney	3 Jan 1868	Jan 9, 1868
BUCHANAN, William H.	Sarah F. Rhoades	11 Mar 1859	Mar 17, 1859
BUFFETT, S. H.	Evalina Ketcham	10 Nov 1870	Nov 17, 1870
BULKLEY, Henry L.	Anna Jones	14 Aug 1861	Aug 22, 1861
BUNKER, Edward S.	Alice Loines	25 Dec 1860	Jan 3, 1861
BURCH, Newbury	Harriet Baker	11 Dec 1861	Jan 30, 1862
BURDETT, George	Libbie Patterson	recently	Sep 6, 1877
BURGHARD, Henry	Alice Beers	22 Feb 1877	Mar 1, 1877
BURMAN, Jacob	Maria Hart	no date	Oct 14, 1858
BURR, Horace B.	Emma Bennette	22 Oct 1868	Oct 29, 1868
BURT, Alfred	Sarah A. Firth	26 Dec 1860	Jan 3, 1861
BURTIS, Abram S.	Mary J. Baker	2 Apr 1861	Apr 25, 1861
BURTIS, Theodore E.	Cornelia M. Simonson	2nd inst	Mar 23, 1865
BUSHNELL, George	Phebe Elizabeth Conklin	no date	Nov 4, 1858
BUSSMAN, Henry	Mary C. Languillette	17 Apr 1872	Apr 25, 1872
CALHOUN, William	Maggie Cunningham	no date	Aug 12, 1858
CAMPBELL, Alexander	Millicent Oliver	26 Jun 1864	Jun 30, 1864
CAMPBELL, Richard C.	Hattie E. Marsh	14 Jan 1875	Jan 21, 1875
CAMPBELL, S. T.	Gracie Snedeker	3 Dec 1874	Dec 10, 1874
CANWAY, Richard	Hannah Davis	Aug 1859	Sep 15, 1859
CARLL, Gilbert E.	Mary E. Oakley	25 Dec 1858	Jan 13, 1859

Groom's Name	Bride's Name	Date of marriage	Date of newspaper
CARMAN, Abram	Phebe E. Doty	28 Sep 1865	Oct 19, 1865
CARMAN, Benjamin J.	Alice Montross	22 Oct 1865	Oct 26, 1865
CARMAN, Henry	Amanda Sprague	no date	Mar 7, 1861
CARMAN, Henry	Kate Hendrickson	1 Dec 1864	Dec 15, 1864
CARMAN, Stephen T.	Louise H. Townsend	29 Feb 1872	Mar 14, 1872
CARMAN, Thomas	Susan Raynor, (Mrs)	28 May 1861	Jun 6, 1861
CARMAN, William E.	Jennie Ackley	23 Jun 1875	Jun 24, 1875
CARMAN, William H.	Margaret A. Stevenson	8 Oct 1865	Oct 19, 1865
CARMEN, Richard	Phebe Maria Denbar	10 Jan 1869	Jan 14, 1869
CARPENTER, Andrew J.	Cornelia L. Ferguson, (Mrs)	20 Apr 1863	Apr 30, 1863
CARPENTER, Benjamin C.	Mary J. Adams	15 Nov 1876	Dec 7, 1876
CARPENTER, James	Lettie A. Lush	8 Jul 1861	Jul 18, 1861
CARPENTER, John D.	Rebecca Vanveghten	10 Jun 1864	Jun 16, 1864
CARPENTER, William	Ella Floyd-Jones	26 Nov 1878	Dec 5, 1878
CARSON, Joseph W.	Maria Birdsall	4 Sep 1871	Sep 7, 1871
CHARLICK, John	Evangeline Craft	6 Aug 1876	Aug 24, 1876
CHARLICK, John	Laura Ketcham	4 Nov 1863	Nov 19, 1863
CHATFIELD, Horace F.	S. Louise Prime	13 Sep 1877	Sep 20, 1877
CHESHIRE, Morris	Mary L. Carpenter	27 Feb 1859	Mar 17, 1859
CHESTER, Charles	Harriet A. Seaman	9 Dec 1869	Feb 10, 1870
CHICHESTER, Abner	Sarah A. Town	26 Jan 1870	Feb 10, 1870
CLAPP, L. Russel	Susie J. Smith	4 Aug 1874	Aug 6, 1874
CLARK, Daniel	Cornelia Rosa Arnold	18 Apr 1860	Apr 26, 1860
CLARK, William Everett	Ann(a) Martin	29 Sep 1863	Oct 1, 1863
CLIFTON, Frank I.	Theresa (Lily) Hall	21 Oct 1874	Oct 29, 1874
CLOCK, Hallet	Ellen D. White	12 Dec 1865	Dec 14, 1865
COBB, Henry N.	Matilda E. Van Zandt	17th inst	May 24, 1860
COCKS, Isaac H.	Mary T. Willets	5 Jun 1859	Jul 7, 1859
COFFEY, John	Ann Elliott	18 Oct 1862	Oct 30, 1862
COLE, Abram J.	--?-- Bendirnagel	last Thurs	May 16, 1878
COLES, Barak G.	Kate E. Cape	26 Apr 1859	May 5, 1859
COLES, Harvey	Rhoda White	15 Dec 1858	Dec 23, 1858
COLYEA, John H.	Mariam S. Jarvis	7th inst	Dec 28, 1865
COMBS, Abram	Charlotte Combs	9 Oct 1860	Nov 1, 1860
COMBS, Durling	Mary S. Dean	19 Nov 1865	Nov 30, 1865
COMBS, George W.	Emma Jane Golder	18 Nov 1868	Nov 26, 1868
COMBS, Henry	Amanda Smith	31 Oct 1869	Nov 4, 1869
COMBS, John B.	Amanda E. Bedell	15 Feb 1877	Feb 22, 1877
COMBS, Nathaniel	Phebe Ann Smith	20th ult	Jan 19, 1865
COMBS, Smith A.	Elizabeth Ann Watts	26 Jan 1868	Feb 13, 1868
COMBS, Stephen	Emily T. Murray	25 Oct 1867	Nov 7, 1867
COMBS, Stephen	Emma Butcher	12 Nov 1867	Nov 21, 1867
COMBS, Valentine L.	Margaret Ann Davison	6 Jun 1865	Jun 15, 1865
COMBS, Valintine	Jane Ann Magee	13 Aug 1863	Aug 20, 1863
COMBS, William	Alice Carman	no date	Dec 3, 1868
CONKLIN, David	Martha A. Baldwin	17 Apr 1861	Apr 25, 1861
CONKLIN, Henry C.	Mary Johnson	29 Sep 1865	Nov 9, 1865
CONKLIN, John M.	Annie A. Ackerly	19 Dec 1867	Jan 2, 1868
CONKLIN, William F.	Sarah E. Hendrickson	27 Apr 1869	Apr 29, 1869
COOK, J. Rogers	Nancy Jagger	no date	Jul 8, 1858
COOK, Joseph S.	Emma Doughty	30 May 1874	Jun 11, 1874
COOPER, Edward	Lydia A. Thomas	14 Jan 1863	Jan 22, 1863
COOPER, Edward H.	Melissa J. Perrow	5 Sep 1875	Sep 23, 1875
COOPER, Samuel	Elizabeth Cornwell	no date	Sep 30, 1858
COPELAND, John	Mary W. Mayhew	24 May 1859	May 26, 1859
CORDNER, James R.	Charlotte E. Randall	6 Oct 1862	Oct 9, 1862
CORNELL, Augustus	Hannah Heaton	30 Dec 1863	Jan 7, 1864
CORNELL, C. E.	Alice Weeks	20 Apr 1872	May 2, 1872

Groom's Name	Bride's Name	Date of marriage	Date of newspaper
CORNELL, Edwin	Susan J. Abrams	2nd inst	Dec 6, 1860
CORNELL, Elbert Thomas	Julia Wilson Barr	29 Nov 1871	Dec 7, 1871
CORNELL, Joseph D.	Mary E. Albro	24 Nov 1860	Nov 22, 1860
CORNELL, Richard	Amelia A. Shaw	13 Feb 1865	Feb 23, 1865
CORNWELL, Alexander	Mary Elizabeth Horton	23 Aug 1862	Aug 28, 1862
CORNWELL, Rufus F.	Jane Brush	15 Jan 1865	Jan 26, 1865
COSTER, William B. G.	Catharine Ann Jackson	1 Jan 1868	Jan 9, 1868
CRANE, John M.	Harriet H. Seabury	7 May 1861	May 9, 1861
CRAVEN, Anthony	Elizabeth Meyer	19 Oct 1864	Oct 27, 1864
CRAWFORD, James M.	Abby E. Smith	2 Feb 1862	Feb 6, 1862
CREED, George H.	Sarah C. Van Duzer	22nd inst	Mar 2, 1865
CREED, James	Carrie Waldron	24 Dec 1861	Jan 2, 1862
CREED, William	Peggy Pearsall	9 Oct 1876	Oct 26, 1876
CROOKER, Simeon	Julia H. Sands	3rd inst	Jul 20, 1865
CROSBY, Samuel R.	Anna Hurd, (Mrs)	4 Apr 1870	Apr 28, 1870
CROSSETTE, J. Fisher	Mary Merrill	4 May 1870	May 26, 1870
CROSSLEY, J--?--	Adelaide (?) Ke-?--	no date	Nov 22, 1877
CROSSMAN, C. Alonzo	Cornelia Denton	13 Jan 1878	Jan 24, 1878
CRUIKSHANK, A. W.	Carrie Macy	18 Sep 1878	Oct 3, 1878
CULVER, William	Rosenar A. Fanning	9th inst	Jan 12, 1860
CURTIS, John B.	Mary Ann Hardy	18 Oct 1860	Oct 25, 1860
DACOSTA, Theodore X.	Annie J. Smith	12 Apr 1864	Apr 21, 1864
DANDIN, Ferdinand F.	Margaret T. O'Brien	4 Mar 1875	Mar 11, 1875
DANES, Edward N.	Anna R. Green	27 Jan 1862	Feb 6, 1862
DARBY, John	Susan E. Wright	3 Feb 1859	Mar 3, 1859
DARBY, William H.	Jane W. Radford	14 Jun 1860	Jun 21, 1860
DAVENPORT, Conklin	Louisa Mott	11 Oct 1874	Oct 22, 1874
DAVENPORT, Lewis	Mary Jane Von Nostrand	17 Jun 1867	Jul 11, 1867
DAVIDSON, Alexander	Mary A. Horton	4 Dec 1864	Dec 22, 1864
DAVIDSON, Charles	Mary Alena Wright	21 Nov 1858	Nov 25, 1858
DAVIDSON, John K. T.	Fannie E. Mersereau	6 Sep 1876	Sep 14, 1876
DAVIES, Addison	Hannah Maria Sprague	25 Jul 1860	Aug 2, 1860
DAVIES, Edward C.	Margaret E. Darragh	16 Jan 1868	Jan 30, 1868
DAVIS, Charles Henry	Helena Van Wyck Southard	28 Sep 1867	Oct 3, 1867
DAVIS, Jeremiah K.	Phebe A. Flemming	11 Mar 1865	Mar 16, 1865
DAVIS, Levi	Eliza Salky	4 Nov 1877	Nov 8, 1877
DAVIS, Stephen VanRenselaer	(Miss) Lupton	Saturday	Mar 19, 1874
DAVIS, William A.	Emily P. James	no date	Aug 12, 1858
DAVISON, John T.	Armenia Pearsall	29 Dec 1869	Jan 6, 1870
DAVISON, Robert H.	Minerva Jane Cornwell	31 Aug 1870	Sep 22, 1870
DAYTON, Charles R.	Sarah Frances Sherry	16 Dec 1858	Dec 23, 1858
DE LANGUILLETTE, George Fridrick	Mary Louise Kock	17 Oct 1869	Oct 21, 1869
DE MOTT, Andrew J.	Hannah P. Hopkins	13 Nov 1867	Nov 21, 1867
DE MOTT, Benjamin B.	Catharine A. Stubbs	2 Jan 1873	Jan 9, 1873
DE MOTT, Charles	Elnora Bedell	20 Jul 1876	Aug 10, 1876
DE MOTT, Daniel	Hannah Hicks	4 Jan 1863	Feb 19, 1863
DE NYSE, Walter N.	Carrie B. Rushmore	11 Feb 1868	Feb 13, 1868
DEAN, Stephen	Elizabeth T. Smith	29 Mar 1870	Apr 7, 1870
DEBBLE, Marshall	Helen Pagan	10th inst	Jun 21, 1860
DECK, Isaiah	C. Vere De Vere, (Lady)	no date	Jun 21, 1860
DECK, Isaiah	Louisa Halpin	no date	Jun 21, 1860
DECK, Isaiah	Madelina De Morveau	no date	Jun 21, 1860
DEMOTT, Elijah P.	Susan Young, (Mrs)	10th inst	Oct 24, 1867
DEMOTT, Jarvis	Hannah E. Dunbar	18th ult	Jan 19, 1865
DEMOTT, John W. (Jr.)	Christiana Sprague	20 Feb 1872	Feb 29, 1872

Groom's Name	Bride's Name	Date of marriage	Date of newspaper
DEMOTT, Sidney	Celia E. Cornell	18 Jan 1863	Feb 19, 1863
DEMOTT, William	Sarah W. Pearsall, (Mrs)	12 Dec 1869	Dec 16, 1869
DEMPSTER, James B.	Elizabeth H. Dalziel	15th inst	Sep 20, 1860
DENNIS, Gilbert	Experience Smith	15 Oct 1860	Nov 1, 1860
DENTON, Alexander	Nettie Keith	13 Oct 1875	Nov 4, 1875
DENTON, Amos	Mary Ann Ludlum	28 Mar 1861	Apr 4, 1861
DENTON, Charles A.	Victoria E. Spillett	15 May 1872	May 23, 1872
DENTON, Charles Wesley	Mary Smith	17 May 1861	May 30, 1861
DENTON, John H. B.	M. Libbie Carman	3 Nov 1872	Nov 7, 1872
DENTON, John Wesley	Orpha A. Wells	11 Mar 1863	Mar 19, 1863
DENTON, Joseph	Elizabeth Raynor	4 Jun 1861	Jun 6, 1861
DEWEY, W. N.	Mary Peterson	6 May 1865	May 11, 1865
DICKENSON, Joseph E.	Matilda Schenck	3 Jul 1867	Jul 11, 1867
DICKERSON, Joseph M.	Martha A. Hildreth	1 Oct 1865	Oct 5, 1865
DICKSON, J.	Anna M. Reeve	20 Apr 1869	May 6, 1869
DILLEN, William H.	Charlotte O. Painter	no date	Sep 23, 1858
DILLER, William A. M.	Mary A. Welles	17 Jun 1863	Jun 25, 1863
DIRKING, Henry	(Mrs. John) Gunzer	24 Oct 1878	Oct 31, 1878
DITMAS, I. Adrian	Helen W. Stoothoff	no date	Jun 9, 1859
DODGE, John	Mary J. Duryea	1st inst	Jan 13, 1859
DOREMUS, Franklin C.	Mary Ann Troward	16 May 1872	May 23, 1872
DORLON, Charles	Arabella Rhodes	1 Jul 1858	Jul 8, 1858
DOTY, Carman	Eliza Ann Wood	17 Sep 1865	Sep 28, 1865
DOUGHTY, Walter K.	Clarissa Bedell	28 Oct 1877	Nov 1, 1877
DOWNING, Edward T.	Adelia M. Bedell	28 Mar 1861	Apr 11, 1861
DOWNING, Frank	Elizabeth Coles	2 Jun 1864	Jun 9, 1864
DOWNING, G. Jackson	Phebe A. Albertson	8 Feb 1861	Feb 28, 1861
DOWNING, Henry	Sarah S. Hurd	17 Nov 1869	Nov 25, 1869
DOWNING, Valentine	Mary Jean Townsend	17 Oct 1867	Oct 24, 1867
DOWNS, George Harvey	Catherine Seimes	17 Mar 1870	Mar 31, 1870
DOWNS, Sylvester	Emeline R. Fanning, (Mrs)	14th inst	Oct 27, 1864
DOXSEY, Romine	Susan Van Wickler	6 Jan 1861	Jan 17, 1861
DOXY, Richardson	Sarah E. Jones	6 Sep 1868	Sep 10, 1868
DRESSING, Fredr.	Elizabeth Yagle	19 Dec 1867	Dec 26, 1867
DRISCOLL, Alexander	Phebe E. Gritman	27 Oct 1861	Nov 28, 1861
DRISCOLL, David	Arethusia Abrams	22 Nov 1871	Nov 30, 1871
DUNBAR, Garret S.	Eunice N. Horton	14 Oct 1872	Nov 7, 1872
DUNBAR, Thomas	Emma J. Seaman	28 Aug 1878	Sep 5, 1878
DUNCKLEE, John B.	Libbie S. Adams	14 Jan 1875	Jan 21, 1875
DUNN, Michael	Emeline Cornell	24 Mar 1874	Apr 2, 1874
DURLAND, George	Phebe J. Young	15 Dec 1863	Dec 24, 1863
DURYEA, Andrew	Matilda Bedell	13 Jun 1869	Jun 17, 1869
DURYEA, Benjamin	Sarah Totten	23 Dec 1869	Feb 10, 1870
DURYEA, John	Cornelia M. Doughty	26 Oct 1867	Nov 14, 1867
DURYEA, John W.	Frances E. Smith	4 Jan 1859	Jan 20, 1859
DURYEA, Robert L. S.	Martha Armenia Abrams	no date	Nov 15, 1860
DURYEA, Whitehead C.	Adelia E. Bedell	12 May 1861	May 16, 1861
EASTMAN, Henry M. W.	Gussie Rushmore	26 Sep 1878	Oct 3, 1878
ECKEL, Fredrick	Mary S. Nix	13 Sep 1871	Sep 14, 1871
EDWARDS, Andrew	Annie Moore	18 Jul 1874	Jul 30, 1874
EDWARDS, Charles	Ann E. Cornelius	no date	Feb 15, 1872
EDWARDS, R. Willett	Magda A. Smith	no date	May 23, 1878
ELDERD, George S.	Jane A. Lewis	29 Oct 1867	Nov 7, 1867
ELDERT, Chas Henry	Margaret Combes	9 Apr 1865	Apr 13, 1865
ELDERT, Elnathan	Alice A. Mott	27th ult	Jul 11, 1867
ELDRED, John E.	Henrietta Leech	16 Jul 1863	Aug 20, 1863

Groom's Name	Bride's Name	Date of marriage	Date of newspaper
ELDRED, Seaman	Sarah L. Vanciclen	28 Aug 1873	Sep 4, 1873
ELLES, Charles M.	Julia Young	25 Jul 1867	Aug 1, 1867
ELLISON, Alanson	Eleanor Pearsall	recently	Sep 6, 1877
ELLISON, Allen H.	Zora Smith	10 Feb 1864	Feb 18, 1864
ELLISON, C. Agustus	Matilda N. Pearsall	26 Mar 1873	Apr 3, 1873
ELLISON, Chas H.	Maria Smith	4 Oct 1864	Nov 3, 1864
ELLISON, Henry	Phebe Ann Kelly	15 Mar 1862	Mar 20, 1862
ELLISON, Isaac	Jessie Jenkins	30 Oct 1877	Nov 8, 1877
EMORY, Frank A.	Theodora Garnett	13 Jun 1864	Jul 7, 1864
EMORY, George W.	Susan E. Searing	19 Dec 1860	Dec 20, 1860
EVANS, Elias	Elizabeth Ann Brewster	9 Aug 1860	Aug 16, 1860
EVERETT, William L.	Mary E. Anthony	2 Jul 1871	Jul 13, 1871
EVERIT, Charles H.	Elizabeth Ludlum	10 Jul 1861	Jul 11, 1861
EVERITT, Benjamin S.	Mary Ann Rider	2 Jun 1859	Jun 9, 1859
FAULKNER, Thomas C.	Sarah E. Smith	1 Jan 1864	Jan 7, 1864
FERN, George	Cornelia R. Willets	7 Sep 1870	Sep 15, 1870
FIELBACH, Philip H. C.	Margaret C. Wilson	27th inst	Jun 3, 1858
FISH, J.G.	Lou Wells	4 Jan 1871	Feb 2, 1871
FLETCHER, James	Lavinia Stringham	31st ult	Jun 8, 1876
FLOWERS, William E.	Martha Watts	16 Sep 1860	Oct 25, 1860
FOGERTY, William	Eliza Jane Baylis	8 Feb 1864	Feb 18, 1864
FOOTE, John H.	Annie M. Lambertson	4 Jun 1864	Jun 30, 1864
FORBEL, George W. L.	Fannie Abrams	13 Mar 1865	Mar 16, 1865
FOREMAN, William	Jennie Hewlett	24 Apr 1873	May 8, 1873
FOSDICK, Lewis I.	M. Eloise Terry	20 Jun 1878	Jun 27, 1878
FOSDICK, Lewis L.	Julia E. Bennet	29 Aug 1861	Sep 5, 1861
FOSTER, Abraham	Frances H. Abrams	31 Oct 1867	Nov 14, 1867
FOSTER, Nat W.	Fanny Miller	no date	Sep 30, 1858
FOSTER, Robert C.	Annie J. Griffin	no date	Oct 17, 1867
FOUNTAIN, Albert D.	Phebe A. Rapelyea	16 Oct 1864	Oct 27, 1864
FOWLER, John B.	Martha Field	24 May 1859	Jun 2, 1859
FOWLER, John Frederick	Grace Baber	16 Jul 1872	Jul 18, 1872
FOWLER, Joseph	Hannah Ann Miller	3 Feb 1864	Feb 11, 1864
FOWLER, Richard	Elizabeth B. Acker	6 Jan 1864	Jan 14, 1864
FOX, John A.	Sarah A. Nostrand, (Mrs)	21st ult	Nov 26, 1868
FOX, John Alfred	Charlotte F. Bedine	31 Aug 1862	Sep 25, 1862
FRANCIS, Oliver	Phebe Jane Akly	3 May 1865	May 11, 1865
FRANKLIN, Charles James	Anna Senska	28 Apr 1872	May 9, 1872
FREAM, Charles Carman	Phebe Noon	22 Mar 1862	Mar 27, 1862
FRECKS, John F.	Phoebe J. Cowenhoven	22 Jun 1858	Jun 24, 1858
FREDERICK, Elias	Sarah E. Frederick	no date	Jan 26, 1860
FREEBORN, Thomas	Orra Clarissa Barnum	13 Sep 1865	Sep 21, 1865
FRIDELL, Benjamin	Frances M. Jones	5 Apr 1868	Apr 9, 1868
FROST, Frank	Alice Combs	26 Oct 1878	Nov 21, 1878
FROST, Platt	Frances Lucinda Pearsall	21 Oct 1860	Nov 1, 1860
FURMAN, Aaron H.	Elizabeth C. Luther	4 Dec 1862	Dec 25, 1862
GALLAGHER, George W.	Emma A. Smith	8 May 1878	May 16, 1878
GARDINER, Alexander	Elizabeth P. Jarvis	29 Dec 1858	Jan 13, 1859
GARDNER, John Morris	Margaret Kelly	13 Mar 1864	Mar 17, 1864
GARRETSON, Garret J.	Eliza L. Eastman	20 Sep 1876	Oct 5, 1876
GARY, Luke	Josephine Proctor, (Mrs)	3 Dec 1869	Dec 9, 1869
GESLAIN, Victor A.	Mary E. Bryers	16 Oct 1873	Nov 6, 1873
GILDERSLEEVE, Moses R.	Sarah Nostrand	26 Apr 1863	May 14, 1863
GILDERSLEEVE, Samuel M.	Harriet G. Jenkens	19 Mar 1865	Mar 23, 1865
GLINSMAN, Henry, Jr.	Louisa Muus	17 Feb 1874	Feb 26, 1874

Groom's Name	Bride's Name	Date of marriage	Date of newspaper
GOFF, William	Julia M. Holdrich	20 Jul 1858	Jul 29, 1858
GOLDEN, Andrew J.	Sarah Elizabeth Spillet	15 Jul 1858	Jul 29, 1858
GOLDEN, Oliver	Mary Louisa Webb	28 Jul 1861	Aug 8, 1861
GOLDEN, William T.	Addie Fleet	15 Mar 1868	Mar 19, 1868
GOLDER, Alfred	Sarah Crooker	5 Mar 1865	Mar 9, 1865
GOLDER, Carman	Hannah Snediker	26 Dec 1858	Dec 30, 1858
GOLDER, Frank	Lottie A. Pettit	19 Nov 1868	Nov 26, 1868
GOLDER, George	Elockey A. Pearsall	no date	Mar 23, 1865
GOLDER, Jacob	Alice A. Dorlon	27 Nov 1867	Dec 12, 1867
GOLDER, Joseph	Elizabeth Nostrand	3rd inst	Oct 11, 1860
GOLDER, W. Edgar	Clara A. Bedell	28 Nov 1878	Dec 5, 1878
GOLDER, Wm. H.	Mary Louisa Rhodes	9 Oct 1865	Oct 19, 1865
GOOD, William H.	Susie A. Wood	23 Oct 1872	Nov 7, 1872
GOODRICH, Charles N.	Helen S. Cook	6th inst	Sep 23, 1858
GORDON, John H.	Theresa A. Newton	1 Jan 1865	Jan 12, 1865
GORMAND, Dennis	Margaret Smith	29 Dec 1864	Jan 5, 1865
GOSLINE, Joseph W.	Phebe C. Bedell	20 Oct 1858	Oct 28, 1858
GRANT, N. B.	Juliett H. Hedges	5 Aug 1858	Aug 12, 1858
GREEN, A. W.	Smith Bannerman, (Mrs)	no date	Jan 19, 1860
GREEN, J. Townsend	Sarah E. Mott	10 Dec 1870	Dec 15, 1870
GRIFFIN, Abram	Huldah Turrell	27 Feb 1878	Mar 7, 1878
GRIFFIN, JR, Abraham	Elizabeth D. Molineaux	16 Dec 1862	Dec 25, 1862
GRIFFIN, Joseph	Jennie H. Lott	7 Dec 1863	Dec 10, 1863
GROB, John N.	Anna Davison	13 Jan 1864	Jan 21, 1864
GUINNE, Almerin	Sarah Lavinia Vermilyea	21st inst	Feb 23, 1860
GUNTHER, Caspar	Elizabeth Horsmann	13 Feb 1868	Feb 20, 1868
HAFF, Stephen	Louisa Nichols	10 Jan 1864	Jan 21, 1864
HAFF, Stephen J.	Antoinette Wicks, (Mrs)	27 Jan 1870	Feb 17, 1870
HAFF, Townsend	Mary Elizabeth Smith	30th ult	Oct 7, 1858
HAFF, William H.	Emma J. Derby	6 Oct 1878	Oct 24, 1878
HAIGHT, John C.	Julia M. Raynor	5 Sep 1877	Sep 20, 1877
HAINE, Maltby	Hannah Case	no date	Jun 9, 1859
HAINES, Isaac S.	Mary A. Jenkins, (Mrs)	11 Jul 1858	Jul 29, 1858
HALL, A. Douglas	Rosalie Littell	27 Sep 1863	Oct 8, 1863
HALL, Daniel	Adeline Webster	25 Dec 1858	Jan 20, 1859
HALL, Ebenezer M.	Julia A. Eldred	10 Jan 1872	Feb 1, 1872
HALL, William	Mary E. Westervelt	7 Mar 1861	Mar 28, 1861
HALL, William J.	Lizzie M. De Mott	13 Nov 1878	Nov 21, 1878
HALSEY, James E.	Lettie A. Hull	12th inst	Jan 19, 1865
HALSEY, William	Susan Bedell	6 Sep 1867	Nov 7, 1867
HARNED, Samuel L.	Rachel A. Bowne	4 Feb 1864	Feb 11, 1864
HAROLD, John	Emma F. Snedeker	21 Dec 1872	Dec 26, 1872
HAROLD, Thomas G.	Martha S. Walker	24 Sep 1859	Sep 29, 1859
HARPER, John	Mary Emma Hirst	4th inst	Oct 19, 1865
HARPER, Philip J. A.	Augusta M. Thorne	29 Jun 1858	Jul 1, 1858
HARRINGTON, Daniel	Ellen D. Hendrickson	6 Mar 1859	Mar 24, 1859
HARRIS, Charles H.	Florence Hall	18 Jun 1867	Jun 27, 1867
HARRIS, Charles H.	Florence Hall	18 Jun 1867	Jul 11, 1867
HARRISON, George W.	Fannie Eabank	no date	Aug 12, 1858
HARRISON, John	Susan J. Bishop	5 Nov 1874	Nov 19, 1874
HARRISON, Wm Henry	Anna Moran	19 Mar 1859	Mar 24, 1859
HART, Alex R.	Carrie E. Snow	7 Nov 1877	Nov 15, 1877
HART, Edmund H.	Isabella Martense Howland	1 Dec 1870	Dec 15, 1870
HARTMAN, Christian	Bernardine Hager	12 Sep 1875	Sep 16, 1875
HARTMER, Charles	Sarah A. Drevile	14 May 1874	May 28, 1874
HARVEY, Martin	Margaret Faye	22 May 1870	May 26, 1870

Groom's Name	Bride's Name	Date of marriage	Date of newspaper
HARWOOD, T. Henry	Jennie Forgie	28 Feb 1868	Mar 5, 1868
HASBROUCK, George W.	Alice M. Cornwell	6 Nov 1872	Nov 14, 1872
HATFIELD, William	Catherine Carman	6th inst	Feb 17, 1859
HATFIELD, William	Catherine Carman	6 Feb 1859	Mar 3, 1859
HATHORN, William H.	Almira A. Hicks	10 Mar 1859	Mar 24, 1859
HAVENS, Charles S.	Nannie M. Williamson	14 Dec 1858	Dec 23, 1858
HAVILAND, Henry M.	Emma A. Skidmore	21 Nov 1878	Nov 28, 1878
HAVILAND, Periam T.	Mary P. Albertson	5 Feb 1868	Feb 13, 1868
HAVILAND, Theodore	Julia M. Dannat	10 Jun 1874	Jun 18, 1874
HAWKINS, Robert F.	Elizabeth Norton (?)	no date	Jan 6, 1859
HAWKINS, Robert F.	Elizabeth Noston (?)	no date	Jan 6, 1859
HAYDEN, T. A.	Elizabeth Coles, (Mrs)	20 Sep 1877	Sep 27, 1877
HAYES, James E.	Addie Bedell	26 Feb 1863	Mar 5, 1863
HEBARD, George W.	Mary F. Foster	6 Oct 1869	Oct 14, 1869
HEDDA, Adam	Susanna Combs	11 Nov 1867	Nov 21, 1867
HEDGES, Willian H.	Susan A. Van Wickler	11 Oct 1870	Nov 3, 1870
HEGEMAN, John V.	Mattie Downing	20 Jan 1870	Jan 27, 1870
HENDERSON, Daniel A.	Grace Richardson	4 Sep 1878	Sep 12, 1878
HENDRICKSON, Abraham	Sarah Shaw	29 Jul 1867	Aug 8, 1867
HENDRICKSON, Assa	Elizabeth Duryea	30 Oct 1861	Nov 14, 1861
HENDRICKSON, Charles A.	Sarah C. Carman	15 Feb 1872	Feb 29, 1872
HENDRICKSON, Daniel R.	Kate Suydam	12 Sep 1872	Sep 26, 1872
HENDRICKSON, James	Mary Fowler, (Mrs)	3 Sep 1860	Sep 6, 1860
HENDRICKSON, James G.	Julia A. Higbie	20 Oct 1867	Nov 7, 1867
HENDRICKSON, James R.	Catherine Jane Baylis	17 Dec 1863	Dec 24, 1863
HENDRICKSON, Jeremiah	Amanda Covert	6 Feb 1874	Feb 12, 1874
HENDRICKSON, John B.	Marietta Hendrickson	no date	Nov 29, 1877
HENDRICKSON, John L.	Lizzie Bailey	24 Mar 1875	Apr 8, 1875
HENDRICKSON, Remsen	Susannah E. Baylis	2 Nov 1867	Dec 12, 1867
HENDRICKSON, Robert C.	Adaline Powell	10 Dec 1861	Mar 6, 1862
HENDRICKSON, Samuel	Sarah A. Carpenter	15 Nov 1865	Dec 7, 1865
HENDRICKSON, Smith	Martha E. Skidmore	23rd inst	Nov 26, 1868
HENGGELER, Jacob	Lydia A. Brush	27 Nov 1862	Dec 4, 1862
HENRY, John	Mary Davidson	23 Oct 1863	Nov 5, 1863
HERBERT, Walter	Ann C. Abrams	20 Oct 1870	Nov 3, 1870
HERBERT, Walter	Phoebe A. Sammis	no date	May 21, 1874
HERBERT, William	Ann Carman	5th inst	Jul 12, 1860
HERMEN, Frank	Phillipene Asslar Zauder	30 Nov 1858	Dec 2, 1858
HEWLETT, James K. Polk	Jennie Curtis	6 Dec 1865	Dec 7, 1865
HEWLETT, John Mitchell	Margaret A. Hentz	25 Oct 1859	Oct 27, 1859
HEWLETT, Oliver T.	Hester Ann Bedell	21 Nov 1861	Nov 28, 1861
HEWLETT, Samuel	Nettie J. McCloud	no date	Sep 28, 1865
HEWLETT, Thomas W.	Libbie Raynor	25 Jun 1878	Jul 4, 1878
HEWLETT, William F.	Mary E. Middlebrooks	25 Mar 1873	Mar 27, 1873
HEWLETT, William H.	Emma Walters	22 Aug 1859	Sep 8, 1859
HICKS, John E.	Mary F. Powell	29 Nov 1871	Nov 30, 1871
HICKS, Willet B.	Hannah S. Nostrand	6th inst	Oct 10, 1867
HIGBIE, A. Burtis	Mary E. Nostrand	26 Nov 1878	Dec 19, 1878
HILDRETH, Albert G.	Mary D. Loper	no date	Aug 26, 1858
HILL, George W.	Emeline Schenk	30 Jan 1872	Feb 1, 1872
HILL, Zlona	Charlotte Coles	16th inst	Nov 30, 1876
HINGLE, Richard	Estelle Ruland	23 Dec 1873	Jan 8, 1874
HOFFMAN, Leonard	Catharine Twiner	15 Feb 1862	Feb 27, 1862
HOGINS, Edward P.	Josephine Raynor	9 Feb 1870	Mar 3, 1870
HOLLINGSWORTH, John G.	Margaret A. Smith, (Mrs)	no date	Jun 17, 1858
HOLTZ, Joseph	Phebe Jane Stillwell	3 Nov 1873	Nov 13, 1873
HOMAN, John	Sally Hammond	last week	Nov 7, 1872
HOMAN, Robert H.	Maria Emma Doty	9 Mar 1868	Apr 2, 1868
HOMAN, Sylvester	Rebecca Smith	15th inst	Jan 19, 1860

Groom's Name	Bride's Name	Date of marriage	Date of newspaper
HOOD, Dennis	Mary Ann Smith	28 Sep 1867	Oct 3, 1867
HOOD, George	Sarah Jane Baldwin	16 May 1859	May 19, 1859
HOOK, Christian	Alice Carman	11 Nov 1863	Dec 10, 1863
HOPPINS, (A.) Stile	Lizzie A. West	no date	Nov 26, 1863
HORSEFORD, Charles L.	Hattie I. Pierce	Tues last	Oct 15, 1863
HORSFIELD, Isreal	Emma Willets	1 May 1869	May 6, 1869
HORSFIELD, William U.	Mary W. Smith	9th inst	Apr 16, 1868
HORTON, Jonathan G.	Bethiah H. Brown, (Mrs)	24 Nov 1870	Dec 8, 1870
HORTON, Salter S.	Victorine Bressieux	19 Jul 1859	Sep 15, 1859
HORTON, Samuel J.	Mary Lavinia Fowler	6 Apr 1864	Apr 21, 1864
HOWELL, Edgar F.	Lucy Lent	27 Dec 1864	Dec 29, 1864
HOYT, Henry M.	Matilda Haight	25 Jan 1864	Jan 28, 1864
HOYT, Purdy B.	Emily Mather	10 Apr 1862	Apr 17, 1862
HUBBS, Amos T.	Margaret S. Budd	no date	Jul 29, 1858
HUBBS, John R.	Esther Robbins	9 Nov 1870	Dec 8, 1870
HUDSON, John Y.	Isabella M. Howe	4 Mar 1861	Mar 7, 1861
HUFFINGTON, John Worthington	Julia Elizabeth Vredenburgh	19 May 1859	May 26, 1859
HULL, Thomas G.	Josie M. Smith	28 Nov 1876	Dec 7, 1876
HULTE, Edward	Ellina Rhodes	no date	Apr 8, 1869
HULTZ, Patrick	Amelia Hultz	27 Jun 1872	Jun 27, 1872
HUMESTOM, Benjamin Franklin	Susan Maria Cromer	16 Mar 1876	May 11, 1876
HUNT, George L.	Maggie Denton	27 Feb 1877	Mar 8, 1877
HUNTER, Robert	Sarah A. Wallace	no date	Aug 12, 1858
HYATT, Thomas B.	Christina Kouwenhoven	13 Dec 1865	Dec 21, 1865
HYDE, Harry	Hannah H. Searing	6 Apr 1876	Apr 13, 1876
IRELAND, John H.	Henrietta C. Smith	55 Sep 1867	Oct 10, 1867
IRISH, Henry	Mary Louisa Griffin	25 Nov 1862	Dec 4, 1862
JACKSON, Charles	Catherine Davison	27 Mar 1863	Apr 9, 1863
JACKSON, John	Mary DeBoise	15 Nov 1867	Nov 28, 1867
JACKSON, Thomas E.	Virginia Bedell	27 Sep 1877	Jan 17, 1878
JACKSON, Townsend A.	Ellana J. Langdon	10 Dec 1868	Dec 24, 1868
JACKSON, William C.	Amelia Burrows	21 Dec 1870	Jan 5, 1871
JACKSON, William H.	Elizabeth J. Jones	22th inst	Jan 30, 1868
JACKSON, William H.	Emma Grover	28 Oct 1867	Nov 7, 1867
JAGGER, William	Mary Elizabeth Seaman	14 Aug 1871	Aug 17, 1871
JAISLE, Christopher	Mary Tully	22 Apr 1860	May 3, 1860
JAMES, Elbert C.	Sarah Maria Bedell	19 Jan 1868	Jan 23, 1868
JAMES, Stephen D.	Mary A. Green	24 Feb 1864	Feb 25, 1864
JEFFREY, Richard	Amelia Williams	31 Mar 1874	Apr 9, 1874
JENKS, Almet Francis	Maud Eleanor Littlejohn	5 Dec 1878	Dec 12, 1878
JESSUP, Louis A.	Frances M. Pearsall	6 Feb 1861	Feb 21, 1861
JOHNSON, A. Ditmars	Phebe Durland	12th inst	Sep 19, 1867
JOHNSON, Benjamin T.	Abbey Jane Golder	24 May 1860	May 31, 1860
JOHNSON, Benjamin T.	Ann Amelia Ackley	12 Jul 1872	Jul 18, 1872
JOHNSON, Clark H.	Ellen A. McNeil	26 Aug 1859	Sep 8, 1859
JOHNSON, Edmund	Mary Combes	1 May 1862	Jun 5, 1862
JOHNSON, Epnetus S.	Amelia Jane Frost	4 Jul 1865	Jul 6, 1865
JOHNSON, F. Asbury	Celeste Story	7 Oct 1874	Oct 22, 1874
JOHNSON, Henry	Ann Elizabeth Seaman	23 Oct 1875	Nov 4, 1875
JOHNSON, Henry Floyd	Jennie Holmstrom	1st inst	Jan 19, 1865
JOHNSON, James	Ann Maria	30 Jul 1865	Aug 10, 1865
JOHNSON, Martin G.	Margaret Nostrand	31 May 1859	Jun 2, 1859
JOHNSON, Oscar C.	Caroline M. Burdett	17th inst	Sep 26, 1867

Groom's Name	Bride's Name	Date of marriage	Date of newspaper
JOHNSON, Stephen	Katie A. Phillips	6 Sep 1868	Sep 10, 1868
JOHNSON, Sylvester	Annie Stine	10 Apr 1878	Apr 25, 1878
JOHNSON, William Henry	Maria Platt, (Mrs)	28 Nov 1860	Jan 10, 1861
JOHNSON, William S.	Harriet W. Townsend	12 Feb 1863	Feb 19, 1863
JONES, Alfred	Margery C. Weeks	26 Oct 1870	Nov 3, 1870
JONES, George Floyd	Nettie Wood	18 Jan 1865	Jan 26, 1865
JONES, J. Hilton	Sarah M. Partridge	7 Nov 1861	Nov 14, 1861
JONES, Richard	Bella Fish	18 Nov 1868	Nov 26, 1868
JORDAN, C. A.	Annie M. Eldert	26 Apr 1860	May 3, 1860
KALDFLEISCH, Frederick W.	Frederica V. Fowler	28 Oct 1858	Nov 4, 1858
KARL, William	Sarah Jane Powell	22 Apr 1878	May 9, 1878
KEELER, William Mathew	Mary Allan Brower	25 Sep 1867	Nov 14, 1867
KEIRSTED, George W.	Margaret King	29 Dec 1864	Jan 5, 1865
KELLER, Gustavus A.	Louise Tucker	no date	Sep 23, 1858
KELLOGG, Charles W.	Lina L. Searing	26 Sep 1876	Oct 5, 1876
KELLUM, Ebenezer	Mary R. Rushmore	8 Jan 1862	Jan 16, 1862
KELLUM, John H.	Christiana Littell	6 Jul 1864	Aug 4, 1864
KELLY, Michael	Eliza Sweeney	13 Nov 1859	Nov 17, 1859
KENNAHAN, John C.	Evangeline Webb	4 Jun 1872	Jun 27, 1872
KENNEDY, Charles H.	Ellen B. Dwight	28 Feb 1860	Mar 8, 1860
KENYON, N. S.	Jennie A. Miller	6th inst	Nov 14, 1867
KETCHAM, Ebenezer	Eliza Southard	17 Jan 1871	Jan 26, 1871
KETCHAM, George A.	Eliza Brown, (Mrs)	no date	May 21, 1874
KETCHAM, George H.	Elvira Terry	14 Dec 1870	Dec 22, 1870
KETCHAM, Isaac S.	Sarah F. Mann	18 Sep 1867	Sep 26, 1867
KETCHAM, Latting C.	Anna E. Jervis	no date	Nov 4, 1858
KETCHAM, Peter	Hannah A. Austin	18 Jan 1859	Jan 20, 1859
KETCHAM, Thomas B.	Ruth A. Sprague	11 Jul 1858	Jul 15, 1858
KETCHUM, Henry E.	Sarah Jane Tilley	17 Jun 1873	Jun 26, 1873
KEYES, John	Margaret Martin	no date	Feb 9, 1860
KILLIN, Edward	Dallie Hewlett	22 Dec 1863	Dec 24, 1863
KIMBALL, James	Julia Pearsall	26th ult	Apr 13, 1865
KIMBALL, James A.	Julia A. Brower	21 Nov 1877	Nov 29, 1877
KINGSLEY, William	Sarah DeSmith	22 Sep 1859	Sep 29, 1859
KIRBY, Charles H.	Julia A. Mathews	3 Jun 1858	Jun 10, 1858
KIRK, John W.	Annie C. Campbell	21 Jun 1863	Jun 25, 1863
KISSAM, George C.	Louise Adriance	16th inst	Apr 25, 1861
KISSAM, George H.	Ellen Galatian Cordray	18th inst	Aug 24, 1865
KNOWLTON, Dexter A. (Jr.)	Mary Louisa Myers	7 Jun 1871	Jun 15, 1871
KORTRIGHT, John	Martha Heartt	29th ult	Apr 13, 1865
KORTWRIGHT, John	Elizabeth Wanser	2 Feb 1864	Feb 4, 1864
LAFETRA, Daniel W.	Emma Hendrickson	23 Oct 1867	Oct 24, 1867
LAING, James B.	Emily Malcolm Ferris	15 Sep 1870	Sep 22, 1870
LANE, John H.	Mary E. Lewis	2 Jun 1871	Jun 15, 1871
LANGDON, Carman S.	Jane M. Simonson	13 Dec 1865	Dec 21, 1865
LANGDON, Joseph B.	Julia Ann Pearsall	26 Dec 1860	Jan 3, 1861
LANGDON, Joseph P.	Harriet A. Eldert	29 Mar 1864	Apr 21, 1864
LANGDON, Stephen	Charlotte Cornell, (Mrs)	13 May 1860	Jun 14, 1860
LARKINS, John P.	Margaret Nolan	30 Jun 1861	Jul 11, 1861
LAROZA, Benjamin S.	Emily V. Leach	28 Dec 1861	Jan 9, 1862
LAROZA, Charles	Alma DeMott	4th inst	Nov 8, 1860
LAWRENCE, A. Effingham	Elizabeth Spooner	4 Jun 1878	Jun 6, 1878
LAWRENCE, J. Burling	Mary Adeline Furman	10 Oct 1861	Oct 24, 1861

Groom's Name	Bride's Name	Date of marriage	Date of newspaper
LAWRENCE, John	Ann Eliza Raynor	22 Jan 1868	Jan 30, 1868
LAWRENCE, Wilson	Lizzie Hover	25 Oct 1859	Nov 3, 1859
LAYTON, Elbert	Sarah A. Grant	25 Sep 1878	Oct 17, 1878
LEA, James N.	Mary R. Duncan	no date	Oct 14, 1858
LEACH, William	Susan Langdon	no date	Jul 7, 1864
LEACH, William R.	M. Augusta Seaman	13 Mar 1878	Mar 21, 1878
LEAVETT, G. Howland	Amelia Willets	5 Oct 1878	Oct 24, 1878
LEEK, Robert	Ann Baylis	13 Mar 1861	Mar 28, 1861
LEGGETT, William H.	Mary E. Beebe	no date	Aug 5, 1858
LESLIE, Frank	Florence Squier	13 Jul 1874	Jul 23, 1874
LEWIS, Lester	Harriet J. Ellis	13 Jul 1861	Aug 1, 1861
LITTLE, Thomas	Eliza Doxy	24 Jan 1869	Jan 28, 1869
LONGMAN, Arthur	Frances Troward	16 Oct 1872	Oct 24, 1872
LOOP, William H. W.	Jennie E. Chapel, (Mrs)	17 Jun 1863	Jun 25, 1863
LOPER, Charles G.	Sarah B. Vancott	27 Jul 1865	Aug 3, 1865
LORD, Theodore A.	Julia L. Jones	no date	Oct 28, 1869
LOSEA, Herman	Martha Hayes	1 Jan 1868	Jan 16, 1868
LOSEA, Leander	Lizzie Conklin	6 Apr 1876	Apr 13, 1876
LOSEA, Richard Edgar	Hannah Smith	27 Nov 1862	Dec 4, 1862
LOSEA, Townsend	Annie Tredwell	14 Mar 1877	Mar 22, 1877
LOSEE, Albert	Maggie Walker	2 Oct 1872	Oct 10, 1872
LOSEE, Oliver	Cornelia A. Bedell	1 Jun 1862	Jun 5, 1862
LOSER, John	Sophia Jagle	2 Feb 1864	Feb 11, 1864
LOSSEE, George W.	Gertrude Golden	14 Nov 1861	Nov 28, 1861
LOTT, Abraham	Susan A. Mott	8 Jan 1862	Jan 16, 1862
LOTT, Charles	Emma T. Mott	5 Jan 1862	Jan 16, 1862
LOWDEN, Abraham R.	Phebe R. Southard	27 Nov 1861	Nov 28, 1861
LOWDEN, George H.	Sarah Prink	16 Sep 1875	Sep 23, 1875
LOWDEN, John J.	Helen J. Wheeler	3 Feb 1869	Feb 11, 1869
LOWDEN, Washington	Esther A. Wood	13 Aug 1863	Aug 20, 1863
LUYSTER, Isaac	Ann Hageman	20 Jan 1864	Jan 28, 1864
MAGAW, John D.	A. Augusta French Rushmore	23 Oct 1872	Oct 31, 1872
MAGEE, John I.	Sadie Brainhard	5 Aug 1875	Aug 12, 1875
MAGEE, John T.	Margaret A. Combes	17 Oct 1861	Nov 7, 1861
MAHAN, Freeman S.	Cornelia Emma Baldwin	24 Feb 1864	Feb 25, 1864
MAIER, Charles	Mary Abrams	1 Jan 1873	Jan 9, 1873
MANOLT, Henry A.	Phebe Ann Powell	16 Feb 1859	Mar 10, 1859
MANWARING, Joseph	Sarah Howard	19 Jan 1864	Jan 28, 1864
MARTIN, Michael	Catherine (or Ellen) Shulteton	17 Nov 1860	Nov 22, 1860
MATHEWS, James J.	Margarette Pine	4 Jul 1858	Jul 29, 1858
MATHEWS, James S.	Rhoda Blydenburgh	12 Aug 1864	Aug 25, 1864
MATHEWS, Vander Water	Celestine E. Smith	4 Oct 1865	Oct 5, 1865
MATSCHAT, P. G. L.	Annie Maria Frederik Rosche	3 Mar 1868	Mar 12, 1868
MAYER, Christian	Sarah Hulse	no date	Sep 3, 1874
MAYHER, Alonzo F.	Addie Handlen	24 May 1860	May 31, 1860
MAYNARD, George W.	Minnie E. Riley	20 Sep 1876	Sep 28, 1876
MCCORMACK, James	Rosetta E. Harvey	6 Nov 1870	Nov 10, 1870
MCCORMICK, Richard C.	Maggie G. Hunt	27th ult	Oct 5, 1865
MCCOUN, Willet	Mary Bedell	25 Dec 1861	Jan 2, 1862
MCCOY, John Gibney	Winifred Garver	20 May 1865	May 25, 1865
MCCRUM, William	Jennie French	26 Apr 1860	May 3, 1860
MCDONOUGH, Toney	Ellen (or Catherine) Shulteton	17 Nov 1860	Nov 22, 1860
MCKINLY, Charles	Mary E. Squires	last Wed	Aug 31, 1865

Groom's Name	Bride's Name	Date of marriage	Date of newspaper
MCMILLAN, George	Julia A. Weeks	5 Nov 1867	Nov 14, 1867
MCMILLIN, John H.	Mary Doxey	22 Apr 1876	May 4, 1876
MCQUEEN, William	Kate Weeks	13 Sep 1872	Sep 26, 1872
MCWILLIAMS, Benard	Sarah Elizabeth Rhodes	6 Jun 1858	Jun 10, 1858
MEAD, Absalom	Harriet A. Robbins	26 Jul 1867	Aug 8, 1867
MERRILL, Benjamin	Josie W. Merrill	28 Apr 1864	May 5, 1864
MERRILL, George	Emma Fitz Randolph Laing	8 Oct 1862	Oct 9, 1862
MERRITT, Smith	Ann M. Barto	26th ult	Apr 13, 1865
MESEROLE, Abraham	Kathryn M. Meserole	9 Dec 1858	Dec 23, 1858
METCALFE, Andrew W.	Kate M. Lee	18 Jan 1875	Jan 21, 1875
MEYERS, Julius George Nichol	Alice Emma Amblerman	25 Dec 1867	Dec 26, 1867
MEYNEN, J. F.	M. Louise Kissam	5 Jan 1859	Jan 13, 1859
MILES, Wm A.	Victorine Wo(r)therspoon	5th inst	Oct 19, 1865
MILLER, Benjamin F.	Elizabeth Ackerly	10 May 1865	May 18, 1865
MILLER, JR., John	Mary Story	1 Jan 1862	Feb 6, 1862
MILLER, Richard B.	Charlotte Baldwin	Wednesday	Apr 9, 1863
MILLER, William S.	Abby Ann Miller	21 Jun 1865	Jun 29, 1865
MILLS, Edwin A.	Mary E. Newton	25th inst	Jan 5, 1865
MILLS, John J.	Sarah Anna Bedell	8 Jan 1868	Jan 16, 1868
MILLS, Joseph	Emma H. Hendrickson	27 Jul 1864	Aug 4, 1864
MILLS, Robert Sidney	Esther Losee	21 Jul 1858	Jul 22, 1858
MITCHELL, --?--	Emma A. Smith (?)	no date	Nov 22, 1877
MITCHELL, George	Mary Hegeman	27 Feb 1861	Mar 14, 1861
MOLLINEUX, John J.	Francis Fowler	14 Feb 1872	Feb 22, 1872
MONTGOMERY, David	Francis Gertrude Pine	14 Jul 1872	Jul 18, 1872
MONTROSS, John H.	Mary E. Abrams	7 Nov 1869	Nov 11, 1869
MOORE, George	Matilda McGill	no date	Feb 13, 1862
MOORE, Herbert H.	Anna E. Webb	18 Dec 1877	Dec 20, 1877
MOORE, William C.	Lucille P. Lu Gar	13 Nov 1872	Nov 21, 1872
MORGAN, John Allen	Jemmima Ann Bayard	21 Sep 1870	Sep 29, 1870
MORLAND, Samuel I.	Ann Ganley	7 Feb 1861	Feb 14, 1861
MORRIS, William H.	Phebe A. Mott	1 Nov 1864	Nov 3, 1864
MORRISON, Windfield Scott	Pati Way	16 Feb 1870	Aug 11, 1870
MORSE, William	Amanda Elizabeth Carman	8 Dec 1867	Dec 26, 1867
MORSE, Zechariah	Phebe Jane Carman	19 Jan 1868	Jan 23, 1868
MOTT, Denton	Ella Reynolds	12 Jan 1868	Jan 23, 1868
MOTT, George	Ellen Shaw	31 Oct 1861	Nov 7, 1861
MOTT, Henry	Emily Shaw	12 Jun 1861	Jul 25, 1861
MOTT, Theodore	Emma Hentz	23 Feb 1864	Feb 25; 1864
MOTT, Thomas	Martha H. Willets	4d 12m 1st	Dec 9, 1869
MOTT, William H.	Sarah W. Alberson	31 May 1865	Jun 8, 1865
MOULD, Richard	Ann Harpell	17 Aug 1858	Sep 9, 1858
MULGANNON, Michael	Bridget Murray	21 Nov 1869	Dec 2, 1869
MUNCEY, Jesse C.	Sarah M. Ketcham	26 Feb 1861	Mar 21, 1861
MURPHY, Peter N.	Fanny Wilson	11 Mar 1863	Mar 19, 1863
MURPHY, William	Martha Pilkington	17th inst	Jul 15, 1858
MURRAY, James	Fanny Flemmings	2nd inst	Jun 14, 1860
MURRAY, James H.	Ellen Tuttle	10 Sep 1865	Sep 21, 1865
MURRAY, Nathaniel	Anna Maria Jackson	1 Oct 1864	Oct 15, 1864
MYERS, Alfred E.	Mary Moffat	3 Jun 1873	Jun 12, 1873
NEALS, Joseph	Fanny Powell	9 Jun 1858	Jun 17, 1858
NEMOIN, Jean Louis	Mary A. Cornell	21 Nov 1874	Dec 3, 1874
NESBITT, Henry I.	Annie Grace	17 Dec 1861	Dec 19, 1861
NEWTON, Isaac	Harriet Gildersleeve, (Mrs)	27 Jan 1870	Feb 3, 1870

Groom's Name	Bride's Name	Date of marriage	Date of newspaper
NEWTON, John W.	Elizabeth Hendrickson	23 Dec 1874	Dec 24, 1874
NIX, George W.	Addie B. Davidson	26 Sep 1877	Sep 27, 1877
NO NAME,	Cunningham, (Mrs)	no date	Aug 9, 1860
NO NAME,	Porter, (Mrs)	no date	Nov 22, 1860
NOHEARN, Ignatius	Catharine Post	3rd inst	Jun 13, 1861
NOLAN, Michael	Catherine Kogan	6 Jan 1878	Jan 31, 1878
NOON, Elbert	Catherine Gritman	23 Aug 1864	Aug 25, 1864
NOON, George D.	Cassie A. Curtis	21 Jan 1872	Jan 25, 1872
NORRIS, William S.	R. Annie Duryea	25 Apr 1877	May 3, 1877
NORTHRUP, Calvin M.	Eliza White	30 Jul 1864	Aug 4, 1864
NORTON, Francis	M. Josephine King	3 Oct 1858	Oct 14, 1858
NORTON, John E.	Esther H. Gildersleeve	18 Nov 1867	Nov 21, 1867
NOSTRAND, Smith	Georgiana Dickinson	2 Jan 1860	Jan 12, 1860
O'BRIEN, John	Indian squaw	ca. 1746	Sep 13, 1860
O'CONNER, William	Bridget Renslla	6 Jul 1861	Aug 1, 1861
ODION, Henry W.	Bertha Spooner	31 Oct 1878	Nov 14, 1878
OLDRIN, Edward, Jr.	Helena Jane McDonald	3 Jul 1867	Jul 18, 1867
OLDRIN, J. Merwin	Clara S. Randall	10 Nov 1869	Nov 18, 1869
OLDS, Daniel S.	Emma Stuart	21 Dec 1863	Jan 7, 1864
OLIVER, Anthony	Esther Ann Thompson	14 Oct 1869	Nov 4, 1869
OLIVER, Arthur D.	Mary F. Moore	6 Nov 1867	Nov 14, 1867
OLIVER, Thos S.	Martha A. Whaley	3 Aug 1864	Aug 11, 1864
ONDERDONK, Benjamin	Caroline Pomeroy	25 Jul 1875	Jul 29, 1875
ONDERDONK, Horatio G.	Anna K. Cortelyou	28 Jan 1859	Feb 3, 1859
OSBORN, Thomas G.	Maria J. Cook	no date	Sep 16, 1858
OVERTON, John C.	Maria Adelia Sherman	no date	Nov 4, 1858
PAFF, George	Charlotte Leonard	15 Aug 1861	Aug 22, 1861
PAFF, George N.	Sarah Amelia Leonard	no date	Dec 27, 1877
PAFF, Townsend D.	Kate Smith	7th inst	Dec 21, 1865
PAGAN, James	Elizabeth Gillen	22nd inst	Dec 6, 1860
PAILING, Richard	Ann Eliza Smith	14 May 1859	May 19, 1859
PALMER, Benjamin W.	Sarah A. Cropsey, (Mrs)	8 Jun 1858	Jun 17, 1858
PALSEY, William	Elizabeth Ann Belknap	30 Dec 1871	Jan 4, 1872
PARKER, William Ayer	Maria Bayard Moore	5 Aug 1874	Aug 13, 1874
PARSON, John	Catherine Miller	no date	Oct 28, 1875
PARSONS, Homer	Lizzie Smith	3 Mar 1874	Mar 5, 1874
PATTERSON, William H.	Ann Augusta Smith	29 Oct 1873	Nov 6, 1873
PEARSALL, Carman	Sarah Eliza Raynor	10 Nov 1865	Nov 16, 1865
PEARSALL, Charles	Mary Ann Wright	1 Sep 1859	Sep 15, 1859
PEARSALL, Charles	Mary Hewlett	16 Oct 1878	Oct 24, 1878
PEARSALL, De Mott	Elizabeth Herkenstein	15 Jun 1873	Jun 19, 1873
PEARSALL, Ed W.	Emma Simonson	1 Nov 1871	Nov 9, 1871
PEARSALL, J. W.	S. Willets	no date	Nov 16, 1865
PEARSALL, Jarvis	Mary Amanda Abrams	25 Dec 1859	Dec 29, 1859
PEARSALL, Joseph	Lydia Rhodes	28 Dec 1862	Jan 8, 1863
PEARSALL, Mahlon F.	Sarah Mann	19 Sep 1870	Sep 29, 1870
PEARSALL, Pierre W.	Nellie Pierce	2 Aug 1861	Aug 8, 1861
PEARSALL, Robert	Mary Wood	28 Mar 1863	May 14, 1863
PEARSALL, W.	Amanda Pearsall	5 Jun 1859	Jun 9, 1859
PEARSALL, W.	Mary Ann Farrington	9 Jul 1865	Jul 13, 1865
PECK, George L.	Fanny C. Fosdick	15 Sep 1864	Sep 22, 1864
PECK, Henry C.	Temmey A. Mills	no date	Aug 26, 1858
PECK, Jonathan	Sarah Elizabeth Searing	20 Feb 1878	Feb 21, 1878
PECKHAM, Zebulon	Susan Smith	8 Oct 1863	Oct 29, 1863
PERRY, Thomas F.	Lucinda Merritt	1 Oct 1865	Oct 5, 1865

Groom's Name	Bride's Name	Date of marriage	Date of newspaper
PETTIT, Charles	Mary Amanda Brower	15 Jan 1862	Jan 23, 1862
PETTIT, Cornell N.	Margaret E. Sprague	19 Jun 1859	Jun 23, 1859
PETTIT, Daniel T.	Emma R. Keator	10 Sep 1872	Sep 12, 1872
PETTIT, Edward G.	Cornelia Lawrence	20 Jun 1867	Jun 27, 1867
PETTIT, Francis	Kate Alvin	22 Mar 1862	Mar 27, 1862
PETTIT, John S.	Sarah E. Simonson	15 Mar 1865	Mar 23, 1865
PETTIT, Stephen B.	Gussie Stout	20 Apr 1864	Apr 28, 1864
PETTIT, Winfield	Ada Carlisle	14 Sep 1870	Sep 22, 1870
PHARAOH, Sylvester	Jerushia Putnam	18 Mar 1861	Mar 28, 1861
PHILLIPS, John Henry	Maria Lewis	18 Apr 1859	Apr 21, 1859
PINDER, Edward	(dau. of Austin) Bellows	23 Nov 1870	Nov 24, 1870
PINE, Albert B.	Emma E. Richards	12 Sep 1867	Sep 19, 1867
PINE, Edward	Susie Cornell	15 May 1871	Jun 15, 1871
PINE, Nicholas	Elsie A. Sylvester	9 May 1875	May 20, 1875
PINE, Smith	Susan Duryea	22 Jan 1868	Jan 30, 1868
PINE, William H.	Mattie M. Randall	19 Aug 1868	Sep 3, 1868
PINKHAM, Joseph	Annie M. Vanderwater	27 Nov 1873	Dec 4, 1873
PITTS, George	Mary Elizabeth James	30 Jun 1863	Jul 9, 1863
PLACE, Daniel S.	Julia Ann Parsons	10 Sep 1861	Sep 19, 1861
PLACE, William S.	Anselina Sprague	21 Nov 1869	Dec 23, 1869
PLATT, Elias S.	Carrie Child	24 Oct 1867	Nov 7, 1867
PLATT, Henry C.	Jennie Dusenberry	1 Jun 1864	Jun 9, 1864
POLLEY, William L.	Joan Hedges	no date	Sep 16, 1858
POPE, Howard A.	Jennie G. Radford	14 Sep 1870	Sep 22, 1870
PORTER, James S.	Mary A. Rowland	no date	May 26, 1859
POST, (Dr)	No name	recently	Aug 9, 1877
POST, Burtsall J.	Anna Gildersleeve	28 Apr 1863	Apr 30, 1863
POST, Jeremiah	Phebe Pearsall	27 Oct 1861	Oct 31, 1861
POST, Mordecai R.	Emma SMITH	19 Jan 1868	Jan 23, 1868
POST, Samuel	Emma Pettit	18 Jun 1872	Jun 27, 1872
POST, William	Mary A. Willis	18 Oct 1877	Nov 8, 1877
POST, Wm. F.	Matilda Knight	no date	Jul 8, 1858
POWELL, Andrew	Phebe Jane Seaman	6 Sep 1865	Sep 14, 1865
POWELL, Andrew J.	Sarah Jane Mulford	20 Apr 1859	Apr 28, 1859
POWELL, Charles A.	Martha W. Smith	7 May 1863	May 14, 1863
POWELL, Charles C.	S. Gertrude Burt	23 Nov 1876	Nov 30, 1876
POWELL, Henry	Lina L. Remsen	6 Mar 1872	Mar 14, 1872
POWELL, Henry	Mary E. Monfort	6 Nov 1867	Nov 14, 1867
POWELL, Henry	Nettie Remsen	25 Oct 1877	Nov 8, 1877
POWELL, James	Cornelia Wood	25 Dec 1860	Dec 27, 1860
POWELL, Richard Giles	Lucy Jane Oliver	19 Aug 1858	Aug 26, 1858
POWELL, Robert	Permelia Snedeker	13 Jul 1858	Jul 15, 1858
POWELL, Stuyvesant	--?-- Wiggins	Thursday	Sep 26, 1878
POWELL, Walt	Kate Maxon	17 Feb 1869	Mar 11, 1869
POWELL, William R.	Maggie Greenfield	21 Apr 1869	Apr 22, 1869
POWERS, Bernard	Kate Taylor	28 Feb 1870	Mar 17, 1870
POWERS, Dennis	Mary Ann Nolan	18 Jul 1858	Jul 22, 1858
PRAY, Elias L.	Prisella A. Prior	22 Nov 1871	Nov 30, 1871
PRAY, William T.	Adelia M. Bardin	8 Nov 1871	Nov 16, 1871
PREAY, John W.	Cordelia A. Rushmore	24 Jan 1859	Jan 27, 1859
PRENTICE, William	Fannie Mirdyth	no date	Aug 26, 1858
PRIDE, Thomas	Elizabeth Mittington	16 Nov 1865	Nov 23, 1865
PROVO, Moses	Amanda Fuller	no date	Feb 3, 1876
PULLIS, John	Antoinette Lowden	18 Nov 1868	Nov 26, 1868
PUNDERSON, George M.	Lucy M. Davis	no date	Aug 12, 1858
PURDY, Seth P.	Sarah E. Smith	6 Mar 1861	Mar 21, 1861
PYE, George H.	Catherine A. Hedges	2 Mar 1863	Apr 2, 1863

Groom's Name	Bride's Name	Date of marriage	Date of newspaper
QUARITIUS, John	Friederica Zeuner	17 Jun 1860	Jun 21, 1860
RAMSDEN, Thomas T.	Emma Wright	22 May 1870	May 26, 1870
RANCE, Thomas	Susan N. Neil	7 May 1859	May 19, 1859
RANDALL, Frank L.	Carrie Estelle Bradley	3 Oct 1877	Oct 11, 1877
RAYNOR, Abraham	Susan Henry	3rd ult	Aug 3, 1865
RAYNOR, Alansen	Charlotte Bedell	4 Jan 1865	Jan 19, 1865
RAYNOR, Bedell D.	Elmira A. Raynor	6 Jan 1870	Jan 13, 1870
RAYNOR, Frances	Elizabeth Raynor	4 Jul 1858	Jul 8, 1858
RAYNOR, Francis	Elizabeth A. Southard	12 Apr 1865	Apr 27, 1865
RAYNOR, George Henry	Marietta Smith	10th inst	Nov 22, 1860
RAYNOR, James B.	Celia Story	29 Dec 1869	Jan 6, 1870
RAYNOR, John	Althusa Combs	7 Aug 1863	Oct 22, 1863
RAYNOR, John F.	Anna A. Rhodes	27 Oct 1869	Nov 11, 1869
RAYNOR, Joseph	Mary P. Verity	3 Nov 1870	Nov 10, 1870
RAYNOR, Joseph	Rachael Nostrand, (Mrs)	24 Nov 1864	Dec 15, 1864
RAYNOR, Moroni	Mary Jane Wilson	8 Oct 1871	Oct 12, 1871
RAYNOR, Oliver	Elizabeth Ann Smith	13 Jan 1864	Jan 21, 1864
RAYNOR, W. M.	Sarah J. Carman	5 Apr 1861	Apr 25, 1861
RAYNOR, William	--?-- Whitmore	recently	Sep 6, 1877
RAYNOR, William H.	Susan Emma Baldwin	24 Oct 1871	Oct 26, 1871
REEVE, Bethnel	Josephine Payne	31 Jan 1859	Feb 10, 1859
REEVE, Walter F.	Jennie Henderson	1 Nov 1877	Nov 8, 1877
RELYEA, Jeremiah J.	Addie Pettit	18 Nov 1863	Nov 26, 1863
REMSEN, John	Josephine Curtis	24 Nov 1875	Dec 2, 1875
REMSON, David F.	Susan Jane Fish	20 Oct 1861	Oct 31, 1861
REMSON, John H.	Marietta Thompson, (Mrs)	3 Feb 1861	Feb 28, 1861
REYNOLDS, John B.	Harriet Post	17 Dec 1864	Dec 22, 1864
RHODES, Abraham D.	Catharine M. Van Sicklen	30 Jan 1868	Feb 6, 1868
RHODES, Alexander R.	Lydia Ann Combs	26th ult	Mar 9, 1865
RHODES, Andreas	Adelia A. Bedell	1 Jan 1873	Jan 9, 1873
RHODES, Andrew	Angeline Baldwin, (Mrs)	19 Nov 1864	Dec 15, 1864
RHODES, Charles W.	H. Agnes Ketcham	10 Nov 1870	Nov 17, 1870
RHODES, Charles William	Mary Elizabeth Mowbray	26 Feb 1861	Feb 28, 1861
RHODES, George H.	Mary Noon	7 Dec 1873	Dec 11, 1873
RHODES, Jacob	Annietta Losea	16 Jan 1862	Jan 23, 1862
RHODES, McDonald H.	Hannah J. Vanvickler	1 Mar 1859	May 5, 1859
RHODES, Thomas	Emma Watts	25 Jan 1873	Apr 24, 1873
RHODES, Thomas H.	Louise T. Dinnin	8 Oct 1870	Oct 13, 1870
RHODES, William H.	Julia E. Watts	24 May 1877	May 31, 1877
RHODES, William L.	Mary A. Jackson	20 May 1863	May 28, 1863
RICHARDSON, Leonard	S. Louisa Cole	24 Jun 1858	Jul 1, 1858
RIDER, George	Susan A. Frost	18 Dec 1862	Jan 8, 1863
RIDER, Silas	Eliza Johnson	14 Oct 1863	Oct 29, 1863
RIDER, William P.	Harriet E. Johnson	12 Jan 1871	Jan 19, 1871
RITCHIE, John Henry	Arabella Mcdowell	24 Jul 1876	Aug 10, 1876
RITCHIE, Joseph	Susan Amelia Combs	10th inst	Dec 28, 1865
ROBBINS, George A.	Annie M. Skidmore	25 Dec 1867	Jan 2, 1868
ROBBINS, John	Selinda E. Smith	no date	Jun 24, 1858
ROBERTS, George H.	Maria Pettit	7 Feb 1877	Feb 15, 1877
ROBINSON, A. S.	Kate A. Weaver	29 Jun 1871	Jul 20, 1871
ROBINSON, Charles K.	Anna McLaughlin	27 Oct 1876	Nov 2, 1876
ROBINSON, Christopher D.	Jennie A. Bennet	25th inst	Apr 2, 1863
ROGERS, Alexander	Sarah E. Moore, (Mrs)	19 Aug 1872	Sep 12, 1872
ROGERS, Henry	Youphenia Cuffee	no date	Aug 5, 1858
ROOF, Stephen W.	Tillie Venn	3 Aug 1864	Aug 11, 1864
ROSE, William	Martha Jane Cornelius	30 Apr 1865	May 11, 1865
ROSS, James	Maria Champion	10 Aug 1858	Aug 19, 1858

Groom's Name	Bride's Name	Date of marriage	Date of newspaper
ROUSE, Fredrick W.	Fannie A. Fanning	17 Oct 1877	Oct 25, 1877
ROUSE, Gilbert	Judy O'Flanegan	no date	Mar 26, 1862
RUDGARD, Henry T.	Ellen Combs	30 Jul 1865	Aug 10, 1865
RUNCIE, John T.	Amelia Cozine	16 Oct 1878	Oct 24, 1878
RUSCO, John S.	Mary E. Johnson	19 Aug 1858	Sep 2, 1858
RUSHMORE, James D.	Katie J. Skidmore	15 Jun 1873	Jun 19, 1873
RUSHMORE, Lewis E.	Ella L. Williams	17 Apr 1878	Apr 18, 1878
RUSHMORE, Thomas T.	Louisa Amelia Mayher	4 Oct 1877	Oct 11, 1877
RUSHMORE, Wilbur F.	Sarah Elizabeth Ketcham	25 Jan 1865	Jan 26, 1865
RUSHMORE, William H.	Fannie A. Snedeker	6 Sep 1865	Sep 7, 1865
RYDER, Lewis C.	Elizabeth Anna Snedeker	2 Mar 1864	Mar 10, 1864
SAHLMULLER, August	Regina Tessercher	18 Feb 1861	Feb 28, 1861
SAMMIS, Ezra N.	Charlotte R. Sammis	no date	Oct 27, 1864
SAMMIS, Seaman	Mary Abrams	24 Aug 1875	Sep 9, 1875
SAMMIS, William	--?-- Wilkins	last Wed	Oct 27, 1864
SAYRES, William J.	Phebe S. Huntting	21 Jun 1865	Jun 29, 1865
SCHELLENGER, David W.	Jennette A. Bassett	no date	Nov 11, 1858
SCHENCK, M. Warren	A. Louisa Bode	no date	Nov 1, 1877
SCHULTZ, Frederick	Jane Louisa Watts	19 Jan 1872	Jan 25, 1872
SCOTT, Francis Vaugh	Ann Eliza Brennin	19 Dec 1869	Dec 23, 1869
SCOTT, George	Mary Ann Kirwan	5 Aug 1858	Aug 12, 1858
SCUDDER, Reuben N.	Josephine Baldwin	1 Sep 1859	Sep 15, 1859
SEABURY, Albert H.	Eliza C. Place	7 Nov 1872	Nov 14, 1872
SEABURY, Albert Hentz	Elizabeth Mollineaux	15 Oct 1862	Oct 23, 1862
SEABURY, Charles H.	Jennie Haff	8 Oct 1877	Oct 11, 1877
SEABURY, John H.	Mattie Sayers	29 Jan 1875	Feb 4, 1875
SEALEY, John E.	Phebe E. Cox	31 Aug 1870	Sep 8, 1870
SEALEY, Sylvester	Martha A. Willets	11 Sep 1872	Sep 19, 1872
SEAMAN, Benjamin H.	Elizabeth Helen Townsend	20 Jan 1863	Jan 22, 1863
SEAMAN, Charles	Amelia E. Walker	3 Nov 1869	Nov 25, 1869
SEAMAN, Charles C.	Phebe Ann Conway	1 Mar 1868	Mar 5, 1868
SEAMAN, Charles H.	Mary E. Post	3 Jan 1864	Jan 14, 1864
SEAMAN, Cornelius	Nancy Stiverson	26th ult	Nov 3, 1859
SEAMAN, Daniel P.	Julia C. Lane	5 May 1872	May 9, 1872
SEAMAN, Franklin P.	Mary V. Hicks	19 Nov 1878	Dec 5, 1878
SEAMAN, Furman R.	Isabella E. Smith	5 Jan 1870	Jan 6, 1870
SEAMAN, James Henry	Martha Jane Jackson	10 Feb 1877	Feb 22, 1877
SEAMAN, John	Elizabeth Jane Robbins	11 Dec 1871	Dec 14, 1871
SEAMAN, John H.	Mary E. Pettit	1 Jun 1875	Jun 17, 1875
SEAMAN, John L.	Mary Jane Smith	20 Nov 1867	Nov 28, 1867
SEAMAN, John W.	Phebe S. Smith	30 Dec 1869	Feb 10, 1870
SEAMAN, Platt W.	Sarah M. Burger	24 Mar 1864	Apr 21, 1864
SEAMAN, Richard J.	Sarah Ann Tappan	23 Jun 1858	Jul 15, 1858
SEAMAN, T. Edward	Anna R. Coon	18 Jan 1870	Jan 20, 1870
SEAMAN, Thomas	Ann A. Von Nostrand	28 Feb 1865	Mar 30, 1865
SEAMAN, Thomas H.	Mary Emma Henderson	15 Apr 1868	Apr 16, 1868
SEAMAN, William Edgar	Josie Anna Van de Water	17 Dec 1878	Dec 26, 1878
SEAMAN, William H.	Mary F. Lane	12 Jan 1868	Jan 16, 1868
SEAMAN, William H.	Sarah E. Post	no date	Mar 19, 1868
SEAMAN, William T.	Hester Jane Gardiner	28 May 1859	Jun 2, 1859
SEAMAN, Zebulon W.	Maria Louisa Platt, (Mrs)	28 Jul 1858	Aug 5, 1858
SEARING, Alfred	Catherine J. Fish	22 Feb 1859	Mar 10, 1859
SEARING, John Alfred	Ella Russell	26 Sep 1876	Oct 5, 1876
SEARING, Samuel V.	Annie A. Searing	3rd inst	May 17, 1860
SEARLES, John E.	Caroline A. Pettit	3 Apr 1862	Apr 10, 1862
SECOR, Theodore	Jenny Unckles	28 Oct 1869	Nov 18, 1869

Groom's Name	Bride's Name	Date of marriage	Date of newspaper
SELOVER, John W.	Sarah E. Bacon	no date	Jan 27, 1859
SHAW, Benjamin	Hester Ann Carman	13 Sep 1865	Sep 21, 1865
SHAW, David	Lydia Shaw	6 Nov 1865	Nov 16, 1865
SHAW, George	Lavinia Sprague	13 Feb 1861	Feb 21, 1861
SHAW, John Henry	Lucy A. Pearsall	27 Nov 1864	Dec 8, 1864
SHAW, Samuel	Sarah Elizabeth Gorman	2nd inst	Aug 10, 1865
SHAW, William	Lydia A. O'Donell	5 Oct 1859	Oct 13, 1859
SHAW, William H.	Martha J. DeMott	3 Nov 1861	Nov 7, 1861
SHAW, William Henry	Elizabeth Ann Raynor	6 Dec 1864	Dec 8, 1864
SHEPHERD, Gilbert W.	Mary E. Cooper	4th inst	Apr 18, 1861
SHERMAN, Samuel J.	Frances A. Cornwell	25 Nov 1863	Dec 3, 1863
SHIPHERD, Jacob R.	Laura E. Hyman, (Mrs)	9 Mar 1878	Mar 21, 1878
SHOTWELL, Hugh W.	Rosamond Pettit	28 Sep 1859	Sep 29, 1859
SIMMONS, Henry	Jane Stevenson	23 Nov 1867	Jan 9, 1868
SIMONSON, Charles M.	Sarah Elizabeth Firth	14 Oct 1874	Oct 22, 1874
SIMONSON, James B.	Jennie Hewlett	13th inst	Aug 20, 1868
SIMONSON, John	Ann Maria Vail	7 Sep 1859	Sep 15, 1859
SIMONSON, John H.	Josie Syler	16 May 1876	Jun 1, 1876
SIMONSON, John H.	Lucinda Davison	2 Mar 1862	Mar 20, 1862
SIPE, A. J.	Mary S. Wells	20 Sep 1858	Oct 21, 1858
SKIDMORE, C. Fred	Lillian Simonson	20 Jun 1877	Jun 28, 1877
SKIDMORE, David	Susan M. Snedeker	26th ult	Aug 3, 1865
SKIDMORE, John	Mary Thorne Bedell	19 Nov 1865	Nov 23, 1865
SKIDMORE, Samuel R.	Mary A. Reed	19 Feb 1863	Feb 26, 1863
SKIDMORE, Willets	Mary H. Ellison	18 Jun 1876	Jun 22, 1876
SKIDMORE, William	Minnie Forgie	7 Sep 1870	Sep 22, 1870
SKILLIN, Henry T.	Sarah Elizabeth Albertson	22 Jun 1864	Jun 30, 1864
SKILLMAN, Francis	Josephine D. Onderdonk	16 May 1865	May 25, 1865
SKINNER, Ezekiel D.	Nettie A. Hallock	9 Feb 1876	Feb 17, 1876
SKINNER, Peter	Kate Philo	24th inst	Dec 1, 1864
SLOSSEN, Henry V.	Alice Vandewater	6 Dec 1865	Dec 21, 1865
SMITH, Abraham H.	Ann Louise Lott	18 Jul 1865	Jul 27, 1865
SMITH, Albert D.	Phebe R. Ketcham	20 Jul 1865	Jul 27, 1865
SMITH, Alfred	Sarah Duryea	26 Dec 1863	Jan 14, 1864
SMITH, Alonzo R.	Phebe Ann Soper	3 Jan 1864	Jan 21, 1864
SMITH, Arrender	Emma Smith	5 Feb 1865	Feb 23, 1865
SMITH, Benjamin F.	Josephine Smith	20 Jul 1875	Aug 12, 1875
SMITH, Calvin L.	Jennie A. Skidmore	16 Feb 1875	Apr 1, 1875
SMITH, Carman	Ellen Raynor	21 Jun 1865	Jul 13, 1865
SMITH, Charles A.	Catharine Coleman	no date	Aug 26, 1858
SMITH, Charles E.	Anna Augusta Layton	7 Dec 1858	Dec 16, 1858
SMITH, Charles E.	Martha Augusta Abrams	4 Nov 1869	Nov 11, 1869
SMITH, Chauncey	Cornelia Ann Mott	8th inst	Jul 19, 1860
SMITH, D. Lowber	Sophia A. Kirkpatrick	13 Feb 1873	Feb 20, 1873
SMITH, Daniel	Sarah Abrams	25 Jan 1865	Feb 9, 1865
SMITH, Daniel A.	Mary C. A. Pearsall	13 Nov 1867	Nov 21, 1867
SMITH, Daniel C.	Charlotte Smith	11 Aug 1858	Aug 19, 1858
SMITH, Daniel D.	Annie D. De Mott	5 Mar 1876	Mar 16, 1876
SMITH, Daniel K.	Hester A. Wright	13 Mar 1865	Apr 27, 1865
SMITH, Egbert T.	Annie M. Robinson	no date	Jun 17, 1858
SMITH, Francis E.	Mary J. Russell	no date	Sep 16, 1858
SMITH, George	Ann T. Smith	17 Apr 1864	Apr 21, 1864
SMITH, George	Hattie A. Pitt	28 Sep 1875	Sep 30, 1875
SMITH, George D.	Georgie Mott	27 Jun 1877	Jul 12, 1877
SMITH, Gilbert H.	Ann Amelia Brower	28 Jun 1863	Jul 9, 1863
SMITH, Henry	Eliza Ann Pettit, (Mrs)	4 Jun 1865	Jun 15, 1865
SMITH, Henry A.	Susie Van Nostrand	18 Oct 1865	Oct 26, 1865
SMITH, Henry J.	Katie Gilbert	24 May 1871	Jun 1, 1871

Groom's Name	Bride's Name	Date of marriage	Date of newspaper
SMITH, Henry Wagner	Mary Wood	18 Jun 1878	Jun 20, 1878
SMITH, Hewlett	Susan Moore	9th inst	Feb 17, 1859
SMITH, Hiram	Charlotte M. Vanvelsor	30 Aug 1865	Sep 7, 1865
SMITH, Holdridge	Lucinda Jackson	12 Nov 1865	Nov 16, 1865
SMITH, Horace B.	Maria Ellison	19 Oct 1873	Nov 6, 1873
SMITH, James	Isabella M. Mott	23 Sep 1860	Oct 4, 1860
SMITH, James	Isabella McMorrow	23rd inst	Sep 27, 1860
SMITH, James T.	Emma B. Moseman	20 Jan 1864	Feb 11, 1864
SMITH, John A.	Augusta Baisley	10 Dec 1863	Dec 24, 1863
SMITH, John B.	Ann Elizabeth Frost	17 Apr 1870	May 5, 1870
SMITH, John H.	Margarette Ann Lane	31 Dec 1870	Jan 5, 1871
SMITH, Martin P.	Sarah A. Smith	31 Jun 1871	Jun 22, 1871
SMITH, Melville A.	Georgiana Curtis	23 Jul 1864	Aug 4, 1864
SMITH, Merritt	Susan A. Jackson	6 Sep 1873	Sep 11, 1873
SMITH, Mordecai A.	Mary A. Smith	28 Sep 1860	Nov 8, 1860
SMITH, Nathaniel	Celestine S. Wilson	30 Mar 1865	Apr 6, 1865
SMITH, Nathaniel	Esther Ann Frost	2 Oct 1878	Oct 24, 1878
SMITH, Raynor R.	Ann Maria Storey	20 Nov 1859	Nov 24, 1859
SMITH, Robert	Caroline Weekes	6 Mar 1873	Apr 10, 1873
SMITH, Robert H.	Martha J. Powell	14 Oct 1860	Nov 1, 1860
SMITH, Sylvester	Margaretta Powell	28 Dec 1864	Jan 5, 1865
SMITH, Sylvester S.	Emma C. Smith	2nd inst	Dec 9, 1869
SMITH, Thomas	Gussie Howland	25 Oct 1865	Nov 9, 1865
SMITH, Thomas	Mary Louisa Prink	17 Jun 1875	Jun 24, 1875
SMITH, Thomas D.	Kate Freyenhagen	13th inst	Sep 21, 1865
SMITH, Thomas L.	Mary Adelaide Pearsall	1 Nov 1864	Nov 3, 1864
SMITH, Tredwell	(Mrs. Charles) Dikeman	no date	Dec 19, 1878
SMITH, Valentine	Charlotte Craft	no date	Nov 30, 1865
SMITH, William H.	Phebe Ann Combs	18 Feb 1870	Feb 24, 1870
SMITH, William H. S.	Mamie H.W. Smith	17 Dec 1873	Dec 25, 1873
SMITH, William T.	Annie Titus	3 Oct 1878	Oct 10, 1878
SNEDEKER, Isaac	Eliza Bailey, (Mrs)	24 Apr 1865	May 4, 1865
SNEDEKER, J. Seymour	S. Jennie Rushmore	9 Sep 1874	Sep 17, 1874
SNEDEKER, S.N.	Jennie E. Hutton	12 Nov 1873	Nov 20, 1873
SNIFFIN, Alpheus L.	Sarah M. McCauly	15 Jun 1858	Jun 24, 1858
SNIPE, --?--	Mary Wells	no date	Oct 14, 1858
SOPER, Carman	Henrietta Bedell	1 Jan 1864	Jan 21, 1864
SOPER, Charles T.	Charlotte Miller	no date	Jun 27, 1872
SOPER, Joseph	Sarah Pettit	2 Oct 1860	Oct 25, 1860
SOREN, Mortense	Metha Emine Lassen	14 May 1874	May 28, 1874
SOUTH, Francis	Marianna Leuba	27 Jun 1878	Jul 4, 1878
SOUTHARD, Albert S.	Martha A. Cheshire	28 Oct 1878	Oct 31, 1878
SOUTHARD, Daniel R.	Lydia A. Golder	23 Dec 1867	Jan 9, 1868
SOUTHARD, Henry	Emma Thomas	5 Oct 1873	Nov 6, 1873
SOUTHARD, John H.	Angeline Carman	14 Jun 1864	Jun 16, 1864
SOUTHARD, Warren	Hattie Wells	11 Mar 1863	Mar 19, 1863
SPOONER, Frank G.	Bertha C. M. Graeve	no date	Oct 21, 1869
SPRAGUE, Benjamin	Edith Smith	31 Mar 1878	Apr 4, 1878
SPRAGUE, Benjamin	Mary Adelaine Denton	13 Mar 1864	Apr 21, 1864
SPRAGUE, Charles W.	Hanna A. Powell	2 Mar 1873	Mar 13, 1873
SPRAGUE, Chauncey T.	Anna Augusta Duryea	10 Jan 1864	Jan 14, 1864
SPRAGUE, Johnathon	E. Hildreth, (Mrs)	9th inst	Aug 19, 1869
SPRAGUE, Welsley	Annie Hegeman	20 Jan 1874	Feb 12, 1874
STEAD, George	Louise M. Rouse	29 Sep 1873	Oct 9, 1873
STERLING, John	Frances Pedner	no date	Jul 15, 1858
STILL, Charles	Eveline Hawkins	no date	Sep 24, 1874
STILL, Smith L.	Anne M. Terry	12 Dec 1858	Jan 6, 1859
STILLINGWORTH, --?--	Loretta Weeks	23 Dec 1868	Dec 31, 1868
STILLWAGON, Thomas	Ianthe Brown	26 Nov 1863	Dec 3, 1863

Groom's Name	Bride's Name	Date of marriage	Date of newspaper
STOOTHOFF, James H.	Kate W. Powell	6 Nov 1867	Nov 21, 1867
STOOTHOFF, William	Emma E. Duryea	1 Jun 1871	Jun 8, 1871
STOOTS, W. Treadwell	Eliza J. Garvin	21 Jul 1877	Aug 2, 1877
STORER, Aaron A.	Caroline Bedell	9 Sep 1865	Sep 21, 1865
STORY, Wilbur	Julia A. Brower	31 Mar 1869	Apr 22, 1869
STRATTON, Charles	Lavinia Warren	last Tues	Feb 12, 1863
STREATOR, Charles	Bridget Brady	no date	Jul 29, 1875
STRINGHAM, James T.	Eliza McQueen	6 Aug 1865	Aug 10, 1865
STUBBS, Edwin S.	Susie E. Coffin	21 Feb 1878	Feb 28, 1878
STULL, Henry	Mamie G. Thompson	26 Mar 1872	Mar 28, 1872
SUFFERT, Anthony	Catherine Jackson	11 Oct 1874	Oct 22, 1874
SWEZY, Samuel	Sally Ann Terry	no date	Aug 26, 1858
SWORDS, Peter	Harriet Maria Bell	11 Oct 1858	Oct 14, 1858
TABER, Charles Corey	Cornelia F. Martin	3 Jun 1858	Jun 10, 1858
TAFT, Andrew E.	Annie. E. Seaman	31 May 1871	Jun 8, 1871
TAGGART, Charles	Amelia Curtis	21 Mar 1869	Mar 25, 1869
TAPPAN, Edward	Hattie Fanning	18 Aug 1868	Aug 20, 1868
TAPPEN, Edgar	Harriet A. Fanning	18th inst	Aug 27, 1868
TATE, John H.	Sarah V. Hicks	19 Dec 1867	Jan 9, 1868
TAYLOR, William Wisner	Olie R. Burtis	27 Jul 1871	Aug 10, 1871
TERRILL, Daniel	Elizabeth Abrams	6 Mar 1862	Mar 20, 1862
TERRY, Charles H.	Ency J. Benjamin	29 Dec 1858	Jan 6, 1859
TERRY, Isaac G.	Emma L. Carman	3 Jan 1878	Jan 10, 1878
TERRY, John I.	Sarah E. Buckley	no date	Jan 27, 1859
TERRY, John T.	Hannah Kinner	11 Jun 1860	Jun 28, 1860
TERRY, Wm.	(Mrs) Cowles	no date	Jul 18, 1872
TERRY, Woodhul	Emily J. Fanning	9 Dec 1858	Dec 16, 1858
THAYER, Jonathan	Phebe Valentine	10 Oct 1870	Nov 3, 1870
THOMAS, Amos	Hattie Sprague	31 Dec 1868	Mar 11, 1869
THOMAS, Sylvester	Malvina Losee	12 Oct 1873	Oct 16, 1873
THOMPSON, Charles L.	Amy E. Corse	13 Oct 1878	Oct 17, 1878
THOMPSON, David H.	Elizabeth A. Pettit	17 Nov 1870	Dec 8, 1870
THOMPSON, Frank	Sarah E. Gardiner	21 May 1870	May 26, 1870
THOMPSON, George M.	Esther Jane Wood	16 Oct 1869	Nov 4, 1869
THORNELL, John T.	Ellen Supple	27 Oct 1867	Nov 7, 1867
TILLY, George E.	Mary Brown	11 Sep 1876	Sep 21, 1876
TIMPSON, Charles S.	Carrie Cruikshank	9 Dec 1874	Dec 17, 1874
TITUS, David N.	Jane Ann Burt	25 May 1859	Jun 2, 1859
TITUS, George P.	Mary Townsend	17 Oct 1867	Oct 24, 1867
TITUS, Stephen	Mary E. Aldrich	no date	Oct 17, 1878
TITUS, Willet H.	Phebe Rogers	18 Jul 1864	Aug 4, 1864
TOSTEVIN, Frederick N.	Harriet Hawkridge	5 Jun 1860	Jul 12, 1860
TOTTON, Isaac	Aramantha Carman	13 Jun 1861	Jun 20, 1861
TOWNSEND, Isaac J.	Cornelia Townsend	6 Dec 1859	Dec 15, 1859
TOWNSEND, John F.	Susie J. Wright	25 Feb 1865	Mar 2, 1865
TOWNSEND, William E.	Harriet Ann Searing	30 Jun 1858	Jul 15, 1858
TOWNSEND, William Effingham	Gertrude Tredwell	28 Dec 1876	Jan 11, 1877
TREADWELL, Charles	Emeline E. Seaman	9 May 1861	May 16, 1861
TREDWELL, Timothy	Anna M. Hewlett	10 Jun 1874	Jun 18, 1874
TREVETT, Isaac Orchard	Emma Frost Harden	no date	Apr 15, 1869
TUTHILL, Samuel H.	Jerusha Ruland	12 Jan 1870	Feb 10, 1870
TWYEFFORT, L. P.	Carrie L. Kleinett	no date	Oct 29, 1868
TYLER, Charles	Ruth J. Conklin	28 Dec 1864	Jan 12, 1865
TYLERS, Edward	Rebecca C. Wright	27th ult	Jan 12, 1865

Groom's Name	Bride's Name	Date of marriage	Date of newspaper
UNDERHILL, Abraham G.	Marietta Jones	6 May 1862	May 15, 1862
UNDERHILL, George W.	Ann R. Treadwell	19 Nov 1863	Nov 26, 1863
UNDERHILL, John F.	Adelia Seaman	29 Oct 1867	Nov 7, 1867
UNDERHILL, John H.	Hattie Cruikshank	13 Dec 1876	Dec 21, 1876
UNDERHILL, John T.	Margaret Ann Hendrickson	9th inst	Feb 3, 1859
URTERMAN, Soloman	Catharine Maria Terrill	6 Mar 1862	Mar 20, 1862
VAIL, Daniel C.	Alma Gildersleeve	1 Feb 1876	Feb 17, 1876
VAIL, Henry M.	Kate R. King	no date	Sep 23, 1858
VALENTINE, Charles A.	Amanda Abrams	1 Jan 1870	Jan 6, 1870
VALENTINE, Clarence K.	Carrie Searing	30 Apr 1878	May 2, 1878
VALENTINE, Eugene	Maggie A. Van Wicklen	5 Mar 1873	Mar 27, 1873
VALENTINE, Ezekiel	Sarah Baker	29 Aug 1869	Sep 2, 1869
VALENTINE, Jackson	Jane L. Shaw	25 Dec 1865	Dec 28, 1865
VALENTINE, James	Francis Jackson	11 Sep 1859	Sep 15, 1859
VALENTINE, Silas T.	Marrianna Downing	11 Oct 1865	Oct 19, 1865
VALENTINE, Stephen, Jr.	Annie Lewis	25 Sep 1878	Oct 10, 1878
VALENTINE, William B.	Alice Hendrickson	13 Oct 1875	Oct 21, 1875
VAN AUSDALL, C.	Lottie Huil	27 Nov 1873	Dec 4, 1873
VAN DEWATER, Archibald	Emma Thorn	4 Nov 1878	Nov 14, 1878
VAN DEWATER, Robert	Elizabeth A. Smith	30 Dec 1861	Jan 2, 1862
VAN DINE, P. H.	Hattie Parsons	16 Jun 1874	Jun 18, 1874
VAN DUZEN, M. B.	M. Belle Terry	27 Jun 1878	Jul 4, 1878
VAN GORDEN, James H.	Clara M. Van Brocklyn	29 Mar 1876	Apr 6, 1876
VAN NOSTRAND, John	Caroline Bradshaw	12 Nov 1858	Nov 18, 1858
VAN NOSTRAND, John S.	Phebe A. H--?--	25 May 1871	Jun 1, 1871
VAN NOSTRAND, William	Betsey Corwin	11 Aug 1858	Aug 19, 1858
VAN NOSTRAND, William	Sarah Van De Water	2 Aug 1877	Aug 9, 1877
VAN NOSTRAND, William Layton	Susie D. Place	2 Dec 1869	Dec 9, 1869
VAN RONK, Cornelius	Mary E. Thompson	25 May 1865	Jul 13, 1865
VAN SICKLEN, Court J.	Annie E. Sammis	no date	Nov 6, 1873
VAN SICKLEN, James	Gertrude R. Lott	2 Aug 1864	Aug 11, 1864
VAN VELSOR, G. B.	Esther Bedell	25 Feb 1864	Mar 3, 1864
VAN WICKLEN, Cornelius	Ruth A. Mott	5 Oct 1865	Oct 19, 1865
VAN WICKLER, John H.	Sarah E. Van Wickler	18 Aug 1872	Aug 22, 1872
VAN WICKLIN, George	Sarah Layton	4 Mar 1861	Mar 28, 1861
VAN WYCK, T. C.	Lizzie Willets	1 Jan 1874	Jan 15, 1874
VANDERBERG, John	Elizabeth Stone, (Mrs)	last Wed	Sep 21, 1865
VANDERGAW, David	Gussie Vail	17th inst	Aug 27, 1868
VANDEWATER, C. Livingston	Nellie Sanders	21 Dec 1875	Dec 30, 1875
VANDEWATER, Daniel	Anna Fleming	9 Jul 1864	Jul 21, 1864
VANDEWATER, Devine H.	J. Louisa Valentine	10 Nov 1877	Nov 29, 1877
VANDEWATER, Edgar H.	Agnes Mott	9 Jun 1863	Jul 2, 1863
VANDEWATER, Peter C.	Mary Libbie Hewlett	6 Oct 1868	Oct 29, 1868
VANNOSTRAND, Aaron	Mary Elizabeth Dunlap	5 May 1859	May 19, 1859
VANNOSTRAND, David L.	Maria Valentine	25 May 1859	Jun 2, 1859
VANNOSTRAND, John H.	Phebe E. Reeve	11 Mar 1863	Mar 19, 1863
VAUGHN, Thomas W.	Mary Jane Denton	29 Jan 1874	Feb 5, 1874
VELSOR, Henry E.	Anna Lewis	19 May 1875	May 27, 1875
VELSOR, Samuel D.	Antoinette Robbins	8 Dec 1871	Dec 14, 1871
VERITY, Charles	Caroline Bedel	20 Dec 1859	Dec 29, 1859
VERITY, James	Susan Hulst	no date	Aug 26, 1858
VERITY, Nelson	Mary D. Ashmond	28 Nov 1867	Dec 5, 1867
VERITY, Richard Henry	Ann Eldred	30 Aug 1863	Sep 10, 1863
VERITY, Wm H.	Sarah E. White	1 Oct 1865	Oct 5, 1865
VICKERS, John	Mary B. Howitt	11th inst	Oct 19, 1865

Groom's Name	Bride's Name	Date of marriage	Date of newspaper
VOGEL, (Rev.)	(Mrs) Jackson	13 Sep 1874	Sep 24, 1874
VOORHEST, James B.	Ann E. Downing	14th ult	Mar 9, 1865
WAGG, George	Mary L. Jetter, (Mrs)	no date	Jun 17, 1858
WALKER, Andrew J.	Harriet S. Satterly	30 Jan 1859	Feb 10, 1859
WALKER, James P.	Maria R. Luther	10 Aug 1858	Aug 19, 1858
WALKER, William R.	Emma Bailey	8 Nov 1871	Nov 16, 1871
WALLACE, George	Mariana Raynor	22 Jul 1871	Aug 24, 1871
WALLACE, Roger	Phebe Ann Brower	22nd inst	Jun 9, 1864
WALSH, Oliver	(Miss) Redfield	8 Jun 1875	Jul 15, 1875
WALTERS, Andrew C.	Bertha E. Verity	16 Oct 1870	Oct 20, 1870
WALTERS, F. B. B.	E. H. Thompson	9 Nov 1859	Nov 10, 1859
WANSER, Gilbert M.	Phebe Cora Smith	2 May 1863	Aug 20, 1863
WANSER, William H.	Iantha K. Smith, (Mrs)	18 Nov 1869	Dec 9, 1869
WASHBURNE, Stephen O.	Libbie L. Hendrickson	23 Feb 1868	Feb 20, 1868
WATERS, Albert	Margaret E. Drummond	24 Aug 1875	Sep 2, 1875
WATKINS, Edwin W.	Emma L. Powell	28 Sep 1864	Oct 6, 1864
WATTS, Elbert H.	Catherine H. Golder	no date	Nov 30, 1865
WATTS, James	Sarah E. Bedell	31 Aug 1865	Oct 19, 1865
WATTS, Sidney	Emma Combs, (Mrs)	no date	Oct 15, 1868
WATTS, Smith P.	Hannah Southard	7 Jun 1865	Jul 27, 1865
WATTS, Valentine	Emma Louisa Mott	27 Jan 1861	Jan 31, 1861
WAY, S. Minor	Mary F. Hingle	21 Feb 1877	Mar 1, 1877
WAY, Walter B.	Elizabeth H. Thompson	11th inst	Oct 19, 1865
WEED, Harvey N.	Eleanor S. Queen, (Mrs)	17 Sep 1867	Sep 26, 1867
WEEKES, Charles A.	Phebe Mollineux	14 May 1861	May 16, 1861
WEEKES, Walter N.	Amy Ann Edwards	3 Feb 1870	Feb 17, 1870
WEEKS, Andrew J.	Julia F. Ayer	7 Sep 1871	Sep 14, 1871
WEEKS, Hiram Luther	Sarah Anna Valentine	24 Nov 1869	Dec 2, 1869
WEEKS, Jacob W.	Ettie W. Frost	12 Nov 1862	Nov 20, 1862
WEEKS, John S.	Josie Foster	2 Jul 1872	Jul 4, 1872
WEEKS, Luther	Maggie W. Rapelyea	17 Feb 1875	Feb 18, 1875
WEEKS, Samuel, Jr.	Angelesca Barnum	29 Jun 1864	Jul 7, 1864
WEEKS, Warren S.	Catherine Baldwin	28 Dec 1859	Jan 5, 1860
WELL, Charles H.	Julia E. Arthur	22 Dec 1858	Jan 6, 1859
WELLER, Augustus N.	Kate Ward Onderdonk	19 Feb 1873	Feb 27, 1873
WELLS, John H.	Sophia E. Terry	no date	Jun 17, 1858
WELLS, Theodore J.	Phebe E. Wilmarth	28 Nov 1878	Dec 5, 1878
WERDEN, Charles M.	Hester Lispenard	12 Feb 1859	Mar 3, 1859
WERNER, Frederick W.	Josephine L. Mersereau	21 Feb 1878	Feb 28, 1878
WERTMER, Christian	Celia Bier, (Mrs)	13 Mar 1878	Apr 25, 1878
WETMORE, Jacob W.	Katie L. Hoagland	28 Nov 1878	Dec 19, 1878
WHALEY, Henry H.	Mary Noon	4 May 1870	May 12, 1870
WHALEY, John	Elizabeth Ellison	21 Aug 1858	Aug 26, 1858
WHALEY, John P.	Henrietta Whealey	23 Oct 1878	Oct 31, 1878
WHALEY, Steven M.	Mary E. Burt	25 Oct 1876	Nov 2, 1876
WHEELER, Henry Augustus	Ann Elizabeth Merritt	17 Apr 1859	Apr 28, 1859
WHEELER, James C.	Annie M. Robinson	4 Oct 1878	Nov 28, 1878
WHETLEUFFER, J.	A. Irene A. Smith	5 Jan 1870	Jan 6, 1870
WHITE, Henry Kirke	Mary Louisa Purdy	18 Apr 1868	Apr 23, 1868
WHITE, James A.	Emma R. Mott	9th inst	Apr 18, 1861
WHITE, John H.	Betsey Jones	no date	Apr 22, 1869
WHITE, William L.	Emma Jane Watts	30 Sep 1863	Oct 22, 1863
WHITLOCK, George	Eliza A. Weekes	1 Mar 1864	Mar 17, 1864
WHITMORE, Willand	Margaret A. Cox	21 Dec 1862	Dec 25, 1862
WHITSON, Charles J.	Eliza Creed	15th inst	Aug 22, 1867
WHITSON, John	Rhoda Vansize	29 Dec 1858	Jan 13, 1859
WHITTEN, George E.	Isabella Pinkham	31 Dec 1863	Jan 14, 1864

Groom's Name	Bride's Name	Date of marriage	Date of newspaper
WICKS, George	Martha A. Wicks	20 Oct 1867	Nov 7, 1867
WICKS, Henry	Joanna F. Walter	no date	Jun 17, 1858
WIGGINS, Henry	Julia E. Lattin	25 Nov 1864	Jan 12, 1865
WIGGINS, Platt	Elizabeth K. Horsfield	no date	Dec 9, 1869
WILKINSON, Joseph	Mary F. Mott	25 Dec 1864	Dec 29, 1864
WILLETS, George P.	Charlotte B. Hill	15 Oct 1868	Oct 22, 1868
WILLETS, James R.	Anna H. Titus	4 Jun 1867	Jun 27, 1867
WILLETS, Joseph H.	M. Louisa Nichols	18th inst	Apr 27, 1865
WILLETS, Oliver	Rebecca Stoddart	29 Sep 1863	Oct 1, 1863
WILLETS, S.	J. W. Pearsall	no date	Nov 16, 1865
WILLETS, William Henry	Mattie Tabor	12th inst	Sep 19, 1867
WILLIAMS, Amos	Annie Smith	recently	Sep 6, 1877
WILLIAMS, Henry B.	Georgianna A. Denton	31 Aug 1865	Sep 7, 1865
WILLIAMS, Isaac	Sarah M. Davis	24 Jul 1859	Jul 28, 1859
WILLIAMS, Philetus A.	Julia E. Combs	5 Jan 1870	Feb 10, 1870
WILLIAMSON, Frederic B.	Julia Harris	7 Jul 1858	Jul 15, 1858
WILLIAMSON, W. J.	Mary M. Lee	30 Nov 1874	Dec 3, 1874
WILLIS, Alpheus A.	Mary R. Mersereau	16 Oct 1873	Oct 23, 1873
WILLIS, Charles E.	Sarah Townsend Minor	13 Dec 1865	Dec 21, 1865
WILLIS, Oscar B.	Mary H. Rhodes	18 Oct 1865	Oct 26, 1865
WILLIS, Peter D.	Hannah C. Rosebel	27 Dec 1863	Jan 7, 1864
WILLIS, Warren	Elizabeth Eugenia Clowes	3 Dec 1873	Dec 11, 1873
WILMARTH, Samuel	Alice J. Walters	2nd inst	Feb 10, 1870
WILMARTH, William H.	Rebecca E. Waring	9 Oct 1869	Dec 9, 1869
WILSON, Samuel	Jennie Lawson	no date	Sep 26, 1878
WILSON, Thomas W.	Abbey A. Baldwin	12 Jun 1859	Jun 23, 1859
WINNER, Thomas	Ann Edwards, (Mrs)	24 Nov 1864	Dec 1, 1864
WLALLENQUEST, Victor	Caroline Verity, (Mrs)	3 Mar 1869	Mar 18, 1869
WOGLOM, John	Caroline Rebecca Weeks	11 Feb 1871	Feb 16, 1871
WOOD, Charles	Cathrine Murray	8 Dec 1858	Dec 23, 1858
WOOD, George	Annie Bedell Franks	Sunday	Mar 15, 1877
WOOD, Henry	Ellen K. Sanders	10 Sep 1865	Sep 14, 1865
WOOD, John E.	Phebe J. Hicks	3 Nov 1872	Nov 7, 1872
WOOD, Joseph	Jane Bedell	8 Feb 1868	Feb 20, 1868
WOOD, Silas J.	Mary Emma Powell	27 Jul 1865	Aug 3, 1865
WOODHULL, Oliver J.	Virginia Warwich	19 Oct 1875	Oct 28, 1875
WORMWORTH, Thomas	Elizabeth Kirsted	14 Apr 1878	Apr 25, 1878
WRIGHT, Dorlan	Mary A. Hewlett	5th inst	Dec 20, 1860
WRIGHT, James C.	Susan A. Bedell	3 Mar 1874	Mar 5, 1874
WRIGHT, John S.	Josephine Searing	21 Dec 1869	Jan 6, 1870
WRIGHT, Joseph	Mary B. Saunders	25 May 1862	Jun 5, 1862
WRIGHT, Powell	Averette Ketcham	7 Apr 1869	Apr 15, 1869
YATES, Bowne E.	Annie E. Johnston	23 Jun 1867	Jul 11, 1867
YOUNG, Charles	Ruth Frick	20 Apr 1863	Apr 30, 1863
YOUNGBLOOD, William	Bell Edwards	10 Dec 1865	Dec 21, 1865
ZENT, Isaac	Mary B. Ruland	27th ult	Aug 8, 1867

Bride's name in upper case, groom's name in lower case. Find information
on the marriage by looking in the listing for grooms.

ABRAMS
  Abrams (3)
  Baldwin
  Bedell
  Cornell
  Driscoll
  Duryea
  Forbel
  Foster
  Herbert
  Johnson
  Maier
  Montross
  Pearsall
  Sammis
  Smith (2)
  Terrill
  Valentine

ACKER
  Fowler

ACKERLY
  Conklin
  Miller

ACKLEY
  Carman
  Johnson

ADAMS
  Carpenter
  Duncklee

ADRIANCE
  Kissam

AKLY
  Francis

ALBERSON
  Mott

ALBERTSON
  Downing
  Haviland
  Skillin

ALBRO
  Cornell

ALDRICH
  Titus

ALVIN
  Pettit

AMBERMAN
  Baukney

AMBLERMAN
  Meyers

ANTHONY
  Everett

ARMSTRONG
  Baxter

ARNOLD
  Clark

ARTHUR
  Well

ASHMOND
  Verity

AUSTIN
  Ketcham

AYER
  Weeks

BABER
  Fowler

BACON
  Selover

BAEDER
  Barton

BAILEY
  Hendrickson
  Snedeker
  Walker

BAISLEY
  Smith

BAKER
  Burch
  Burtis
  Valentine

BALDWIN
  Conklin
  Hood
  Mahan
  Miller
  Raynor
  Rhodes
  Scudder
  Weeks
  Wilson

BANNERMAN
  Green

BARDIN
  Pray

BARNUM
  Freeborn
  Weeks

BARR
  Cornell

BARTO
  Merritt

BASSETT
  Baylis
  Schellenger

BAYARD
  Morgan

BAYLIS
  Fogerty
  Hendrickson (2)
  Leek

BEDEL
  Verity

BEDELL
  Abrams (2)
  Adams
  Brower
  Combs
  De Mott
  Doughty
  Downing
  Duryea (2)
  Golder
  Gosline
  Halsey
  Hayes
  Hewlett
  Jackson
  James
  Losee
  McCoun
  Mills
  Raynor
  Rhodes
  Skidmore
  Soper
  Storer
  Van Velsor
  Watts
  Wood
  Wright

BEDINE
Fox

BEEBE
Leggett

BEERS
Burghard

BELKNAP
Palsey

BELL
Swords

BELLOWS
Pinder

BENDIRNAGEL
Cole

BENJAMIN
Terry

BENNET
Fosdick
Robinson

BENNETT
Alden
Bell

BENNETTE
Burr

BERRY
Austin
Brooks

BIER
Wertmer

BIRDSALL
Carson

BISHOP
Harrison

BLYDENBURGH
Mathews

BODE
Schenck

BOND
Brower

BOWNE
Harned

BRADLEY
Randall

BRADSHAW
Van Nostrand

BRADY
Allen
Streator

BRAINHARD
Magee

BRENNIN
Scott

BRESSIEUX
Horton

BREWSTER
Evans

BROWER
Abrams
Bedell
Brower
Keeler
Kimball
Pettit
Smith
Story
Wallace

BROWN
Bedell
Horton
Ketcham
Stillwagon
Tilly

BROWNSON
Bisland

BRUSH
Cornwell
Henggeler

BRYERS
Geslain

BUCKLEY
Terry

BUDD
Hubbs

BURDETT
Johnson

BURGER
Seaman

BURROWS
Jackson

BURT
Bailey
Powell
Titus
Whaley

BURTIS
Taylor

BUTCHER
Combs

CAMPBELL
Kirk

CAPE
Coles

CARLISLE
Pettit

CARMAN
Abrams
Brush
Combs
Denton
Hatfield (2)
Hendrickson
Herbert
Hook
Morse (2)
Raynor
Shaw
Southard
Terry
Totton

CARPENTER
Cheshire
Hendrickson

CASE
Haine

CHAMPION
Ross

CHAPEL
Loop

CHESHIRE
Southard

CHILD
Platt

CLOWES
Willis

COFFIN
Stubbs

COLE
  Richardson

COLEMAN
  Smith

COLES
  Downing
  Hayden
  Hill

COMBES
  Eldert
  Johnson
  Magee

COMBS
  Abrahams
  Abrams
  Combs
  Frost
  Hedda
  Raynor
  Rhodes
  Ritchie
  Rudgard
  Smith
  Watts
  Williams

CONGER
  Bennett

CONKLIN
  Barto
  Bushnell
  Losea
  Tyler

CONWAY
  Seaman

COOK
  Goodrich
  Osborn

COON
  Seaman

COOPER
  Shepherd

CORDRAY
  Kissam

CORNELIUS
  Baylis
  Bowers
  Edwards
  Rose

CORNELL
  Allen
  DeMott
  Dunn
  Langdon
  Nemoin
  Pine

CORNWELL
  Abrams (2)
  Brewer
  Cooper
  Davison
  Hasbrouck
  Sherman

CORSE
  Thompson

CORTELYOU
  Onderdonk

CORWIN
  Ackerly
  Van Nostrand

COVERT
  Hendrickson

COWENHOVEN
  Frecks

COWLES
  Terry

COX
  Sealey
  Whitmore

COZINE
  Runcie

CRAFT
  Abrams
  Charlick
  Smith

CREED
  Whitson

CROMER
  Humestom

CROOKER
  Golder

CROPSEY
  Palmer

CRUIKSHANK
  Timpson
  Underhill

CUFFEE
  Rogers

CUNNINGHAM
  Calhoun
  No name

CURTIS
  Hewlett
  Noon
  Remsen
  Smith
  Taggart

DALZIEL
  Dempster

DANIELS
  Ames

DANNAT
  Haviland

DARRAGH
  Davies

DAVIDSON
  Henry
  Nix

DAVIS
  Canway
  Punderson
  Williams

DAVISON
  Combs
  Grob
  Jackson
  Simonson

DEAN
  Combs

DEBOISE
  Jackson

DEEMS
  Adams

DE MORVEAU
  Deck

DE MOTT
  Hall
  Smith

DEMOTT
  Abrams
  Baldwin
  Bedell

Box
  LaRoza
  Shaw

DENBAR
  Carmen

DENTON
  Baldwin
  Crossman
  Hunt
  Sprague
  Vaughn
  Williams

DERBY
  Haff

DESMITH
  Kingsley

DE VERE
  Deck

DICKINSON
  Nostrand

DIKEMAN
  Smith

DINNIN
  Rhodes

DIX
  Bowditch

DORLON
  Golder

DOTY
  Carman
  Homan

DOUGHTY
  Cook
  Duryea

DOWNING
  Hegeman
  Valentine
  Voorhest

DOXEY
  McMillin

DOXSEY
  Brower

DOXY
  Little

DRAKE
  Bouker

DREVILE
  Hartmer

DRUMMOND
  Waters

DUNBAR
  Barteau
  Bishop
  DeMott

DUNCAN
  Lea

DUNLAP
  VanNostrand

DURLAND
  Johnson

DURYEA
  Dodge
  Hendrickson
  Norris
  Pine
  Smith
  Sprague
  Stoothoff

DUSENBERRY
  Platt

DWIGHT
  Kennedy

EABANK
  Harrison

EASTMAN
  Garretson

EDWARDS
  Benjamin
  Weekes
  Winner
  Youngblood

ELDERT
  Jordan
  Langdon

ELDRED
  Hall
  Verity

ELLIOTT
  Coffey

ELLIS
  Lewis

ELLISON
  Skidmore
  Smith
  Whaley

ESSENS
  Abrahams

FAIRWEATHER
  Boardman

FANNING
  Culver
  Downs
  Rouse
  Tappan
  Tappen
  Terry

FARNHAM
  Abbott

FARRINGTON
  Pearsall

FAYE
  Harvey

FERGUSON
  Carpenter

FERRIS
  Laing

FIELD
  Fowler

FIRTH
  Burt
  Simonson

FISH
  Jones
  Remson
  Searing

FLEET
  Golden

FLEMING
  Vandewater

FLEMMING
  Box
  Davis

FLEMMINGS
  Murray

FLOYD-JONES
  Carpenter

FORGIE
  Harwood
  Skidmore

FOSDICK
  Peck

FOSTER
  Hebard
  Weeks

FOWLER
  Hendrickson
  Horton
  Kaldfleisch
  Mollineux

FRANCIS
  Abrams

FRANKS
  Wood

FREDERICK
  Frederick

FRENCH
  McCrum

FREYENHAGEN
  Smith

FRICK
  Young

FROST
  Bedell (2)
  Johnson
  Rider
  Smith (2)
  Weeks

FULLER
  Provo

FURMAN
  Lawrence

GANLEY
  Morland

GARDINER
  Seaman
  Thompson

GARNETT
  Emory

GARVER
  McCoy

GARVIN
  Stoots

GILBERT
  Smith

GILDERSLEEVE
  Newton
  Norton
  Post
  Vail

GILFILLAN
  Bell

GILLEN
  Pagan

GOLDEN
  Lossee

GOLDER
  Combs
  Johnson
  Southard
  Watts

GORMAN
  Shaw

GRACE
  Nesbitt

GRAEVE
  Spooner

GRANT
  Layton

GREEN
  Danes
  James

GREENFIELD
  Powell

GRIFFIN
  Foster
  Irish

GRISWOLD
  Bellows

GRITMAN
  Driscoll
  Noon

GROVER
  Jackson

GUNZER
  Dirking

HAFF
  Seabury

HAGEMAN
  Luyster

HAGER
  Hartman

HAIGHT
  Hoyt

HALL
  Brenton
  Clifton
  Harris (2)

HALLOCK
  Skinner

HALPIN
  Deck

HAMMOND
  Homan

HANDLEN
  Mayher

HARDEN
  Trevett

HARDY
  Curtis

HARPELL
  Mould

HARRIS
  Williamson

HART
  Burman

HARVEY
  McCormack

HAVILAND
  Ballou

HAWKINS
  Still

HAWKRIDGE
  Tostevin

HAYES
  Losea

HEARTT
  Kortright

HEATON
  Cornell

HEDGES
  Grant
  Polley
  Pye

HEGEMAN
  Mitchell
  Sprague

HENDERSON
  Reeve
  Seaman

HENDRICKSON
  Baylis
  Carman
  Conklin
  Harrington
  Hendrickson
  LaFetra
  Mills
  Newton
  Underhill
  Valentine
  Washburne

HENRY
  Raynor

HENTZ
  Hewlett
  Mott

HERKENSTEIN
  Pearsall

HEWLETT
  Foreman
  Killin
  Pearsall
  Simonson
  Tredwell
  Vandewater
  Wright

HICKS
  De Mott
  Hathorn
  Seaman
  Tate
  Wood

HIGBIE
  Hendrickson

HIGHFIELD
  Abrams

HILDRETH
  Dickerson
  Sprague

HILL
  Willets

HINGLE
  Ashdown
  Way

HIRST
  Harper

HOAGLAND
  Wetmore

HOLDRICH
  Goff

HOLMSTROM
  Johnson

HOPKINS
  De Mott

HORSFIELD
  Wiggins

HORSMANN
  Gunther

HORTON
  Cornwell
  Davidson
  Dunbar

HOVER
  Lawrence

HOWARD
  Manwaring

HOWE
  Hudson

HOWITT
  Vickers

HOWLAND
  Hart
  Smith

HUIL
  Van Ausdall

HULL
  Halsey

HULSE
  Mayer

HULST
  Verity

HULTZ
  Hultz

HUNT
  McCormick

HUNTTING
  Sayres

HURD
  Crosby
  Downing

HUTTON
  Snedeker

HYMAN
  Shipherd

JACKSON
  Abrams
  Coster
  Murray
  Rhodes
  Seaman
  Smith (2)
  Suffert
  Valentine
  Vogel

JAGGER
  Allen
  Cook

JAGLE
  Loser

JAMES
  Bedell
  Davis
  Pitts

JARVIS
  Colyea
  Gardiner

JAYNE
  Baylis

JENKENS
  Gildersleeve

JENKINS
  Ellison
  Haines

JERVIS
  Ketcham

JETTER
  Bower
  Wagg

JOHNSON
  Alexander
  Conklin
  Rider (2)
  Rusco

JOHNSTON
  Yates

JONES
  Bulkley
  Doxy
  Fridell
  Jackson
  Lord
  Underhill
  White

KE-?--
  Crossley

KEATOR
  Pettit

KEITH
  Denton

KELLY
  Ellison
  Gardner

KETCHAM
  Bennett
  Buffett
  Charlick
  Muncey
  Rhodes
  Rushmore
  Smith
  Wright

KING
  Keirsted
  Norton
  Vail

KINNER
  Terry

KIRKPATRICK
  Smith

KIRSTED
  Wormworth

KIRWAN
  Scott

KISSAM
  Alliger
  Meynen

KLEINETT
  Twyeffort

KNIGHT
  Post

KOCK
  De Languillette

KOGAN
  Nolan

KOUWENHOVEN
  Hyatt

LAING
  Merrill

LAMBERTSON
  Foote

LANE
  Seaman (2)
  Smith

LANGDON
  Abrams
  Jackson
  Leach

LANGUILLETTE
  Bussman

LASSEN
  Soren

LATTIN
  Wiggins

LAWRENCE
  Alexander
  Pettit

LAWSON
  Wilson

LAYTON
  Smith
  Van Wicklin

LEACH
  LaRoza

LEE
  Metcalfe
  Williamson

LEECH
  Eldred

L'HOMMEDIEU
  Abrams

LENT
  Howell

LEONARD
  Paff (2)

LEUBA
  South

LEWIS
  Elderd
  Lane
  Phillips
  Valentine
  Velsor

LISPENARD
  Werden

LITTELL
  Hall
  Kellum

LITTLEJOHN
  Jenks

LOINES
  Bunker

LOPER
  Hildreth

LOSEA
  Rhodes

LOSEE
  Mills
  Thomas

LOTT
  Griffin
  Smith
  Van Sicklen

LOWDEN
  Pullis

LUDLUM
  Denton
  Everit

LU GAR
  Moore

LUPTON
  Davis

LUSH
  Bedell
  Carpenter

LUTHER
  Furman
  Walker

MCCABE
  Bishop

MCCAULY
  Sniffin

MCCLOUD
  Hewlett

MCDONALD
  Oldrin

MCDOUGALL
  Banks

MCDOWELL
  Ritchie

MCGILL
  Moore

MCLAUGHLIN
  Robinson

MCMORROW
  Smith

MCNEIL
  Johnson

MCQUEEN
  Stringham

MACY
  Cruikshank

MAGEE
  Combs

MAGINNIS
  Baldwin

MANN
  Ketcham
  Pearsall

MARSH
  Campbell

MARSHALL
  Brear

MARTIN
  Ayres
  Clark
  Keyes
  Taber

MATHER
  Hoyt

MATHEWS
  Kirby

MAXON
  Powell

MAYHER
  Brown
  Rushmore

MAYHEW
  Copeland

MERRILL
  Crossette
  Merrill

MERRITT
  Perry
  Wheeler

MERSEREAU
  Davidson
  Werner
  Willis

MESEROLE
  Meserole

MEYER
  Craven

MIDDLEBROOKS
  Hewlett

MILLER
  Baylis
  Brower
  Foster
  Fowler
  Kenyon
  Miller
  Parson
  Soper

MILLS
  Peck

MINOR
  Willis

MIRDYTH
  Prentice

MITTINGTON
  Pride

MOFFAT
  Myers

MOLINEAUX
  Griffin

MOLLINEAUX
  Seabury

MOLLINEUX
  Weekes

MONFORT
  Bedell
  Powell

MONTROSS
  Carman

MOORE
  Bedell
  Birdsall
  Edwards
  Oliver
  Parker
  Rogers
  Smith

MORAN
  Harrison

MOSEMAN
  Smith

MOTT
  Bedell
  Bishop
  Davenport
  Eldert
  Green
  Lott (2)
  Morris
  Smith (3)
  Van Wicklen
  Vandewater
  Watts
  White
  Wilkinson

MOWBRAY
  . Rhodes

MULFORD
  Powell

MURRAY
  Auld
  Combs
  Mulgannon
  Wood

MUUS
  Glinsman

MYERS
  Knowlton

NEIL
  Rance

NEWTON
  Gordon
  Mills

NICHOLS
  Haff
  Willets

NIX
  Eckel

NOLAN
  Larkins
  Powers

NOON
  Baldwin
  Fream
  Rhodes
  Whaley

NORTON
  Hawkins

NOSTON
  Hawkins

NOSTRAND
  Fox
  Gildersleeve
  Golder
  Hicks
  Higbie
  Johnson
  Raynor

O'BRIEN
  Dandin

O'DONELL
  Shaw

O'FLANEGAN
  Rouse

OAKLEY
  Carll

OLIVER
  Campbell
  Powell

ONDERDONK
  Skillman
  Weller

ORR
  Bedell

OVERTON
  Allen

PAGAN
  Debble

PAINTER
  Dillen

PARSONS
  Brinckerhoff
  Place
  Van Dine

PARTRIDGE
  Jones

PATTERSON
  Boyden
  Burdett

PAYNE
  Reeve

PEARSALL
  Abrams (2)
  Creed
  Davison
  DeMott
  Ellison (2)
  Frost
  Golder
  Jessup
  Kimball
  Langdon
  Pearsall
  Post
  Shaw
  Smith (2)
  Willets

PECK
  Armstrong

PEDNER
  Sterling

PERROW
  Cooper

PETERSON
  Dewey

PETTIT
  Birdwall
  Brower
  Golder
  Post
  Relyea
  Roberts
  Seaman
  Searles
  Shotwell
  Smith
  Soper
  Thompson

PHILLIPS
  Johnson

PHILO
  Skinner

PHRANER
  Bergen

PIERCE
  Horseford
  Pearsall

PILKINGTON
  Murphy

PINCKNEY
  Benedict

PINE
  Bellows
  Mathews
  Montgomery

PINKHAM
  Whitten

PITT
  Bedell
  Smith

PLACE
  Seabury
  Van Nostrand

PLATT
  Johnson
  Seaman

POMEROY
 Onderdonk

PORTER
 No name

POST
 Baldwin
 Nohearn
 Reynolds
 Seaman (2)

POWELL
 Bedell
 Hendrickson
 Hicks
 Karl
 Manolt
 Neals
 Smith (2)
 Sprague
 Stoothoff
 Watkins
 Wood

PRIME
 Chatfield

PRINK
 Lowden
 Smith

PRIOR
 Pray

PROCTOR
 Gary

PURDY
 White

PUTNAM
 Pharaoh

QUEEN
 Weed

RADFORD
 Darby
 Pope

RANDALL
 Cordner
 Oldrin
 Pine

RAPELYEA
 Fountain
 Weeks

RAYNOR
 Carman
 Denton
 Haight
 Hewlett
 Hogins
 Lawrence
 Pearsall
 Raynor (2)
 Shaw
 Smith
 Wallace

REDFIELD
 Walsh

REED
 Skidmore

REEVE
 Dickson
 VanNostrand

REMSEN
 Adams
 Baylis
 Powell (2)

RENSLLA
 O'Conner

REYNOLDS
 Mott

RHOADES
 Buchanan

RHODES
 Abrams
 Bedell
 Brower
 Dorlon
 Golder
 Hulte
 McWilliams
 Pearsall
 Raynor
 Willis

RICHARDS
 Pine

RICHARDSON
 Henderson

RIDER
 Bedell
 Brower
 Everitt

RILEY
 Maynard

ROBBINS
 Brush (2)
 Hubbs
 Mead
 Seaman
 Velsor

ROBINSON
 Benjamin
 Smith
 Wheeler

ROGERS
 Bracken
 Titus

ROSCHE
 Matschat

ROSEBEL
 Willis

ROUSE
 Stead

ROWLAND
 Porter

RULAND
 Hingle
 Tuthill
 Zent

RUSHMORE
 Bromfield
 De Nyse
 Eastman
 Kellum
 Magaw
 Preay
 Snedeker

RUSSELL
 Searing
 Smith

RYERSON
 Bedell
 Birdsall

SALKY
 Davis

SAMMIS
 Herbert
 Sammis
 Van Sicklen

SANDERS
 Vandewater
 Wood

SANDS
  Crooker

SATTERLY
  Walker

SAUNDERS
  Wright

SAYERS
  Seabury

SCHENCK
  Dickenson

SCHENK
  Hill

SCOTT
  Bevetland

SEABURY
  Crane

SEAMAN
  Brower
  Brown
  Chester
  Dunbar
  Jagger
  Johnson
  Leach
  Powell
  Taft
  Treadwell
  Underhill

SEARING
  Emory
  Hyde
  Kellogg
  Peck
  Searing
  Townsend
  Valentine
  Wright

SEIMES
  Downs

SENSKA
  Franklin

SHAW
  Cornell
  Hendrickson
  Mott (2)
  Shaw
  Valentine

SHEARMAN
  Beekwith

SHERMAN
  Overton

SHERRY
  Dayton

SHULTETON
  Martin
  McDonough

SIMONSON
  Abrams
  Burtis
  Langdon
  Pearsall
  Pettit
  Skidmore

SKIDMORE
  Haviland
  Hendrickson
  Robbins
  Rushmore
  Smith

SMITH
  Allen
  Althause
  Beare
  Bedell
  Clapp
  Combs (2)
  Crawford
  DaCosta
  Dean
  Dennis
  Denton
  Duryea
  Edwards
  Ellison (2)
  Faulkner
  Gallagher
  Gormand
  Haff
  Hollingsworth
  Homan
  Hood
  Horsfield
  Hull
  Ireland
  Losea
  Mathews
  Mitchell
  Paff
  Pailing
  Parsons
  Patterson
  Peckham
  Post
  Powell
  Purdy
  Raynor (2)

Robbins
Seaman (3)
Smith (8)
Sprague
Van DeWater
Wanser
Wanser
Whetleuffer
Williams

SNEDEKER
  Bennett
  Campbell
  Harold
  Powell
  Rushmore
  Ryder
  Skidmore

SNEDIKER
  Golder

SNOW
  Hart

SOPER
  Bedell
  Smith

SOUTHARD
  Abrams
  Davis
  Ketcham
  Lowden
  Raynor
  Watts

SPADER
  Belcher

SPILLET
  Golden

SPILLETT
  Denton

SPOONER
  Balfour
  Lawrence
  Odion

SPRAGUE
  Abrams
  Bedell
  Carman
  Davies
  DeMott
  Ketcham
  Pettit
  Place
  Shaw
  Thomas

SQUIER
  Leslie

SQUIRES
  McKinly

STEVENSON
  Carman
  Simmons

STILLWELL
  Holtz

STINE
  Johnson

STIVERSON
  Seaman

STODDART
  Willets

STONE
  Albro
  Vanderberg

STOOTHOFF
  Ditmas

STOREY
  Smith

STORY
  Johnson
  Miller
  Raynor

STOUT
  Pettit

STRINGHAM
  Bedell
  Fletcher

STUART
  Olds

STUBBS
  De Mott

SUPPLE
  Thornell

SUTPHIN
  Bowden

SUYDAM
  Hendrickson

SWEENEY
  Kelly

SYLER
  Simonson

SYLVESTER
  Pine

TABOR
  Willets

TAPPAN
  Seaman

TAYLOR
  Baker
  Brown
  Powers

TERRIL
  Brush

TERRILL
  Urterman

TERRY
  Fosdick
  Ketcham
  Still
  Swezy
  Van Duzen
  Wells

TESSERCHER
  Sahlmuller

THOMAS
  Bedell
  Cooper
  Southard

THOMPSON
  Bellamy
  Oliver
  Remson
  Stull
  Van Ronk
  Walters
  Way

THORN
  Van Dewater

THORNE
  Harper

TILFORD
  Beatty

TILLEY
  Allen
  Ketchum

TITUS
  Smith
  Willets

TOTTEN
  Duryea

TOWN
  Chichester

TOWNSEND
  Carman
  Downing
  Johnson
  Seaman
  Titus
  Townsend

TREADWELL
  Underhill

TREDWELL
  Losea
  Townsend

TROWARD
  Doremus
  Longman

TUCKER
  Keller

TULLY
  Jaisle

TURRELL
  Griffin

TUTTLE
  Murray

TWINER
  Hoffman

UNCKLES
  Secor

VAIL
  Simonson
  Vandergaw

VALENTINE
  Thayer
  VanNostrand
  Vandewater
  Weeks

VAN BROCKLYN
  Van Gorden

VANCICLEN
  Eldred

VANCOTT
  Loper

VANDERWATER
  Pinkham

VAN DE WATER
  Beach
  Seaman
  Van Nostrand

VANDEWATER
  Slossen

VAN DUZER
  Creed

VAN NOSTRAND
  Smith

VAN SICKLEN
  Rhodes

VANSIZE
  Whitson

VANVEGHTEN
  Carpenter

VANVELSOR
  Smith

VANVICKLER
  Rhodes

VAN WICKLEN
  Valentine

VAN WICKLER
  Doxsey
  Hedges
  Van Wickler

VAN ZANDT
  Cobb

VENN
  Roof

VERITY
  Borst
  Raynor
  Walters
  Wlallenquest

VERMILYEA
  Guinne

VON NOSTRAND
  Davenport
  Seaman

VREDENBURGH
  Huffington

WALDRON
  Creed

WALKER
  Harold
  Losee
  Seaman

WALLACE
  Hunter

WALTER
  Wicks

WALTERS
  Hewlett
  Wilmarth

WANSER
  Kortwright

WARING
  Wilmarth

WARREN
  Stratton

WARWICH
  Woodhull

WATTS
  Combs
  Flowers
  Rhodes (2)
  Schultz
  White

WAY
  Morrison

WEAVER
  Robinson

WEBB
  Golden
  Kennahan
  Moore

WEBSTER
  Hall

WEEKES
  Baldwin
  Smith
  Whitlock

WEEKS
  Cornell
  Jones
  McMillan
  McQueen
  Stillingworth
  Woglom

WELLES
  Diller

WELLS
  Denton
  Fish
  Sipe
  Snipe
  Southard

WEST
  Hoppins

WESTERVELT
  Hall

WHALEY
  Oliver

WHEALEY
  Whaley

WHEELER
  Lowden

WHITE
  Clock
  Coles
  Northrup
  Verity

WHITMORE
  Raynor

WHITNEY
  Bryant

WICKS
  Haff
  Wicks

WIGGINS
  Powell

WILKINS
  Sammis

WILLETS
  Bergen
  Cocks
  Fern
  Horsfield
  Leavett
  Mott
  Pearsall
  Sealey
  Van Wyck

WILLIAMS
  Jeffrey
  Rushmore

WILLIAMSON
  Havens

WILLIS
  Post

WILMARTH
  Wells

WILSON
  Fielbach
  Murphy
  Raynor
  Smith

WO(R)THERSPOON
  Miles

WOOD
  Doty
  Good
  Jones
  Lowden
  Pearsall
  Powell
  Smith
  Thompson

WRIGHT
  Abrams
  Darby
  Davidson
  Pearsall
  Ramsden
  Smith
  Townsend
  Tylers

YAGLE
  Dressing

YOUNG
  DeMott
  Durland
  Elles

ZAUDER
  Hermen

ZEUNER
  Quaritius

Name	Age	Date of death	Date of newspaper
ABBOTT, Alvan Summerfield	13y 7m	no date	Feb 19, 1874
ABBOTT, Daniel	76	29 Jul 1858	Aug 5, 1858
ABBOTT, H. P. (Mrs.)	32	9 May 1864	May 12, 1864
ABERCROMBIE, Mary E.	56y 1m	15 Aug 1874	Aug 20, 1874
ABERY, John	no age	Thursday	Sep 17, 1874
ABRAMS, (son of Ezekiel)	10m	3 Sep 1872	Sep 12, 1872
ABRAMS, (son of John)	5m	12 Aug 1873	Aug 14, 1873
ABRAMS, (son of John)	1m	30 Aug 1874	Sep 3, 1874
ABRAMS, Alvin Herbert	3y 6m 7d	11 Sep 1864	Oct 6, 1864
ABRAMS, Drusilla	1y 5m	8 Aug 1868	Aug 20, 1868
ABRAMS, Elijah	no age	11 Jul 1878	Jul 25, 1878
ABRAMS, Elizabeth	15	1 Mar 1876	Mar 9, 1876
ABRAMS, George	15	10 Feb 1875	Feb 18, 1875
ABRAMS, Gertrude P.	3d	18 Dec 1869	Dec 30, 1869
ABRAMS, Hannah	73	4 Sep 1870	Sep 15, 1870
ABRAMS, Henrietta	no age	29 Feb 1864	Mar 10, 1864
ABRAMS, Hollet	70	3 Apr 1872	May 2, 1872
ABRAMS, Jane	93y 3m	21 Aug 1864	Aug 25, 1864
ABRAMS, Jennie	no age	23 Apr 1869	Apr 29, 1869
ABRAMS, John Henry	16	10 Feb 1862	Feb 20, 1862
ABRAMS, Jonathan	ca. 70	5th inst	Jul 19, 1860
ABRAMS, Josephine	child	16 Feb 1878	Feb 28, 1878
ABRAMS, Mary Ann	55	21 Oct 1863	Oct 29, 1863
ABRAMS, Mervin	6th y	2nd inst	Nov 9, 1865
ABRAMS, Samuel	16m	24th inst	Aug 31, 1865
ABRAMS, Samuel	1y 1m	20 Jul 1872	Jul 25, 1872
ABRAMS, Sarah	70	3 Jul 1871	Jul 6, 1871
ABRAMS, Whitehead	73y 20d	7 Nov 1863	Nov 26, 1863
ABRAMS, Wilson B.	1y 4m	8 Aug 1868	Aug 20, 1868
ABRICROMBIE, I. I.	73	3rd inst	Jan 11, 1877
ACKER, Martha R.	26y 5m 18d	12 Aug 1872	Aug 15, 1872
ACKER, Nicholas	66th y	3rd inst	Mar 16, 1865
ACKERLY, Faith	8	2 Nov 1874	Nov 5, 1874
ACKERLY, Ione Down	27	27 Oct 1874	Nov 5, 1874
ACKERLY, Isabelle	2	25 Oct 1874	Nov 5, 1874
ACKERLY, Ruth	6	22 Oct 1874	Nov 5, 1874
ACKERMAN, Harriet J.	54	19 Apr 1869	May 6, 1869
ACKERMAN, J. Montague	9m 7d	20 Aug 1871	Aug 24, 1871
ACKERMAN, James	47y 5m 6d	22 Sep 1864	Oct 6, 1864
ADAMS, (son of George W.)	infant	1 Nov 1875	Nov 4, 1875
ADAMS, Cornelius Alexander	4m 20d	11 Sep 1865	Sep 14, 1865
ADAMS, Elizabeth	89	22 Mar 1872	Mar 28, 1872
ADAMS, Mary Ann	64y 10m 15d	17 May 1873	May 29, 1873
ADAMS, Thomas W.	6m	5th inst	Aug 9, 1860
ADAMS, Walter C.	5y 4m 4d	7 Jan 1864	Jan 14, 1864
ADAMS, Washington	45	3 May 1862	May 8, 1862
AIKENS, Joseph	50	no date	Feb 9, 1871
AITKEN, R. F.	55	25 Aug 1858	Sep 9, 1858
AKLEY, Addie Louise	11m 25d	11 Oct 1873	Oct 16, 1873
AKLEY, Jane	89y 5m	1 Aug 1875	Aug 5, 1875
AKLEY, John	74	11 Oct 1862	Oct 23, 1862
AKLEY, John H.	13y 2d	9 Nov 1867	Nov 14, 1867
ALBERTSON, Thomas W.	no age	6 May 1874	May 14, 1874
ALBIN, William H.	35y 1m	11 Jul 1872	Jul 18, 1872
ALBRO, Ann	75y 1m 9d	30 Sep 1875	Oct 7, 1875
ALBURTIS, John	75	14 Apr 1870	Apr 21, 1870
ALDRIDGE, Ira	no age	no date	Aug 15, 1867
ALLEN, (widow of William)	68	14 Feb 1865	Mar 2, 1865
ALLEN, Benjamin W.	no age	no date	Dec 31, 1874

Name	Age	Date of death	Date of newspaper
ALLEN, Carrie A.	18	9 Jun 1876	Jun 15, 1876
ALLEN, David William	49	9 Sep 1859	Sep 15, 1859
ALLEN, Deborah Rhinelander	83	15 Feb 1877	Feb 22, 1877
ALLEN, Elise	85	3 Dec 1858	Dec 16, 1858
ALLEN, John	54	11 Sep 1865	Sep 14, 1865
ALLEN, John	no age	16 Sep 1870	Oct 13, 1870
ALLEN, John C.	no age	yesterday	Nov 1, 1860
ALLEN, Josephine	34	4 Jan 1877	Jan 18, 1877
ALLEN, Mary H.	47	24th inst	Mar 1, 1860
ALLEN, Phebe	76y 10m 16d	29 Nov 1863	Dec 3, 1863
ALLEN, Richard K.	92y 7m	25 Oct 1868	Oct 29, 1868
ALLEN, Samuel	no age	29 Sep 1874	Oct 1, 1874
ALLIARE, Cornelia	75	no date	Jan 27, 1859
ALLIMAND, John E.	73	18 Feb 1861	Feb 21, 1861
ALTHONS, Elizabeth	81	10 Oct 1865	Oct 26, 1865
ALTHOUSE, Thomas E.	32y 11m	17 Mar 1863	Mar 26, 1863
AMBERMAN, Cornelius	73y 2d	31 Dec 1863	Feb 4, 1864
AMBERMAN, William Henry	2	23 Mar 1874	Mar 26, 1874
AMES, Charles Eugene	2y 7m 3d	8 Sep 1864	Sep 15, 1864
AMES, Robert	12y 6m	17 Jan 1872	Jan 25, 1872
ANDERSON, George	no age	7 Aug 1875	Aug 12, 1875
ANDERSON, Jonathan	71	5 Jun 1878	Jun 13, 1878
ANDERSON, Lettie Dell	2y 2m 13d	27 Dec 1873	Jan 1, 1874
ANDERSON, Robert G.	2y 7m	4 May 1864	May 12, 1864
ANDERTON, Dorinda	17	15 Apr 1869	Apr 22, 1869
ANDREWS, Charity	25	14 Nov 1865	Nov 16, 1865
ANDREWS, James Ward	11y 1m 17d	11 Aug 1875	Aug 19, 1875
ANDREWS, Margaret	65y 4m 4d	17 Nov 1876	Nov 23, 1876
ANGEL, (Mrs. Samuel)	30	no date	Nov 4, 1858
ANTHONY, Adam	94	4 Nov 1872	Nov 7, 1872
APPLEBY, George S.	17y 8m 20d	28 Apr 1873	May 1, 1873
APPLEBY, R. Anna	49m 6m 19d	25 Jun 1878	Jun 27, 1878
ARCHAMBAULT, (dau. of Matilda)	3	29 Oct 1865	Nov 2, 1865
ARCHAMBAULT, Matilda	no age	29 Oct 1865	Nov 2, 1865
ARCHER, Hanna A.	59	21 Dec 1873	Dec 25, 1873
ARESON, Mary S.	9	4 Jan 1859	Jan 13, 1859
ARMSTRONG, John	no age	21st inst	May 26, 1864
ARMSTRONG, Joseph	1y 8m 15d	28 Apr 1876	May 4, 1876
ARMSTRONG, Margaret	no age	14 Jul 1858	Jul 29, 1858
ARMSTRONG, Mary J.	23y 10m	6th inst	Nov 8, 1860
ARMSTRONG, Samuel	76	27 Aug 1858	Sep 2, 1858
ARNOLD, Charles B.	no age	no date	Mar 3, 1870
ARNOLD, Mary	110	25th ult	Oct 10, 1867
ASHMEAD, (dau. of Henry)	4	Thursday	May 31, 1877
ASHMOND, Sarah	71	no date	Jan 10, 1878
ASHMOND, Sarah A.	71y 21d	27 Oct 1877	Nov 1, 1877
ATCHISON, (Mrs Sandy A.)	no age	Monday	Nov 29, 1877
ATKINS, William	no age	no date	Mar 12, 1874
AUERBACH, Adelaide	13	26 Aug 1861	Aug 29, 1861
AUERBACH, Julius	56y 8m	28 Aug 1878	Sep 5, 1878
AUMULLER, Elizabeth	102y 14d	17 Aug 1870	Aug 25, 1870
AXLER, (Mrs.)	no age	yesterday	Aug 2, 1860
AYLIFF, James E.	59	2 Nov 1878	Nov 7, 1878
AYRES, Jane	61	9 Dec 1861	Dec 12, 1861
BABBITT, George R.	52y 11m	9 Feb 1869	Feb 18, 1869
BABCOCK, Benjamin	no age	29 Dec 1870	Jan 5, 1871
BABCOCK, Charles	65	19 May 1859	May 26, 1859

Name	Age	Date of death	Date of newspaper
BABCOCK, Mary F.	no age	22nd ult	Jan 5, 1871
BADGER, (Mrs)	62	Friday	Sep 13, 1877
BADGER, David J.	64y 9m 14d	13th inst	Oct 20, 1864
BAILEY, Christina	64	18 Feb 1876	Feb 24, 1876
BAILEY, John	16th y	9 Jan 1870	Jan 13, 1870
BAIRD, Eddie	7	5 Feb 1877	Feb 15, 1877
BAISLEY, David	82y 2m 3d	19 Jan 1875	Jan 28, 1875
BAISLEY, Sarah	81y 2m	2 Dec 1878	Dec 12, 1878
BAKEMAN, Eva	67	16 Nov 1873	Nov 20, 1873
BAKER, Asa	88th y	7th inst	Jun 21, 1860
BAKER, Bazil	no age	Jan	Feb 24, 1859
BAKER, John	3y 6m	30 Jul 1873	Aug 7, 1873
BAKER, Lewis	2	12 Jul 1873	Jul 17, 1873
BAKER, Treadwell	59	24 Jul 1867	Aug 1, 1867
BAKER, William	33	15th inst	Aug 22, 1867
BALDWIN, (son of Thomas)	3	recently	Dec 27, 1877
BALDWIN, (wife of Stephen)	ca. 60	8 Sep 1864	Sep 15, 1864
BALDWIN, Adeline	29	24 Aug 1870	Sep 1, 1870
BALDWIN, Barbara	20	11 Jan 1869	Jan 14, 1869
BALDWIN, Carrie	infant	22 Jul 1865	Aug 10, 1865
BALDWIN, Catherine	18y 2m	18th inst	Nov 21, 1861
BALDWIN, Charles	58	28 May 1863	Jul 2, 1863
BALDWIN, Clarissa	24y 3m 17d	20 Aug 1873	Aug 28, 1873
BALDWIN, Elbert W.	51	2 Jan 1868	Jan 23, 1868
BALDWIN, Elisha B.	43y 9m 23d	25 Aug 1868	Aug 27, 1868
BALDWIN, Elizabeth	ca. 80	2 May 1864	May 12, 1864
BALDWIN, Emeline	1m 9d	7 Oct 1868	Oct 15, 1868
BALDWIN, Etta	1y 20d	20 Aug 1869	Sep 2, 1869
BALDWIN, Gideon	69	26 Jan 1861	Jan 31, 1861
BALDWIN, Gilbert	no age	Wed last w	Jul 4, 1867
BALDWIN, Hannah	21	3 Aug 1859	Aug 11, 1859
BALDWIN, Hannah Ann	ca. 21	29th ult	Sep 8, 1864
BALDWIN, Jonathan	80	27 Dec 1859	Dec 29, 1859
BALDWIN, Lockey	70	6 Feb 1861	Feb 14, 1861
BALDWIN, Loraner	84	8 Jan 1875	Jan 14, 1875
BALDWIN, Mary Ann	47	1 Feb 1861	Feb 14, 1861
BALDWIN, Michael	78	21st inst	Jun 24, 1858
BALDWIN, Moses S.	37	Thur last w	Jan 18, 1877
BALDWIN, Peter	34	1st inst	Jul 20, 1865
BALDWIN, Samuel	27	6 Sep 1872	Sep 12, 1872
BALDWIN, Sarah	75	27 Jul 1867	Aug 15, 1867
BALDWIN, Sarah	72	25 Apr 1870	Apr 28, 1870
BALDWIN, Susan	76	8 Mar 1865	Mar 16, 1865
BALDWIN, Thomas	31	9 Sep 1861	Sep 12, 1861
BALDWIN, Thomas	77	8 Feb 1872	Feb 15, 1872
BALDWIN, William	77y 11m 19d	31 Mar 1863	Apr 2, 1863
BALL, Walter W.	19	17 Feb 1878	Feb 21, 1878
BALSTEN, Charles	no age	no date	Mar 11, 1875
BANCKER, Sarah Ann	73nd y	no date	Dec 19, 1878
BANE, John	56	17 Sep 1876	Sep 21, 1876
BANE, William	64	28 Aug 1865	Aug 31, 1865
BANGS, Nathan	84	Sat	May 8, 1862
BARBOUR, Charles J.	27y 6m	11 Oct 1869	Oct 21, 1869
BARIO, P. C.	51	14 Dec 1858	Dec 23, 1858
BARKER, Clarence E.	24	18 Jul 1878	Jul 25, 1878
BARKER, Lydia Stewart	no age	10 Jul 1865	Jul 13, 1865
BARKER, Mary	78y 4m 11d	1 Apr 1872	Apr 4, 1872
BARKER, Thomas	78	3 May 1869	May 6, 1869
BARNES, (Mrs W. E.)	no age	Thursday	Jan 4, 1877
BARNES, George	50	28 Jul 1874	Jul 30, 1874

Name	Age	Date of death	Date of newspaper
BARNETT, Charles Edward	2y 6m	23 Oct 1876	Oct 26, 1876
BARNETT, Mary B.	9	14 Jan 1877	Jan 18, 1877
BARNETT, Rosie	no age	13 Dec 1876	Dec 14, 1876
BARNIHER, Louisa	38	1 Feb 1871	Feb 9, 1871
BARNUM, Charles	55	28 Jun 1875	Jul 29, 1875
BARON, Edmund	28	6th inst	May 14, 1863
BARRON, Joseph	40	10 Mar 1869	Mar 18, 1869
BARRON, Thomas	no age	31 Aug 1875	Sep 16, 1875
BARTEAU, Frank C.	no age	29 Nov 1876	Dec 7, 1876
BARTHOLOMEW, James R.	68	20 Oct 1878	Oct 24, 1878
BARTO, Benjamin F.	6y 7m	28 Jan 1864	Feb 4, 1864
BARTO, Mary	74y 2m 3d	3 Dec 1868	Dec 10, 1868
BARTO, Peter C.	no age	20 Dec 1858	Dec 30, 1858
BARTO, Robert T.	no age	3 weeks ago	Aug 2, 1877
BARTO, Sarah J.	22y 3m 6d	11 Mar 1865	Mar 23, 1865
BARTO, Smith	75	31 Aug 1865	Sep 7, 1865
BARTON, Sarah	94y 2m	25 Aug 1871	Aug 31, 1871
BASKET, Elizabeth	62	11 Aug 1863	Aug 13, 1863
BASSET, Herman G.	no age	last Mon	Jul 26, 1860
BATES, Martin	56	23 Dec 1875	Dec 30, 1875
BAUERS, John	no age	23 Feb 1864	Mar 17, 1864
BAURS, Michael	no age	25 Aug 1862	May 21, 1863
BAVER, Caroline	74	24 Mar 1877	Mar 29, 1877
BAXTER, Nancy	no age	22nd inst	Apr 2, 1863
BAYLES, John	no age	26 Jan 1870	Feb 3, 1870
BAYLEY, George M.	30	19 Nov 1863	Nov 26, 1863
BAYLIS, B. (Mrs)	no age	no date	Dec 16, 1875
BAYLIS, Daniel	75th y	20 Jul 1878	Jul 25, 1878
BAYLIS, Elizabeth Frances	no age	6th inst	Jul 20, 1865
BAYLIS, Jesse	8m	12 Aug 1863	Aug 20, 1863
BAYLIS, John	13y 8m	7th inst	Jun 16, 1864
BAYLIS, Samuel Arthur	6m 11d	9 Jul 1864	Jul 14, 1864
BAYLIS, Sarah	no age	7th inst	Jul 20, 1865
BAYLIS, Warren	15	last Sat	Jan 27, 1870
BEACH, Elias J.	no age	Friday	May 24, 1877
BEACH, Kate Vandewater	23	15 Jun 1875	Jun 17, 1875
BEACORN, (son of Edward)	7m	15 Feb 1876	Feb 24, 1876
BEACORN, (son of Frank)	2	30 Jun 1874	Jul 9, 1874
BEAM, Robert Anderson	6m 20d	17 Aug 1873	Aug 21, 1873
BEARDSLEY, Wilobut	78y 5m	1 Aug 1872	Aug 15, 1872
BEARE, Henry	81	5 Nov 1876	Nov 9, 1876
BEBEE, Daniel	90	3 Dec 1870	Dec 8, 1870
BECKHORN, (dau. of George W.)	infant	24 Jul 1858	Aug 5, 1858
BECKWITH, J. K.	59	28 May 1873	Jun 5, 1873
BECON, Andrew	no age	recently	Oct 4, 1877
BEDELL, (Mrs. Stephen C.)	no age	20 Oct 1874	Oct 22, 1874
BEDELL, (child of Elbert A.)	ca. 3m	18 Jun 1871	Jun 22, 1871
BEDELL, (dau. of Elbert)	infant	10 Jul 1858	Jul 15, 1858
BEDELL, (dau. of Elijah)	2	28 Aug 1870	Sep 1, 1870
BEDELL, (dau. of James)	4	16 Jan 1865	Jan 19, 1865
BEDELL, (dau. of John)	10m	2 Sep 1877	Sep 6, 1877
BEDELL, (son of Jordan)	3	27 Jan 1868	Feb 6, 1868
BEDELL, Abram	66y 7m 16d	21 Dec 1872	Dec 26, 1872
BEDELL, Amelia	80	22 Jun 1861	Jun 27, 1861
BEDELL, Ann	45y 10m	24 Feb 1864	Mar 3, 1864
BEDELL, Ann	85	12 Sep 1865	Sep 14, 1865
BEDELL, Ann	5w	21 Aug 1874	Aug 27, 1874
BEDELL, Cassindra	30	15 May 1859	May 19, 1859
BEDELL, Catharine A.	54	9 Aug 1875	Aug 12, 1875
BEDELL, Catherine	41y 3m 10d	8th inst	Feb 23, 1865

| | DEATHS | Date of | Date of |
Name	Age	death	newspaper
BEDELL, Catherine Elizabeth	18y 4m	10 Sep 1874	Sep 24, 1874
BEDELL, Charles Lent, Jr.	no age	17 Dec 1876	Dec 21, 1876
BEDELL, Cornelia	25	19 Jun 1861	Jun 27, 1861
BEDELL, Daniel	25	29 May 1865	Jun 15, 1865
BEDELL, Daniel	4w	1 Oct 1869	Oct 14, 1869
BEDELL, Daniel	74y 4m 2d	14 Jan 1872	Jan 25, 1872
BEDELL, Edgar S.	10m 7d	23 Mar 1875	Mar 25, 1875
BEDELL, Elias	75	17th inst	Feb 23, 1860
BEDELL, Fannie	ca. 10m	30 Jun 1860	Jul 5, 1860
BEDELL, Fanny	75	17 May 1877	May 24, 1877
BEDELL, George S.	3	26th ult	Jan 19, 1865
BEDELL, Grace	65	1 Dec 1877	Dec 6, 1877
BEDELL, Hannah	78y 11m 24d	20 Oct 1874	Oct 22, 1874
BEDELL, Hannah A.	60y 9m	4 Mar 1872	Mar 7, 1872
BEDELL, Hannah Elizabeth	45	3 Jan 1872	Jan 11, 1872
BEDELL, Harriet Louisa	20	6 Jul 1863	Jul 9, 1863
BEDELL, Hezekiah	79y 7m	18 Jul 1865	Jul 27, 1865
BEDELL, Hiram	39	5 Jan 1864	Jan 7, 1864
BEDELL, Jacob Morton	56	27 Sep 1865	Oct 5, 1865
BEDELL, James H.	20	14 Dec 1871	Dec 21, 1871
BEDELL, Jane A.	92	7 Jul 1867	Jul 11, 1867
BEDELL, John	82	3 Oct 1863	Oct 8, 1863
BEDELL, John Montfort	9y 9m 9d	27 Jul 1872	Aug 15, 1872
BEDELL, Joseph	59th y	17 Nov 1869	Dec 2, 1869
BEDELL, Josephine	21y 5m	22 Jan 1865	Jan 26, 1865
BEDELL, Lydia	62y 8m 16d	15 Aug 1870	Aug 18, 1870
BEDELL, Mary	92y 12d	3 Mar 1874	Mar 5, 1874
BEDELL, Mary C.	6m 24d	10th inst	Jul 12, 1860
BEDELL, Mary Emma	19y 5m 17d	26 May 1864	Jun 9, 1864
BEDELL, Mary Jane	21	20 Feb 1864	Mar 17, 1864
BEDELL, Mary Lillie	6m 29d	29 Jul 1868	Aug 6, 1868
BEDELL, Mary R.	3y 1m	5 Sep 1876	Sep 7, 1876
BEDELL, Minnie	3	7 May 1875	May 13, 1875
BEDELL, Mott	no age	5 Feb 1878	Feb 14, 1878
BEDELL, Phebe Cortelyou	no age	7 Jun 1865	Jun 15, 1865
BEDELL, Richard	59y 4m	3 Oct 1867	Oct 10, 1867
BEDELL, Richard	69	27 Dec 1870	Jan 5, 1871
BEDELL, Samuel A.	22	6 Sep 1873	Sep 11, 1873
BEDELL, Sarah Rebecca	50y 5m 6d	9 Nov 1873	Nov 13, 1873
BEDELL, Seaman	89	11 Aug 1870	Aug 18, 1870
BEDELL, Stephen	75	23 Sep 1861	Sep 26, 1861
BEDELL, Stephen	49y 2m	22 May 1873	May 29, 1873
BEDELL, Stephen C.	88th y	last Sun	Jul 15, 1875
BEDELL, Stephen C.	88th y	11 Jul 1875	Jul 15, 1875
BEDELL, Sylvanus	77y 6m 27d	29 Oct 1878	Oct 31, 1878
BEDELL, Sylvester, Jr.	11m	30 Nov 1875	Dec 2, 1875
BEDELL, Treadwell	no age	15 Jun 1864	Jul 7, 1864
BEDELL, Walter J.	2y 6m	3 Sep 1877	Sep 6, 1877
BEDELL, William	84	25 Nov 1868	Dec 24, 1868
BEEBE, William Arthur	3m	2 Oct 1858	Oct 14, 1858
BEERE, Mary	44	4th inst	Jan 9, 1862
BEERS, Elizabeth	3	24 Jul 1874	Jul 30, 1874
BEERS, Hector	50	30 Jul 1875	Aug 5, 1875
BEETHAM, (Mrs.)	no age	6 Apr 1859	Apr 7, 1859
BELKNAP, Oraette Augusta	no age	no date	Aug 12, 1858
BELL, Horace M.	3	11 May 1863	May 14, 1863
BELL, John R.	38	17 Aug 1864	Aug 25, 1864
BELLAMY, George	68y 3m 22d	25 Dec 1869	Dec 30, 1869
BELLER, (Dr.)	no age	no date	Aug 29, 1872
BELLOWS, Emma Ellen	infant	16th inst	Jul 20, 1865

Name	Age	Date of death	Date of newspaper
BELLOWS, William H.	23	31 Oct 1862	Nov 13, 1862
BEMSEN (or REMSEN), Jeremiah	ca. 70	6th inst	Jul 20, 1865
BENEDICT, Eugene	71	21 Aug 1858	Sep 2, 1858
BENJAMIN, L. R.	no age	28 Sep 1875	Oct 7, 1875
BENNET, Barnardus J.	4	16 Apr 1862	Apr 24, 1862
BENNET, Henry C.	41	13 Nov 1862	Nov 20, 1862
BENNET, Jane Elizabeth	42	10 Feb 1859	Feb 17, 1859
BENNET, Lydia Selina	40y 3m 6d	19th inst	Oct 19, 1865
BENNETT, Albert	1y 8m	5 Apr 1874	Apr 9, 1874
BENNETT, Andrew Mercein	59	29 Jun 1873	Jul 3, 1873
BENNETT, Benjamin	60	10 Apr 1861	Apr 18, 1861
BENNETT, Daniel	75	30 May 1874	Jun 4, 1874
BENNETT, Ditmars	no age	no date	Sep 1, 1870
BENNETT, Elizabeth	40	23 Apr 1865	Apr 27, 1865
BENNETT, G. Striker	51	4 May 1872	May 9, 1872
BENNETT, John	no age	last Thurs	Nov 29, 1877
BENNETT, John	74	19 Dec 1878	Dec 26, 1878
BENNETT, John, Jr.	72nd y	5 May 1872	May 9, 1872
BENNETT, Lillian	child	no date	Aug 20, 1874
BENNETT, Mary Ann	69	3 Jun 1878	Jun 13, 1878
BENNETT, Remson	63y 1m 12d	25 Dec 1875	Dec 30, 1875
BENSON, James	83	24 Jan 1872	Feb 1, 1872
BERDSALL, Jerusha	no age	21 Mar 1859	Mar 24, 1859
BERG, Philip Gustave	17y 6m	2 Apr 1878	Apr 4, 1878
BERGEN, Charles M.	27y 1m 2d	11 Jan 1870	Jan 13, 1870
BERGEN, Charles W.	7m	8 Jul 1860	Jul 12, 1860
BERGEN, Daniel	47y 6m 24d	19th inst	Apr 23, 1863
BERGEN, James	5	no date	Jul 29, 1858
BERGEN, James	no age	9 Feb 1861	Feb 14, 1861
BERGEN, John	85y 9m 9d	13th inst	Feb 23, 1865
BERGEN, John	no age	13 Apr 1875	Apr 22, 1875
BERGEN, John G.	no age	18th inst	Jul 25, 1867
BERGEN, Mary Ann	54y 9m 23d	31 Oct 1868	Nov 12, 1868
BERGEN, Sarah	85	24 Aug 1868	Sep 3, 1868
BERGEN, Victor Barsalon	no age	16 Aug 1868	Aug 27, 1868
BERGMANN, Emily	no age	Fri	Jul 12, 1860
BERRIAN, Charles	no age	no date	Aug 24, 1871
BERRIAN, Era L.	2y 7m 21d	3 Sep 1871	Sep 14, 1871
BERRIEN, William	67	23 Jan 1861	Jan 31, 1861
BERRY, Charles	73rd y	17 Mar 1878	Mar 21, 1878
BETHUNE, Joanna	92	Saturday	Aug 9, 1860
BETTS, John	45	31 May 1874	Jun 4, 1874
BILLS, Henry C.	no age	Sat/Sun	Feb 19, 1863
BIRCH, James	ca. 70	6 May 1864	Jun 9, 1864
BIRDSALL, Samuel	71	9 Dec 1871	Dec 14, 1871
BIRDSELL, Eugene Wallace	6m 28d	4 Aug 1872	Aug 15, 1872
BISHOP, (daughter of James)	3	9 Aug 1859	Aug 18, 1859
BISHOP, Harvey	no age	Monday	Nov 15, 1877
BISHOP, Julia Adeline	16	26 Nov 1873	Nov 27, 1873
BISHOP, Phebe M.	52y 2d	21 Mar 1869	Mar 25, 1869
BISHOP, Richard	no age	no date	Nov 18, 1858
BISHOP, Richard	no age	no date	Nov 25, 1858
BISHOP, Sarah	18	19 Nov 1873	Nov 27, 1873
BIXBY, Horatio N.	no age	last Thur	Jan 23, 1862
BLACK, Z. M. P.	54	10th inst	Jan 16, 1868
BLAIR, Adel	37y 1m	7th inst	Jul 13, 1865
BLANKMAN, Jane A.	no age	no date	Oct 25, 1860
BLISSON, Mary E.	12y 7m 26d	12 Sep 1874	Oct 22, 1874
BLOM, (male)	no age	last Sat	Jul 22, 1875
BLOODGOOD, Nathaniel	54	16 Mar 1859	Mar 24, 1859

Name	Age	Date of death	Date of newspaper
BLOOMFIELD, John Lefferts	1y 1m	1 Jul 1865	Jul 6, 1865
BLOOMFIELD, John W.	68	22 Nov 1871	Dec 21, 1871
BLUME, Ethalena	1y 2w	8 Oct 1872	Oct 10, 1872
BLYDENBURGH, Isaac	64	20th inst	Oct 14, 1869
BOCHL, William	51	no date	Apr 19, 1877
BOERUM, (Mr.)	no age	Friday	Aug 3, 1876
BOERUM, Barnett	no age	11 Aug 1861	Aug 15, 1861
BOERUM, Jacob B.	52	6 Apr 1861	Apr 11, 1861
BOERUM, Maria Jane	49y 8m 3d	24th ult	Oct 4, 1860
BOGARDUS, Irving	25	28 Mar 1876	Mar 30, 1876
BOGART, Frederick T.	23	4 Jun 1877	Jun 7, 1877
BOGART, John	no age	last Fri	Jun 10, 1858
BOGART, William H.	52nd y	12 May 1878	May 16, 1878
BOHL, Ernst	no age	no date	Sep 1, 1870
BOKEE, David A.	no age	last week	Mar 22, 1860
BOLSTEN, Christian	no age	no date	Mar 11, 1875
BOND, Emma	5m 14d	17 Dec 1868	Dec 24, 1868
BOND, Stephen	50	15th inst	Aug 24, 1865
BOOTH, Charles Isaac	4m 7d	12 Aug 1864	Aug 18, 1864
BORLAND, Louisa H.	55y 8m 18d	22 May 1863	May 28, 1863
BORNE, John Philip	no age	last Aug	Dec 9, 1869
BORST, Abby Jane	24y 7m	23 Apr 1873	May 1, 1873
BORUM, Samuel	ca. 40	9 Sep 1878	Sep 19, 1878
BOSWORTH, George	no age	16 Feb 1875	Feb 18, 1875
BOSWORTH, Royal	66y 11m 12d	23 Oct 1865	Oct 26, 1865
BOURDETT, Elizabeth	42y 2m 8d	3 Mar 1874	Mar 26, 1874
BOURDETTE, (son of Peter)	no age	15 Dec 1874	Dec 17, 1874
BOURDETTE, Frank M.	3m 14d	24 Apr 1872	May 2, 1872
BOUTON, Abm.	no age	Sat/Sun	Feb 19, 1863
BOUTON, James D.	55y 10d	29th ult	Dec 12, 1867
BOWDEN, Charlotte F.	3m	11 Feb 1864	Feb 18, 1864
BOWER, Henry	75	21 Jun 1878	Jun 27, 1878
BOWER, Margaret	9	14 Aug 1876	Aug 17, 1876
BOWER, Mary Frances	7m	25 Mar 1870	Mar 31, 1870
BOWHACK, Sophia	16y 11m 2w	16 Nov 1863	Nov 26, 1863
BOWLEY, Harmon S.	4y 11m 11d	8 Jan 1877	Jan 11, 1877
BOWNE, Josiah Q.	5y 11m	14 Jun 1858	Jul 8, 1858
BOWNE, Mary	1 1/2	12 Jun 1858	Jul 8, 1858
BOWNE, Walter	72	30 Oct 1877	Nov 15, 1877
BOX, (ch. of Frank)	14d	25 Mar 1872	Mar 28, 1872
BOYCE, Elizabeth A.	26y 9m	23 Jun 1877	Jun 28, 1877
BOYCE, Lulu	10m	28 Aug 1877	Aug 30, 1877
BOYD, John L.	51st y	31 Dec 1859	Jan 5, 1860
BOYD, Samuel	no age	last week	Mar 22, 1860
BOYLE, John A.	33	Sat	Feb 26, 1863
BRADLEE, Eliza	84	4 Feb 1875	Feb 11, 1875
BRADLEE, Samuel	29y 6m 13d	5th inst	Oct 13, 1864
BRADLEE, Samuel	89	2 Aug 1867	Aug 8, 1867
BRADLEE, Thomas	89y 3m	19 Feb 1878	Mar 7, 1878
BRADLEY, Edward W.	no age	25 Feb 1876	Mar 2, 1876
BRADLEY, Rachel	65	3rd inst	Mar 5, 1868
BRADLEY, Richard	no age	25 Sep 1861	Sep 26, 1861
BRADY, John A.	46	Monday	Sep 13, 1877
BRADY, Philip	ca. 49	Sat	Apr 25, 1872
BRAINIE, John	8y 9m 1d	24 Apr 1865	Apr 27, 1865
BRAMWELL, Harold	22	last Thur	Aug 22, 1878
BRANCH, Richard	ca. 70	25 Mar 1864	Apr 7, 1864
BREED, Amos	60	25th ult	Feb 9, 1860
BREEN, Mary	79	21 Jun 1878	Jun 27, 1878
BREEN, Peter	30	no date	May 31, 1860

Name	Age	Date of death	Date of newspaper
BRENNAN, (Mr.)	no age	Wednesday	Jun 25, 1874
BRENTON, Elizabeth	67	30 Mar 1875	Apr 1, 1875
BREWATER, Henrietta	20	30 Nov 1867	Dec 5, 1867
BREWER, Gilbert	ca. 33	5th inst	May 10, 1860
BREWER, John	no age	19 Sep 1877	Oct 4, 1877
BREWER, Mary Emma	6m	29 Aug 1875	Sep 2, 1875
BREWSTER, Charles	15	18 Sep 1871	Sep 21, 1871
BREWSTER, Ruth	63	15 Apr 1876	Apr 27, 1876
BREWSTER, Townsend	60	5 Jan 1874	Jan 8, 1874
BRICE, Eliza	17	27 Feb 1865	Mar 2, 1865
BRIGGS, (5 children of Luther)	no age	last Fri	Feb 16, 1860
BRIGGS, (two brothers)	no age	last Sat	May 15, 1862
BRIGHAM, Josephine	37	3 Jul 1873	Jul 10, 1873
BRINCKERHOFF, Elbert A.	89th y	5 Mar 1875	Mar 11, 1875
BRINCKERHOFF, Elizabeth Nostrand	83	1 Jan 1874	Jan 7, 1875
BRINCKERHOFF, Rebecca	92	11 Sep 1861	Sep 19, 1861
BRINKERHOFF, Phebe Bogart	52	23 Mar 1861	Apr 4, 1861
BRITT, Patrick	ca. 80	last Sat	Feb 5, 1874
BROCKET, Maurice	21	14th	Apr 23, 1863
BROCKETT, Charlotte E.	18y 6m	1 Aug 1865	Aug 10, 1865
BRODERICK, David C.	no age	no date	Oct 13, 1859
BRODERICK, Patrick	no age	12 Jun 1874	Jun 18, 1874
BROMFIELD, Edward M.	no age	25 Nov 1875	Dec 2, 1875
BROOKS, Merritt S.	22	29 Oct 1865	Nov 2, 1865
BROWER, Anna J.	infant	10 Oct 1869	Oct 14, 1869
BROWER, Daniel	no age	22 Jul 1867	Aug 1, 1867
BROWER, Elisha	77	17 Jun 1877	Jun 21, 1877
BROWER, Kezia	51	last Tue	Jul 20, 1865
BROWER, Parmenus	75	19 Apr 1869	Apr 22, 1869
BROWER, Sarah Amelia	4y 3m	12th inst	Aug 18, 1864
BROWER, Sarah E.	33	8 Feb 1864	Feb 11, 1864
BROWN, (Mrs.)	38	last Tue	Dec 14, 1865
BROWN, (male)	no age	1 Aug 1875	Aug 5, 1875
BROWN, Adelia	7m	5 Sep 1875	Sep 16, 1875
BROWN, Anthony	22	20 May 1875	May 27, 1875
BROWN, Charlotte A.	23	16 Oct 1872	Oct 24, 1872
BROWN, Edward	62	no date	Jan 10, 1861
BROWN, Edwin	6m 15d	16 Dec 1865	Dec 21, 1865
BROWN, George Henry	ca. 7	Tuesday	Aug 22, 1867
BROWN, Harry	13	1 Apr 1875	Apr 15, 1875
BROWN, John	5y 6m 20d	21 Oct 1876	Oct 26, 1876
BROWN, Maggie	1y 2m 15d	5 Jul 1878	Jul 11, 1878
BROWN, Rebecca K.	13y 11m	15 Jun 1863	Jun 18, 1863
BROWN, Susan	57	2 May 1868	May 7, 1868
BROWN, Sylvester	3y 5m 7d	7 Oct 1876	Oct 12, 1876
BROWN, Thomas	3m 18d	18 Jul 1871	Jul 20, 1871
BROWN, William	55	21 May 1877	May 24, 1877
BROWN, William F.	2m	11 Jul 1876	Jul 13, 1876
BROWN, William H.	no age	9th inst	Sep 24, 1874
BROWN, William H.	no age	12 Sep 1874	Sep 24, 1874
BROWN, William Henry	26	11 Apr 1859	Apr 21, 1859
BROWNELL, Thomas C.	89	13 Jan 1865	Jan 19, 1865
BRUENINGHAUSEN, Adele	1y 6m 8d	28 Nov 1870	Dec 8, 1870
BRUENMAN, Joseph	58	22 Sep 1874	Sep 24, 1874
BRUSH, Israel	84	no date	Jun 9, 1859
BRYANT, Lloyd	71	10 Jan 1870	Jan 13, 1870
BUCHANAN, Wm. Henry	no age	last Sat	Aug 15, 1872
BUCHMAN, John	24	28 Jun 1874	Jul 9, 1874

Name	Age	Date of death	Date of newspaper
BUCKLEY, (dau. of A. C.)	no age	29 Apr 1870	May 5, 1870
BUHLER, Julia Rosa	1	15 Feb 1878	Feb 21, 1878
BUKOWAKI, Albert	no age	Wednesday	Jul 22, 1875
BULMER, Elizabeth	51y 8m 5d	28 Jan 1878	Jan 31, 1878
BUNCE, Edmund A.	no age	14th inst	Mar 21, 1872
BUNCE, Sidney	no age	30th ult	Sep 14, 1865
BUNGER, Frederic	no age	no date	Jun 17, 1858
BURCH, George	19	1 Nov 1871	Nov 9, 1871
BURCHARD, John	no age	Mon last wk	Jan 19, 1860
BURDELL, Elizabeth A.	45	2 Jan 1861	Jan 10, 1861
BURDETT, Henry S.	10m 6d	16 Mar 1869	Mar 25, 1869
BURDETT, Phebe	60	24 Aug 1861	Aug 29, 1861
BURDETTE, Sarah Jane	46	18 Aug 1865	Aug 24, 1865
BURGER, James Guion	69y 2m 2d	4 Dec 1878	Dec 12, 1878
BURGESS, Robert	no age	9th inst	Nov 21, 1872
BURKE, Denis	no age	no date	Sep 13, 1860
BURKE, John	no age	no date	Dec 22, 1870
BURKHARDT, Henry	60	29 Dec 1874	Jan 7, 1875
BURKHART, (2 ch.)	no age	no date	Feb 1, 1872
BURKHART, (Mr.)	no age	no date	Feb 1, 1872
BURNS, (4 ch of Thomas)	no age	no date	Jan 4, 1873
BURR, (captain of oyster sloop)	no age	Wednesday	Mar 29, 1860
BURR, Eliza Frances	no age	16 Sep 1870	Sep 29, 1870
BURROWS, Caroline	47	10 Mar 1862	Mar 13, 1862
BURT, Ann	86	20 Apr 1862	Apr 24, 1862
BURT, Carrie	10y 5m	15 Apr 1874	Apr 30, 1874
BURT, Mary	84y 6m	20 Aug 1876	Aug 24, 1876
BURT, Richard	79	11 Nov 1873	Nov 13, 1873
BURT, Samuel	50y 5m 9d	27 Dec 1868	Dec 31, 1868
BURT, Smith	69y 9m 2d	1 Sep 1870	Sep 8, 1870
BURT, William Sanford	50	6 Oct 1874	Oct 8, 1874
BURTIS, Charles Seward	10m 11d	4 Aug 1863	Aug 20, 1863
BURTIS, Cornelia	10m 26d	25 Jul 1875	Jul 29, 1875
BURTIS, Elizabeth	81	15th inst	Mar 12, 1863
BURTIS, Jacob H.	76	17 Jun 1873	Jul 10, 1873
BURTIS, James R.	76	16 Sep 1876	Sep 21, 1876
BURTIS, Phebe F.	68	1 Feb 1871	Feb 9, 1871
BURTIS, Sarah	no age	4 Sep 1864	Sep 15, 1864
BURTON, Charles	11m	31 Aug 1868	Sep 3, 1868
BURTON, Edward N.	21y 4m 14d	1 Aug 1872	Aug 15, 1872
BURTON, William Evans	b. 1802	last Fri	Feb 16, 1860
BUSSING, Elizabeth	61y 1m 3d	16 Mar 1874	Mar 26, 1874
BUSSMAN, Harry	1	18 Aug 1874	Aug 20, 1874
BUSWELL, Charles A.	5y 6m	23 Aug 1868	Aug 27, 1868
BUTLER, Benjamin F.	63	8 Nov 1858	Dec 9, 1858
BUTLER, Frances	no age	14 Jun 1874	Jun 25, 1874
BUTLER, Jared Sengar	5y 4m	16 Mar 1876	Mar 23, 1876
BUTTERWORTH, (Rev.)	no age	no date	Mar 14, 1861
BYER, Nelson	no age	last Fri	Oct 10, 1872
BYRNE, Agnes Annie	14y 11m 10d	24 May 1876	May 25, 1876
CAFFRY, Thomas	99	22 Nov 1864	Dec 1, 1864
CAHILL, Francis	6	6 Oct 1876	Nov 9, 1876
CAHILL, John P.	10	3 Nov 1876	Nov 9, 1876
CAHILL, Lawrence Jr.	4	4 Nov 1876	Nov 9, 1876
CAHILL, Patrick	28	Tuesday	Jun 15, 1871
CAHILL, William	8	7 Nov 1876	Nov 9, 1876
CAIRNS, William, Jr.	65	no date	Oct 11, 1860

Name	Age	Date of death	Date of newspaper
CALAHAN, Bernard	no age	4 Feb 1875	Feb 11, 1875
CALKINS, J. P.	36	1 Sep 1862	Sep 4, 1862
CALLAHAN, Thomas	12	28 Sep 1878	Oct 3, 1878
CAMMAN, Herman	no age	5 Nov 1878	Nov 7, 1878
CAMPBELL, Eliza	64	20 Apr 1859	Apr 28, 1859
CAMPBELL, Elvira	3y 6m	1st inst	Mar 16, 1865
CAMPBELL, Lizzie	3w 4d	14 Sep 1875	Sep 16, 1875
CAMPBELL, Mellie M.	29y 11m	23 Nov 1865	Nov 30, 1865
CANFIELD, (dau. of Harry)	3w	1 Nov 1876	Nov 9, 1876
CAREY, Thomas G.	no age	no date	Jul 7, 1859
CARHER, Edward	ca. 50	4th inst	Aug 15, 1867
CARLE, Silas	75	16 Jan 1861	Jan 24, 1861
CARLL, Cornelia E.	no age	5 Oct 1863	Oct 15, 1863
CARLL, Margaret	91	last Sat	Jul 18, 1878
CARLL, Selah	92y 2m	30th ult	Dec 8, 1864
CARMAN, (dau. of Stephen)	3m 18d	27 Jun 1864	Jun 30, 1864
CARMAN, (male)	3m	16 Oct 1867	Oct 24, 1867
CARMAN, Abagail	84y 7m 3d	22 Mar 1875	Apr 1, 1875
CARMAN, Ada M.	2y 7m 16d	no date	Jan 10, 1878
CARMAN, Adeline	1y 3m 7d	10 Sep 1863	Oct 15, 1863
CARMAN, Amanda	20y 20d	9 Mar 1864	Mar 24, 1864
CARMAN, Ambrose	2y 6m	1 Nov 1873	Nov 6, 1873
CARMAN, Angeline	63	4 Feb 1874	Feb 5, 1874
CARMAN, Ann	88y 2d	8 Jan 1876	Jan 13, 1876
CARMAN, Carrie	4y 5m	18 Nov 1873	Nov 20, 1873
CARMAN, Clarence S.	4y 6m 5d	3 Dec 1867	Dec 12, 1867
CARMAN, Coles	6y 6m 5d	7 Oct 1870	Oct 13, 1870
CARMAN, Elisha	14	7 Nov 1865	Nov 16, 1865
CARMAN, Eliza	84	no date	Sep 10, 1868
CARMAN, Elizabeth	67	12 Oct 1858	Oct 21, 1858
CARMAN, Ella Frances	11m 4d	14 Mar 1864	Mar 24, 1864
CARMAN, George Otto	2	22 Apr 1865	Apr 27, 1865
CARMAN, John	76th y	12 Jan 1864	Jan 28, 1864
CARMAN, John	57	20 Feb 1870	Feb 24, 1870
CARMAN, Josephine	3y 8m 19d	21 Dec 1863	Dec 24, 1863
CARMAN, Mary Ann	5y 5m 11d	3 Nov 1873	Nov 6, 1873
CARMAN, Nelson	2y 6m	19 Sep 1870	Sep 22, 1870
CARMAN, Phebe	87y 4m	28 Mar 1878	Apr 4, 1878
CARMAN, Thomas	81y 2m 12d	29 Aug 1873	Sep 4, 1873
CARMAN, Timothy	85	25 Aug 1871	Aug 31, 1871
CARMAN, William	40	28 Feb 1862	Mar 6, 1862
CARMAN, William S.	44	26 Mar 1870	Mar 31, 1870
CARMEN, Benjamin	no age	4 Feb 1875	Feb 11, 1875
CARMICHAEL, Susan A.	53	6 Aug 1868	Aug 13, 1868
CARNIA, John	2m 14d	24 Oct 1873	Nov 6, 1873
CARPENTER, (Mrs. Jacob)	no age	last Fri	Feb 1, 1872
CARPENTER, Alletta	71	27 Jan 1861	Jan 31, 1861
CARPENTER, Benjamin	74y 2m	25 Aug 1875	Sep 2, 1875
CARPENTER, Ditmars	1m 8d	4 Aug 1864	Aug 11, 1864
CARPENTER, Elizabeth	71	3rd inst	Sep 8, 1864
CARPENTER, Fanny	95	28 Nov 1874	Dec 3, 1874
CARPENTER, George	54y 1m 19d	26th inst	Oct 5, 1865
CARPENTER, George Henry	5m 14d	11 Mar 1863	Mar 19, 1863
CARPENTER, Increase	19y 4m 1d	18 Jul 1858	Jul 22, 1858
CARPENTER, Jane	77	23 Mar 1878	Apr 11, 1878
CARPENTER, John S.	79y 1m 19d	23 Jan 1877	Feb 1, 1877
CARPENTER, Latting C.	ca. 50	7th inst	Oct 17, 1867
CARPENTER, Mary	62	28 Jan 1869	Feb 4, 1869
CARPENTER, Miriam	40	25 Sep 1875	Sep 30, 1875
CARPENTER, Sarah S.	70y 4m	13 Nov 1872	Nov 21, 1872

                                         DEATHS
Name   Age   Date of   Date of
                                               death   newspaper

---

CARPENTER, Sarah Scaring   3y 9m 19d   12 Jul 1858   Jul 22, 1858
CARPENTER, Smith   no age   26th   Jul 6, 1876
CARPENTER, William S.   18   3 Mar 1877   Mar 8, 1877
CARR, Elizabeth   no age   no date   Nov 18, 1858
CARR, Ella B.   ca. 4m   9th inst   Aug 18, 1864
CARRAGHAN, Michael   25   Thursday   Jul 11, 1872
CARRIGAN, Mary   no age   4 Jul 1872   Jul 11, 1872
CARROLL, Thomas   1y 6m   18 Jul 1872   Jul 25, 1872
CARROLL, William Henry   15y 11m 23d 16 Oct 1867   Oct 24, 1867
CARTER, (son of Thomas)   ca. 11   no date   Mar 14, 1872
CARTER, J. P. (Mrs)   no age   last Tues   Nov 7, 1872
CARTER, Minnie B.   no age   19 Jan 1861   Jan 24, 1861
CARY, Isaac   62   19 Sep 1873   Sep 25, 1873
CASE, Betsy   92y 3m   7d 8 Feb 1874   Feb 26, 1874
CASE, John   42   23 Oct 1865   Oct 26, 1865
CASE, Peggy   103   last week   Oct 20, 1870
CASEY, John   65   5th inst   Nov 14, 1867
CASEY, John   65   26 Aug 1873   Aug 28, 1873
CASSIDY, Ellen (or Mary)   ca. 50   yesterday   Mar 11, 1875
CASTERDAY, Christian   no age   no date   Oct 10, 1867
CATO (colored slave)   no age   8 Mar 1859   Mar 10, 1859
CATON, Velina C.   16   13 Jan 1859   Jan 20, 1859
CEGAL, Charles   no age   1 Mar 1872   Mar 14, 1872
CHAMBERS, Fanny B.   no age   no date   Nov 16, 1871
CHAPIN, Reily   40th y   2 Dec 1863   Dec 10, 1863
CHAPMAN, Austin   79   31 Dec 1858   Jan 6, 1859
CHAPMAN, Sarah   72   7 Feb 1861   Feb 14, 1861
CHAPPELL, Wallace D.   4   17 Oct 1859   Oct 20, 1859
CHARLICK, (child of John)   6w   5 Feb 1870   Feb 10, 1870
CHARLICK, (dau. of John)   8   last week   Feb 13, 1862
CHARLICK, Henry   ca. 60   16 Oct 1864   Oct 20, 1864
CHARLICK, Jennie   4m 15d   31 Jan 1872   Feb 8, 1872
CHARLICK, Laura   24   5 Feb 1870   Feb 10, 1870
CHARLICK, Oliver   63   30 Apr 1875   May 6, 1875
CHARLICK, Ruth   33   11th inst   Mar 15, 1860
CHARLICK, Ruth Ella   14y   16 Sep 1872   Sep 19, 1872
CHARLICK, Thomas I. L.   7y 5d   2 Jun 1860   Jun 14, 1860
CHARLICK, Willet   no age   15 Jun 1869   Jun 17, 1869
CHARLICK, Willet   58y 6m   15 Jun 1869   Jun 24, 1869
CHASE, Elizabeth Maria   22   20 Dec 1874   Dec 24, 1874
CHEESEMAN, Deborah M.   76y 6m 20d 24 Aug 1868   Aug 27, 1868
CHEIVERS, Edward   54   11 Sep 1870   Sep 22, 1870
CHERRY, Abram   ca. 60   14th inst   Jul 25, 1878
CHICHESTER, (dau. of Platt)   ca. 12   last week   Dec 29, 1864
CHICHESTER, (son of Platt)   ca. 14   last week   Dec 29, 1864
CHICHESTER, Benjamin   22   8 Mar 1860   Mar 15, 1860
CHICHESTER, George W.   11   4 Oct 1865   Oct 19, 1865
CHICHESTER, Ketcham   no age   27 Jan 1877   Feb 15, 1877
CHICHESTER, Rachel   77   15 Jun 1872   Jun 20, 1872
CHICHESTER, William   50y 9m   3d 22 Sep 1865   Oct 19, 1865
CHIVERS, Thomas   no age   4 Feb 1874   Feb 26, 1874
CHOATE, Rufus   60   13 Jul 1859   Jul 21, 1859
CHRISTY, E. P.   no age   21 May 1862   May 29, 1862
CHRISTY, John   no age   Monday   Mar 14, 1872
CLAPER, George Creamer ·   7y 11m   6d 3 Sep 1875   Sep 9, 1875
CLARK, (wife of Thomas)   no age   22 Dec 1858   Dec 30, 1858
CLARK, Andrew J.   37   20 Dec 1872   Dec 26, 1872
CLARK, Anna B.   77   Saturday   Jul 12, 1877
CLARK, Edward L.   20th y   19 Feb 1860   Apr 19, 1860
CLARK, Elisha   50   2 May 1873   May 8, 1873

Name	Age	Date of death	Date of newspaper
CLARK, Francis A.	26	26 May 1859	Jun 2, 1859
CLARK, John	63	28 Jan 1861	Feb 7, 1861
CLARKE, Caroline Matilda	no age	22 Feb 1864	Mar 3, 1864
CLARKSON, Charles	no age	4 Sep 1861	Sep 12, 1861
CLELAND, Julia	86y 4m 10d	15 Jul 1878	Jul 18, 1878
CLEMENT, Sarah E.	63	28th ult	Jul 11, 1867
CLINTON, William	52	29 Apr 1875	May 6, 1875
CLOONAN, James	no age	20th ult	Aug 1, 1872
CLOWES, Charles Augustus	8y 2d	1 Sep 1867	Sep 5, 1867
CLOWES, Edward A.	74y 5m 18d	27 Nov 1867	Nov 28, 1867
CLOWES, Gerardus	74	31st ult	Sep 14, 1865
CLOWES, Justina Louisa	1y 1m 5d	10 Sep 1867	Sep 12, 1867
CLOWES, Lizzie Whitman	5y 11m 25d	1 Jul 1858	Aug 12, 1858
CLOWES, Lydia	6y 10d 23d	22 Nov 1867	Nov 28, 1867
CLOWES, Mary S.	76	22 Oct 1875	Oct 28, 1875
CLOWES, Saah	71y 7m 5d	12 Aug 1874	Aug 20, 1874
CLYDE, (Mrs.)	no age	Saturday	May 31, 1860
COAKLEY, Joseph	3m	6 Jul 1878	Jul 11, 1878
COBB, Edward	57	3 Jul 1873	Jul 10, 1873
COBEY, Catherine	64	21st inst	Jul 4, 1867
COCK, Elizabeth Hicks	59	1st mo, 2d	Jan 5, 1865
COCK, Freddie	4y 6m	6 Aug 1864	Aug 11, 1864
COCK, Isaac S.	55	21 Aug 1864	Sep 1, 1864
COCK, Rachel	74th y	7 Dec 1867	Dec 12, 1867
COFFIN, William J.	no age	Saturday	Sep 13, 1877
COGGSWELL, Theodore A.	no age	last Thurs	Nov 29, 1877
COGSWELL, Theodore J.	33	22 Nov 1877	Nov 29, 1877
COHORT, (dau. of Jerome)	14	12th inst	Sep 20, 1860
COLE, (Mrs. Abram J.)	no age	Sunday	May 16, 1878
COLE, Seymour	4y 11m 27d	18 Oct 1867	Oct 24, 1867
COLES, Daniel	50	2 Oct 1865	Oct 5, 1865
COLES, George D.	64	26 Dec 1858	Jan 13, 1859
COLES, Jacob	74	30 Nov 1871	Dec 7, 1871
COLES, John M.	75	24 Mar 1878	Mar 28, 1878
COLES, Joshua	56	28 Oct 1863	Oct 29, 1863
COLES, Lydia Anna	3y 7m	16th inst	Mar 22, 1860
COLES, Samuel	93	29 Nov 1875	Dec 2, 1875
COLES, Thomas	77	26 Jan 1859	Feb 3, 1859
COLLINS, David	no age	16 Jul 1877	Aug 2, 1877
COLLINS, James	no age	Wednesday	Aug 22, 1878
COLYER, (male)	no age	Monday	Nov 15, 1860
COLYER, Andrew	ca. 35	Monday	Oct 25, 1860
COLYER, Caroline E.	19	12 Dec 1864	Jan 5, 1865
COLYER, George F.	21y 9d	5 Nov 1874	Nov 12, 1874
COLYER, Jacob	58	23 May 1865	Jun 1, 1865
COMBES, Henry	ca. 30	18th	Apr 23, 1863
COMBS, (son of Augusta)	9m	5 Mar 1875	Mar 11, 1875
COMBS, (three dau. of John)	no age	no date	Jun 7, 1877
COMBS, Alexander	75	11 Dec 1858	Dec 16, 1858
COMBS, Annie E.	26	8 Oct 1862	Oct 16, 1862
COMBS, Betsy	79	27 Apr 1877	May 10, 1877
COMBS, Delia	39	7 Apr 1877	Apr 12, 1877
COMBS, Elbert Alva	4y 8m 8d	29 May 1877	May 31, 1877
COMBS, Jarvis	39	30 Mar 1862	Apr 10, 1862
COMBS, Jarvis	80	2 Oct 1876	Oct 5, 1876
COMBS, Joseph	20	1 Apr 1863	Apr 9, 1863
COMBS, Mary	ca. 79	6 Mar 1863	Mar 26, 1863
COMBS, Mary Labelle	9y 3m	1 Jun 1877	Jun 7, 1877
COMBS, Mattie Augusta	2y 10m	21 May 1877	May 24, 1877
COMBS, Michael	78y 10m 22d	3 Oct 1867	Oct 10, 1867

Name	Age	Date of death	Date of newspaper
COMBS, Oliver	53	28 Jan 1865	Feb 2, 1865
COMBS, Phebe	71	11 Aug 1870	Aug 18, 1870
COMBS, Prudence	72y 10d	no date	Feb 20, 1873
COMBS, William	ca. 70	14th inst	Sep 20, 1860
COMES, Smith	3y 3m 19d	26 Mar 1876	Mar 30, 1876
CONDRON, James	no age	last Sat	May 26, 1870
CONKLIN, Andrew J.	no age	no date	Nov 9, 1871
CONKLIN, Edgar	no age	no date	Jul 15, 1875
CONKLIN, Elbert C.	14	14 Jul 1867	Jul 18, 1867
CONKLIN, Gamaliel	77y 9m	8 Oct 1877	Oct 18, 1877
CONKLIN, Harold Clifford	11m 2d	15 Apr 1876	Apr 20, 1876
CONKLIN, Henry A.	73rd y	15 Jul 1878	Jul 25, 1878
CONKLIN, Joseph W.	no age	17 Sep 1869	Nov 11, 1869
CONKLIN, Lewis W.	72	17 Sep 1876	Sep 21, 1876
CONKLIN, Nathan W.	65y 2m 26d	28th ult	Mar 9, 1865
CONKLIN, Sabrina	70y 7m 15d	20 Aug 1868	Sep 3, 1868
CONKLIN, Theodore W.	29y 10m 2d	18 Dec 1874	Dec 24, 1874
CONKLIN, Zephaniah	68	21 Apr 1872	May 2, 1872
CONLAN, Catherine	no age	10th inst	Mar 1, 1860
CONLIN, James Laycock	11m	no date	Aug 1, 1867
CONNER, Michael	22y 5m	3 Jan 1863	Feb 12, 1863
CONNER, William	35	10 Sep 1876	Sep 14, 1876
CONNOLLY, Julia	10	7 Mar 1872	Apr 11, 1872
CONNOLLY, Patrick	no age	Sunday	Mar 22, 1877
CONNOR, Martin	24	4 Dec 1860	Dec 13, 1860
CONRAD, William	no age	last Sun	May 9, 1872
COOK, (Mrs. Charles)	70	25 Dec 1873	Jan 8, 1874
COOK, (mother of S. T. Cook)	no age	Monday	Mar 22, 1860
COOK, Benjamin C.	30	26 Oct 1862	Nov 6, 1862
COOK, Edwin B.	62	11 Mar 1868	Apr 2, 1868
COOK, Jacob A.	9	20 Apr 1868	Apr 30, 1868
COOK, Matilda	33	8 Aug 1864	Aug 18, 1864
COOK, Richard L.	no age	ca. 10d ago	Sep 13, 1877
COOK, Robert L.	no age	Saturday	Aug 16, 1877
COOK, Theodore	21	recently	Aug 25, 1870
COOK, William Edgar	1y 1m	8 Aug 1858	Aug 12, 1858
COOKE, Purcell	no age	24 Dec 1860	Dec 27, 1860
COOMES, Cora Wagner	8m	16 Aug 1877	Aug 23, 1877
COOPER, (wife of late Thomas)	no age	15 Oct 1859	Nov 24, 1859
COOPER, Edward Jessup	6m 4d	17 Sep 1873	Oct 2, 1873
COOPER, Edwin Osborne	15y 9m 24d	27th inst	Oct 5, 1865
COOPER, Elbert	no age	last Thurs	Sep 14, 1876
COOPER, Grace Glorianna	3y 1m 18d	3 Jun 1871	Jun 8, 1871
COOPER, John B. L.	51	9 Apr 1872	May 9, 1872
COOPER, Leonard	no age	1 Sep 1873	Sep 4, 1873
COOPER, Samuel	41y 10m 23d	9 Oct 1867	Oct 10, 1867
COOPER, Sarah Bedell	77th y	19 Dec 1869	Dec 23, 1869
COOPER, Thomas	65	3 Aug 1858	Sep 2, 1858
COOPER, William	73	no date	Sep 16, 1858
CORBIN, Nathan	no age	last Fri	May 3, 1877
CORDES, Caston	59y 10m 21d	2 Feb 1875	Feb 11, 1875
CORNAGA, John	75	16 Sep 1861	Sep 19, 1861
CORNELIUS, (dau. of Zephaniah)	infant	25 Sep 1875	Sep 30, 1875
CORNELIUS, Anna	15y 8m	18 Jul 1874	Jul 30, 1874
CORNELIUS, Edward Ellsworth	4	6 Mar 1875	Mar 11, 1875
CORNELIUS, Herbert	3m 21d	19 Aug 1871	Aug 24, 1871
CORNELIUS, John	40	8 Jan 1865	Feb 9, 1865
CORNELIUS, Lot	no age	4 Oct 1878	Oct 10, 1878
CORNELIUS, Phebe Ella	11m 15d	28 Sep 1867	Oct 24, 1867

DEATHS

Name	Age	Date of death	Date of newspaper
CORNELIUS, R. J.	ca. 65	16 Jul 1872	Aug 1, 1872
CORNELIUS, Ruth	82y 6m 3d	24 Jul 1873	Aug 21, 1873
CORNELIUS, Sarah	56y 7m	12 Oct 1865	Nov 23, 1865
CORNELIUS, Tecumseh Sherman	8y 2m 24d	18 May 1877	May 24, 1877
CORNELIUS, William	58y 8m 13d	16 Nov 1865	Nov 23, 1865
CORNELL, Catherine	91y 10m	27 Feb 1864	Mar 3, 1864
CORNELL, Charity	80	19 Mar 1875	Mar 25, 1875
CORNELL, Clarence Weeks	1m 11d	19 May 1873	May 29, 1873
CORNELL, Hannah	80	1 Aug 1868	Aug 13, 1868
CORNELL, Hannah	75	30 Jul 1868	Aug 20, 1868
CORNELL, Harry Lafetra	no age	4 Apr 1877	Apr 12, 1877
CORNELL, Henry E.	55	28 Dec 1859	Dec 29, 1859
CORNELL, Ida	7y 2m 26d	12 Nov 1867	Nov 14, 1867
CORNELL, Isaac M.	80y 25d	1 Mar 1873	Mar 13, 1873
CORNELL, James G.	71	25 May 1875	May 27, 1875
CORNELL, Jeffrey	80	19 Oct 1865	Oct 26, 1865
CORNELL, John	2y 1m 2d	12 Oct 1867	Oct 17, 1867
CORNELL, Lawrence	10m 2d	24 Aug 1874	Aug 27, 1874
CORNELL, Louis	49y 7m 15d	15th inst	Jan 23, 1868
CORNELL, Oliver	81	23 Jan 1865	Feb 2, 1865
CORNELL, Willie A.	3y 2m	14 Jun 1873	Jun 26, 1873
CORNER, Charles G.	no age	no date	Jan 10, 1878
CORNING, Almira P. (nee DENTON)	no age	22nd inst	Aug 29, 1867
CORNISH, Maria	3m 26d	21st inst	Jun 27, 1867
CORNWALL, Mary E.	38	10 Mar 1878	Mar 14, 1878
CORNWELL	young	no date	Jul 5, 1860
CORNWELL, Abagail	73	25 Dec 1861	Jan 16, 1862
CORNWELL, Elmer	5m	24th ult	Feb 2, 1860
CORNWELL, George G.	1y 5m 5d	10 Sep 1864	Sep 15, 1864
CORNWELL, Hannah N.	71	28 Jan 1861	Feb 7, 1861
CORNWELL, Joel F.	4y 3m 29d	5 Jan 1877	Jan 25, 1877
CORNWELL, Margaret Motilda	18y 11m 5d	no date	Oct 14, 1858
CORNWELL, Maria	73y 7m 24d	4 Dec 1877	Dec 6, 1877
CORNWELL, Mariah	67	26 Oct 1865	Nov 16, 1865
CORNWELL, Mary Josephine	16y 7m	10 Apr 1860	Apr 12, 1860
CORNWELL, Phebe	85	10 May 1861	May 16, 1861
CORNWELL, Phebe M.	2y 10d	14 Feb 1873	Feb 20, 1873
CORNWELL, Sarah Elizabeth	4y 6m	8th inst	Jul 12, 1860
CORSE, (son of Gilbert)	2m	2 Jan 1873	Jan 9, 1873
CORSE, (son of Silas)	3m	26 Dec 1872	Jan 9, 1873
CORSE, Caroline Amelia	32	18 Jan 1872	Jan 25, 1872
CORSE, Charles	41y 8m	20 Nov 1877	Nov 22, 1877
CORSE, Charles	41y 8m	no date	Jan 10, 1878
CORSE, David	67y 4m 15d	28 Mar 1873	Apr 3, 1873
CORSE, Gilbert	61	4 Sep 1871	Sep 7, 1871
CORSE, Hanna	31	2 Jun 1873	Jun 5, 1873
CORSE, Ida	2	15 Feb 1872	Feb 22, 1872
CORSE, Kate C.	23rd y	16th inst	Aug 24, 1865
CORSE, Titus	68	4 Jul 1876	Jul 6, 1876
CORSER, George	45y 8m	1st inst	Oct 19, 1865
CORSTER, (ch. of Emery E)	2m	28 Jul 1872	Aug 1, 1872
CORSTER, (dau. of Emory)	no age	25 Jan 1876	Jan 27, 1876
CORSTER, Ophelia	2y 6m 22d	22 Aug 1872	Aug 29, 1872
CORTELYOU, Eliza	no age	23 Dec 1865	Dec 28, 1865
CORTELYOU, Mary A.	no age	13 Oct 1869	Oct 21, 1869
CORTELYOU, Peter	55th y	11th inst	Nov 14, 1867
CORTES, John	68	5 May 1870	May 12, 1870
CORWIN, Polly	no age	Nov 1874	Dec 3, 1874
CORWITH, Silas	74	no date	Dec 23, 1858

Name	Age	Date of death	Date of newspaper
COSTER, (dau. of Emory)	6m	9 Jul 1878	Jul 11, 1878
COSTER, Josephine	4m	2 Feb 1874	Feb 5, 1874
COUGHLAN, John	no age	15th inst	Jan 26, 1871
COUGHLIN, Stephen	19	24 Feb 1874	Feb 26, 1874
COURTNEY, (Mrs.)	no age	Monday	Aug 22, 1878
COURTNEY, Daniel	60	26 Nov 1873	Dec 4, 1873
COVERT, Catherine P.	58y 7m 11d	24th inst	Apr 2, 1863
COVERT, Eunice	74	22 Feb 1863	Feb 26, 1863
COVERT, James D.	1y 4m 6d	11 Apr 1876	Apr 13, 1876
COVERT, Mary A.	5m	26th ult	Jul 11, 1867
COVERT, Thomas H.	21	17 Sep 1867	Sep 26, 1867
COWENHOVAN, Susan L.	38	31 Dec 1858	Jan 13, 1859
COX, Francis Esquarall	1	7 Aug 1858	Aug 19, 1858
COX, Peter	no age	no date	Sep 1, 1870
COX, Stephen	2	no date	Apr 26, 1877
CRAFT, Mary	no age	no date	Sep 1, 1870
CRAFT, Sarah A.	41	27th inst	Jan 30, 1868
CRAFT, Simon	75	23 Oct 1865	Oct 26, 1865
CRAMPTON, Eliza M.	1y 5m	17 Mar 1876	Mar 23, 1876
CRAMPTON, Martha	54y 11m 13d	1 Oct 1877	Oct 4, 1877
CRAMPTON, Martha R.	55	no date	Jan 10, 1878
CREED, Abby	46	no date	Jul 29, 1858
CREED, Anna	18	last Tue	Aug 31, 1865
CRITTENDEN, John J.	77	26 Jul 1863	Jul 30, 1863
CRIZIER, Catherine	22	29 Aug 1872	Sep 12, 1872
CROLEY, Martin	no age	Sunday	Sep 3, 1874
CROMALLS, Alice	6	26 Mar 1875	Apr 1, 1875
CROMWELL, Charles	no age	last Tues	Jun 28, 1860
CROOK, Charles	no age	13 Aug 1874	Aug 20, 1874
CROOK, Margaret	77	26 Mar 1878	Mar 28, 1878
CROOKER, John	29	6 Dec 1867	Dec 12, 1867
CROOKER, Sally	74	2nd inst	Aug 20, 1868
CROONIN, Dennis	no age	no date	Feb 3, 1870
CROSS, Abram	10d	1 Sep 1873	Sep 4, 1873
CROSS, Frances A.	no age	4 Sep 1877	Sep 6, 1877
CROSSMAN, Charles	71y 17d	17 Feb 1872	Feb 22, 1872
CROSSMAN, Elizabeth R.	15y 10m 11d	9 Nov 1868	Nov 12, 1868
CROSSMAN, Emily A.	no age	9 Nov 1870	Nov 17, 1870
CROSSMAN, Harriet E.	8	31 Oct 1859	Nov 3, 1859
CROSSMAN, Harriet I.	61y 2m 27d	27 Feb 1872	Feb 29, 1872
CROSSMAN, Mary G.	64	3 Dec 1878	Dec 12, 1878
CROSSMAN, Mary R.	34y 10m	25 May 1874	May 28, 1874
CROSSMAN, Milton	33y 5m	12 Jul 1871	Jul 13, 1871
CROSSMAN, Susan	32(62? 82?)	10 Nov 1864	Nov 17, 1864
CROWELL, Thomas H.	no age	16 Dec 1870	Dec 22, 1870
CROWLEY, James J.	no age	Tuedsay	Jul 11, 1878
CROWLEY, Martin	no age	30 Aug 1874	Sep 3, 1874
CROWLEY, Martin	no age	Sunday	Sep 3, 1874
CROWTHER, Thomas	no age	Sep	Nov 15, 1877
CRUIKSHANK, Robert M.	22	11 Oct 1877	Oct 18, 1877
CRUM, Sarah	no age	no date	Dec 17, 1874
CUMBERLAND, Joseph	no age	no date	Sep 1, 1870
CUMMING, John G.	no age	no date	Oct 31, 1878
CUNNINGHAM, Eva	16	19 Feb 1872	Feb 22, 1872
CUNNINGHAM, Frederick	19	25 Mar 1870	Mar 31, 1870
CURLEY, (Mr.)	no age	no date	Aug 6, 1874
CURRAN, Charles	no age	Sat	Jul 12, 1860
CURRAN, Edward	no age	14 Aug 1878	Aug 22, 1878
CURRY, Barney	no age	no date	Aug 11, 1870
CURTIS, Adelaida	1	28 Apr 1862	May 1, 1862

Name	Age	Date of death	Date of newspaper
CURTIS, Albert	6m	1 Aug 1861	Aug 8, 1861
CURTIS, Alfred	29	15 Aug 1862	Aug 21, 1862
CURTIS, Sarah	82	14 Jan 1875	Jan 21, 1875
CURTIS, William	no age	no date	Sep 1, 1870
CURTISS, Patience	68	16 Jun 1861	Jun 20, 1861
CUTTER, Sarah	no age	29 Aug 1858	Sep 9, 1858
CUTTING, Charlotte	45	5 Mar 1874	Mar 12, 1874
DAILE, Cheresa	68	6 Nov 1876	Nov 9, 1876
DALTON, John	no age	Saturday	Dec 20, 1860
DALY, Katie	child	27th ult	Mar 11, 1875
DANIELS, Jerome	no age	Thursday	Apr 26, 1877
DARBY, Caroline	48th y	30 May 1865	Jun 8, 1865
DARE, David	21	12 Sep 1858	Oct 14, 1858
DARLAND, Elias	no age	30 Sep 1869	Oct 14, 1869
DARLING, (Mr.)	no age	17th inst	Nov 26, 1868
DAUCH, Barbara	52y 1m 25d	29 Oct 1871	Nov 2, 1871
DAUCH, Eva J.	84y 3m 12d	13 Apr 1877	May 3, 1877
DAULTON, Mary	100	3rd inst	Aug 22, 1878
DAVEE, William	no age	last Sun	Sep 26, 1878
DAVIDSON, Maria	71	25 Sep 1874	Oct 1, 1874
DAVIES, Walter Ernest	19	14 Sep 1873	Sep 18, 1873
DAVIS, (Capt)	no age	30th ult	Sep 16, 1875
DAVIS, (child of Oliver)	4	25 Aug 1861	Aug 29, 1861
DAVIS, Aaron	ca. 60	no date	Jan 14, 1864
DAVIS, Ann Augusta	15	1 Oct 1870	Oct 6, 1870
DAVIS, Benjamin	100y 1m	no date	Feb 29, 1872
DAVIS, Charles	21	31 Dec 1869	Jan 6, 1870
DAVIS, Charlie C.	10m	28 Oct 1871	Oct 26, 1871
DAVIS, Margaret	45y 5m	27 Mar 1877	Mar 29, 1877
DAVIS, Margaret Louisa	10y 21d	30 Nov 1868	Dec 3, 1868
DAVIS, Samuel	55	17 Apr 1864	Apr 21, 1864
DAVIS, Samuel	59	18 Jun 1872	Jun 27, 1872
DAVIS, William H.	24	9 Oct 1869	Oct 14, 1869
DAVIS, William Henry	7m	28 Jul 1864	Aug 4, 1864
DAVISON, Amelia	69y 10m 17d	11th inst	Jan 23, 1868
DAY, Catharine	ca. 72	27 Aug 1869	Sep 2, 1869
DAY, William	no age	yesterday	Aug 9, 1860
DAYMON, Barney	no age	3 Nov 1858	Nov 4, 1858
DAYMON, Mary Jane	no age	11 Jan 1864	Jan 21, 1864
DAYTON, (Mrs. Robert H.)	68	6 Jan 1878	Jan 17, 1878
DEAN, John	82	3 Oct 1870	Oct 13, 1870
DEAN, Rufus B.	64	21 Jan 1877	Feb 1, 1877
DEAN, William	60	10 Jun 1876	Jun 15, 1876
DEARY, Charles	30	26 May 1859	Jun 2, 1859
DE BEVOISE, John R.	79th y	7 Jun 1878	Jun 13, 1878
DE BRUSSAY, Thomas	no age	2 Jul 1858	Jul 8, 1858
DEGRATF, Jeremiah	64	26 Nov 1871	Dec 7, 1871
DEGRAW, Morris F.	11	25 Jan 1878	Jan 31, 1878
DE KAY, Eliza.	16	30 Nov 1860	Dec 6, 1860
DELAFIE, (dau. of John)	no age	last Mon	Jul 26, 1860
DELAFIELD, (male)	85	Saturday	Feb 18, 1875
DELAFIELD, (male)	81	Monday	Feb 18, 1875
DELAFIELD, (male)	83	Tuedsay	Feb 18, 1875
DELAHANTY, Patrick	no age	2 Jul 1858	Jul 8, 1858
DELANEY, William	no age	10th inst	Dec 16, 1875
DE LANGUILLETT, Louis H. W.	2	24 Aug 1872	Aug 29, 1872
DEL ESCOSURA, Virginia (nee JOHNSON)	no age	10 Jan 1873	Jan 16 ,1873

Name	Age	Date of death	Date of newspaper
DELMORE, John	no age	Fri last w	Feb 5, 1874
DE MILT, Henry	no age	22 Feb 1875	Feb 25, 1875
DEMOTT (dau. of Alfred & Lydia)	no age	9 Apr 1869	Apr 15, 1869
DE MOTT, Ann	62	22nd inst	Sep 27, 1860
DE MOTT, Charles	73	no date	Dec 30, 1858
DE MOTT, David	54y 6m 24d	6 Aug 1870	Aug 11, 1870
DE MOTT, David	63y 9m 17d	9 Nov 1874	Nov 12, 1874
DE MOTT, Elizabeth	61	3 Aug 1868	Aug 13, 1868
DEMOTT, Hewlett	76	13 Apr 1878	Apr 18, 1878
DEMOTT, Isaac	63y 10m 6d	16 Jan 1877	Jan 18, 1877
DE MOTT, James	25th y	29 Dec 1862	Jan 8, 1863
DE MOTT, John	82	last Thur	Jul 28, 1864
DE MOTT, John	94	29 Jan 1865	Feb 2, 1865
DE MOTT, John Isaac	19y 9m 22d	15 Sep 1873	Sep 18, 1873
DE MOTT, Lydia A.	34y 4m	11 Oct 1872	Oct 17, 1872
DEMOTT, M. Amelia	17y 7m 16d	3 Nov 1878	Nov 7, 1878
DE MOTT, Marian	90	9 Jun 1873	Jun 19, 1873
DE MOTT, Michael	no age	last Monday	Oct 7, 1869
DE MOTT, Susie Adelia	1y 2m	23 Aug 1874	Aug 27, 1874
DE MOTT, Theodore	14	25 Oct 1865	Oct 26, 1865
DE MOTT, Thomas C.	8y 8m 24d	24 Feb 1876	Mar 2, 1876
DENNIS, Burnat	no age	15 May 1876	May 25, 1876
DENNIS, Daniel	8m	2nd inst	Sep 14, 1865
DENNIS, Jacob	63	23 Jan 1878	Jan 31, 1878
DENNIS, William	55	1 May 1865	May 4, 1865
DENTON, (Mrs Charles C.)	no age	last Thurs	Sep 14, 1876
DENTON, (dau. of Benjamin)	1m	18 Apr 1876	Apr 20, 1876
DENTON, Alfred Greenleaf	2m	12 Oct 1873	Oct 16, 1873
DENTON, Alice Maud	1y 3m	3 Jan 1864	Jan 14, 1864
DENTON, Ann	75	17 Feb 1878	Feb 21, 1878
DENTON, Annie	24y 25d	19 Oct 1876	Oct 26, 1876
DENTON, Arthur	9m	8 Dec 1874	Dec 10, 1874
DENTON, Charles	78	16 Jul 1878	Jul 18, 1878
DENTON, Daniel	no age	no date	Sep 1, 1870
DENTON, Elizabeth	ca. 70	no date	Feb 3, 1859
DENTON, Frank Halstead	2	17 Jan 1861	Jan 24, 1861
DENTON, George W.	38	19 Oct 1878	Oct 24, 1878
DENTON, Grace Estella	6y 8m 8d	6 Jan 1864	Jan 14, 1864
DENTON, Henrietta	8y 7m	28 Apr 1865	May 4, 1865
DENTON, James G.	56	28 Jan 1876	Feb 3, 1876
DENTON, John L.	33rd y	no date	Feb 3, 1870
DENTON, Leonard S.	11y 2m 19d	8 Jan 1864	Jan 14, 1864
DENTON, Lewis, Jr	36	1 Dec 1877	Dec 6, 1877
DENTON, Mariam	2m	7 May 1864	May 12, 1864
DENTON, Mary	80y 4m	30 Aug 1873	Sep 4, 1873
DENTON, Mary Catherine	4m 10d	10th inst	Aug 18, 1864
DENTON, Mary E.	18	16 Nov 1863	Nov 19, 1863
DENTON, Mary Emma	12y 6m	8 Feb 1862	Feb 13, 1862
DENTON, Nehemiah	14y 2m 21d	17 Oct 1860	Oct 18, 1860
DENTON, Phebe	86	7 Feb 1861	Feb 14, 1861
DENTON, Rebecca	94y 10d	20 Sep 1870	Sep 29, 1870
DENTON, Sarah	69	last Sat	Oct 13, 1864
DENTON, Sarah	76	13th inst	Feb 23, 1865
DENTON, Susan	10y 1m	16 Apr 1876	Apr 20, 1876
DENTON, William	6m	22 Aug 1874	Aug 27, 1874
DENTON, William B.	4y 10m	16 Mar 1876	Mar 23, 1876
DENTON, William F.	16	28 Sep 1862	Oct 2, 1862
DENYSE, Isaac	80y 2m 16d	1 Feb 1877	Feb 8, 1877
DE NYSE, Sarah Hegerman	72y 9m 2d	1 Jul 1877	Jul 5, 1877

Name	Age	Date of death	Date of newspaper
DERBY, Edgar Mortimer	21y 5m	25 Mar 1874	Apr 2, 1874
DERBY, Lydia Emma	25y 6m 16d	22 Jan 1876	Jan 27, 1876
DERBY, Marietta	39	12 Apr 1872	Apr 18, 1872
DERBY, Mary S. Place	86th y	19 Nov 1867	Nov 21, 1867
DERBY, Orlando A.	25y 6m 6d	18 Sep 1871	Sep 21, 1871
DERBY, William	67	17th inst	Feb 23, 1860
DERBY, Zephaniah	75y 6m 3d	29 Nov 1869	Dec 2, 1869
DEVEREUX, Sally Ann	no age	17 Jul 1858	Jul 22, 1858
DE WITT, John	2y 18d	4 Oct 1873	Oct 9, 1873
DEWITT, Thomas	83	18 May 1874	May 21, 1874
DICKINSON,	no age	27 May 1874	Jun 4, 1874
DICKINSON, Margaret Kemble	75th y	6 Apr 1878	Apr 11, 1878
DICKSON, Wade	10	4 Aug 1861	Aug 15, 1861
DICKSON, Walter B.	21	22 Aug 1861	Aug 29, 1861
DIETER, Mitchell	10m	24 Aug 1874	Aug 27, 1874
DIKEMAN, (Mrs.)	85th y	13 Sep 1874	Sep 24, 1874
DIKEMAN, Charles	58	18 Jun 1871	Jun 22, 1871
DIKEMAN, Charles	20	11 Dec 1878	Dec 19, 1878
DIKEMAN, Eugene	infant	no date	Aug 19, 1858
DIKEMAN, Freelove	84y 7m 14d	13 Sep 1874	Sep 17, 1874
DIKEMAN, Susanna E.	48y 3m	27 Mar 1875	Apr 1, 1875
DIKEMAN, Tunis	32	6 Jun 1865	Jun 15, 1865
DIKEMAN, William Rushmore	4y 8m 4d	25 Jan 1864	Jan 28, 1864
DILAMAR, Jacques	no age	14 Feb 1874	Feb 26, 1874
DITMARS, Dow	90th y	20 Jun 1860	Jul 5, 1860
DIXON, William	1y 9d	4 Sep 1873	Sep 11, 1873
DODD, Peter F.	ca. 50	3 Jul 1872	Jul 18, 1872
DODD, Sarah Elizabeth	19y 11m 10d	last Fri	Dec 20, 1860
DODGE, Eliza	73	21 Apr 1872	May 9, 1872
DODGE, Isaac	96	20 Sep 1877	Sep 27, 1877
DODGE, William H. H.	27	5 Feb 1864	Feb 11, 1864
DODWORTH, Thomas J.	86	29th ult	May 11, 1876
DOMINICK, J.	no age	no date	Jul 15, 1875
DONAHUE, James	ca. 40	29th inst	Dec 7, 1871
DONAHUE, John	2m 1d	7 Mar 1876	Mar 16, 1876
DONAHUE, Mary	1m 27d	29 Feb 1876	Mar 9, 1876
DONCORT, (child of Alfred)	infant	no date	Jul 15, 1858
DONCOURT, Annie	12	13 Apr 1875	Apr 15, 1875
DONELSON, Andrew Jackson	no age	4 Jul 1871	Jul 6, 1871
DONLAN, James	17	Monday	Dec 13, 1877
DONNELLY, (dau. of James)	infant	10 Oct 1875	Oct 14, 1875
DONNELLY, Ellen	no age	23 Nov 1870	Dec 1, 1870
DONNELLY, Thomas	no age	Fri	Feb 12, 1863
DONNOLAN, William	1y 6m	19 Jul 1871	Jul 27, 1871
DONNOLLY, (Mr.)	no age	22 Jan 1874	Jan 29, 1874
DONOHUE, John	no age	last week	Jul 18, 1872
DONOHUE, Joseph	a boy	Sunday	Jun 7, 1877
DONOLON, Peter	2y 7d	2 Jun 1874	Jun 11, 1874
DONOVAN, James	27y 6m	23 Nov 1868	Dec 3, 1868
DOOLEY, John	32	29 Jan 1872	Feb 1, 1872
DOOLEY, Margaret	46	11 Mar 1876	Mar 16, 1876
DOONAN, (son of Patrick)	3m	24 Aug 1876	Aug 31, 1876
DORIAN, Margaret	82	23 Sep 1875	Oct 7, 1875
DORLAN, Joseph	78	17th	Apr 23, 1863
DORLAND, Rachael	no age	28 May 1858	Jun 3, 1858
DORLON, Carman	69	26th inst	Sep 27, 1860
DORLON, Jane	61y 4m	19 Jan 1877	Jan 25, 1877
DORLON, Martha	74y 3m 6d	5 Apr 1868	Apr 9, 1868
DORLON, Samuel	77	11 Jan 1862	Jan 16, 1862
DORLON, Thomas	ca. 85	16 Mar 1864	Mar 24, 1864

Name	Age	Date of death	Date of newspaper
DOSCEY, Son	21	30 Nov 1877	Dec 6, 1877
DOTY, Elizabeth	75	1 Mar 1873	Mar 13, 1873
DOTY, John	3	26 Sep 1875	Oct 7, 1875
DOTY, John H.	3	22 Jun 1858	Jun 24, 1858
DOUD, Emily A.	25y 2m 4d	24 Oct 1874	Nov 5, 1874
DOUGHERTY, Catherine	56	14 Sep 1867	Sep 19, 1867
DOUGHERTY, J. (Mrs.)	no age	last eve	Aug 2, 1860
DOUGHERTY, John	49	5 Aug 1864	Aug 25, 1864
DOUGHERTY, John	22	26 Jun 1876	Jul 6, 1876
DOUGHTY, Cornelius D.	58y 3m 10d	19 Oct 1876	Oct 26, 1876
DOUGHTY, Ellen Wyckoff	68	15 Apr 1861	Apr 18, 1861
DOUGHTY, John	ca. 22	no date	Dec 8, 1859
DOUGHTY, Margaret A.	54y 5m 19d	29 Jun 1877	Jul 5, 1877
DOUGHTY, Samuel	76	20th inst	Sep 27, 1860
DOUGLAS, Elizabeth	no age	Tue	Jan 12, 1860
DOUGLASS, George	no age	31 Jan 1862	Feb 6, 1862
DOUGLASS, Joseph	no age	Monday	Dec 17, 1874
DOW, Jacob	70	28 Nov 1874	Dec 10, 1874
DOWNEY, Joanna	80	no date	Jun 6, 1878
DOWNING, Daniel	no age	17 Jun 1863	Jun 25, 1863
DOWNING, George	92y 3m 3d	3 Mar 1873	Mar 6, 1873
DOWNING, Samuel B.	74y 9m	14 Nov 1876	Nov 16, 1876
DOWNS, John	86	no date	Jan 25, 1872
DOXEY, Ruth Emily	16	1 May 1865	May 25, 1865
DOXIE, Mary	50	26 Feb 1869	Mar 11, 1869
DOXSEY, John	23	5 Sep 1868	Sep 10, 1868
DOYLE, Catherine	45	30 May 1874	Jun 4, 1874
DOYLE, Edward	no age	4 Jul 1869	Dec 9, 1869
DOYLE, James	no age	20 May 1861	May 23, 1861
DRAKE, Lana	2y 8m	23 Mar 1868	Mar 26, 1868
DRAVEL, Richard	40	9 Apr 1865	Apr 13, 1865
DUFFEE, James	16	11 Aug 1878	Aug 15, 1878
DUFFY, John	22	Sunday	Mar 1, 1877
DUFFY, Patrick	no age	16 May 1874	May 21, 1874
DUHAIN, Evelina D.	22	22 Jun 1858	Jun 24, 1858
DUKOL, John	no age	28 Nov 1871	Dec 7, 1871
DUNBAR, (Mrs)	60	21 Mar 1870	Mar 24, 1870
DUNBAR, James	70y 7m	26 Jan 1878	Jan 31, 1878
DUNBAR, Smith	40y 10m 12d	23 Oct 1871	Oct 26, 1871
DUNLEAVY, Mary Anna	22	5 May 1876	May 18, 1876
DUNN, (5 ch. of Edward)	no age	no date	Mar 3, 1870
DUNN, (wife of Edward)	no age	no date	Mar 3, 1870
DUNN, Edward	no age	no date	Mar 3, 1870
DUNN, Henry Augustus	5m	23 Nov 1868	Nov 26, 1868
DUNN, John	no age	Thursday	Aug 22, 1878
DUNN, John V.	20y 9m 22d	31 May 1864	Jul 7, 1864
DUNN, Michael	no age	no date	Jul 29, 1875
DUPIGNAC, (child of William)	infant	6 Feb 1864	Feb 11, 1864
DURAT, Sarah M.	ca. 56	last Fri/Sa	Nov 29, 1860
DURLAN, Robert R.	no age	8 Nov 1859	Nov 10, 1859
DURLAND, Betsey	76y 6m	21 Sep 1872	Sep 26, 1872
DURLAND, Mary	67	2 Feb 1868	Feb 6, 1868
DURLAND, William	no age	23 Mar 1874	Apr 2, 1874
DURYEA, (wife of Garret)	ca. 40	12th inst	Mar 15, 1860
DURYEA, Abraham J.	ca. 28	18 Mar 1864	Mar 24, 1864
DURYEA, Abram	74th y	7 Dec 1878	Dec 12, 1878
DURYEA, Ada F.	2y 1m 12d	30 Jul 1875	Aug 5, 1875
DURYEA, Adelia A.	no age	no date	Jan 10, 1878
DURYEA, Adelia E. (nee BEDELL)	36y 8m 5d	11 Aug 1876	Aug 17, 1876

Name	Age	Date of death	Date of newspaper
DURYEA, Charles F.	23	19 Aug 1877	Aug 30, 1877
DURYEA, Edward R.	3	23 Apr 1875	May 6, 1875
DURYEA, Elizabeth	84	4 Nov 1865	Nov 16, 1865
DURYEA, Ella T.	8m 1d	12 Sep 1872	Sep 26, 1872
DURYEA, Elvira B.	6m 29d	31 Jul 1868	Aug 6, 1868
DURYEA, Eva C.	3m 8d	7 Jul 1876	Jul 13, 1876
DURYEA, Ida	2y	29 Jul 1870	Aug 11, 1870
DURYEA, Jane	70	10 Feb 1870	Feb 24, 1870
DURYEA, Jemima	88	11 Nov 1862	Nov 20, 1862
DURYEA, Mamie	no age	23 Sep 1875	Sep 30, 1875
DURYEA, Pamelia	30y 10m 2d	14 Jan 1868	Jan 23, 1868
DURYEA, Peter	60y 23d	1st inst	Apr 5, 1860
DURYEA, Phebe	68	27 Aug 1865	Aug 31, 1865
DURYEA, Phebe	66y 22d	4 Jul 1867	Jul 11, 1867
DURYEA, Phebe	19	4 Nov 1868	Nov 12, 1868
DURYEA, Whitehead	no age	no date	Jan 10, 1878
DURYEA, Whitehead C.	28	26 Oct 1868	Oct 29, 1868
DURYEA, William Cooper	1y 4m	26 Jun 1863	Jul 9, 1863
DURYEA, Willie	no age	no date	Jan 10, 1878
DURYEE, Joseph Woodward	5m 17d	4 Feb 1864	Feb 11, 1864
DYKE, Charles	85	30 Jul 1871	Aug 3, 1871
EAGAN, Ann F.	84	31 Jul 1872	Aug 15, 1872
EAGER, Nancy Floyd	30	no date	Sep 30, 1858
EARLY, Daniel	no age	Saturday	Aug 18, 1870
EASTMAN, Cordelia	34y 4m	24 Oct 1868	Oct 29, 1868
EASTMAN, Johathan	61	9 Mar 1868	Mar 19, 1868
EBERHARDT, Jacob	ca. 16	Saturday	Jul 15, 1875
EDMOND, Robert	58	5 Apr 1864	Apr 14, 1864
EDWARDS, (Mr)	no age	recently	Mar 3, 1870
EDWARDS, (Mrs)	no age	recently	Mar 3, 1870
EDWARDS, (child)	no age	recently	Mar 3, 1870
EDWARDS, (son of Andrew)	infant	2 May 1875	May 6, 1875
EDWARDS, Addie	1y 1m 4d	31 Jul 1873	Aug 7, 1873
EDWARDS, Albert B.	45	26 Dec 1873	Jan 1, 1874
EDWARDS, Amy	61y 8m 6d	22 Oct 1865	Oct 26, 1865
EDWARDS, Bedell	50	15 Apr 1859	Apr 21, 1859
EDWARDS, Clarissa B.	25	19 Dec 1873	Dec 25, 1873
EDWARDS, George	45	no date	Apr 29, 1875
EDWARDS, Gouverneur	74y 8m 10d	20th inst	May 26, 1870
EDWARDS, Henrietta	19	7 Dec 1861	Dec 12, 1861
EDWARDS, John	68	2 Apr 1868	Apr 9, 1868
EDWARDS, Laura L.	27y 2m	8 May 1878	May 9, 1878
EDWARDS, Nathaniel	no age	21st inst	May 29, 1862
EDWARDS, Phebe A.	44y 10m	25 Nov 1877	Nov 29, 1877
EDWARDS, Rachael L.	55y 11m	no date	Sep 1, 1864
EDWARDS, Sarah	31y 7m 6d	12 Nov 1876	Nov 16, 1876
EDWARDS, Thomas	62	11 Mar 1869	Mar 18, 1869
EDWARDS, William	infant	24 Sep 1878	Sep 26, 1878
EDWARDS, William H.	2y 8m 24d	25 Aug 1864	Sep 1, 1864
EDWARDS, William Henry	30	18 Oct 1862	Oct 23, 1862
EGER, --?--	no age	last week	Jul 18, 1872
EHLERS, John	45	5 Jul 1875	Jul 8, 1875
EICHLER, Margaret	81	22 Dec 1878	Dec 26, 1878
EIGHMEGH, Ann	ca. 40	26 fifth mo	Jun 9, 1864
ELDERD, Ellen A.	25y 4m	15 Mar 1878	Mar 21, 1878
ELDERED, Phebe	77y 3m 21d	25 Aug 1871	Aug 31, 1871
ELDERT, Harriet	53y 2m 13d	24 Jun 1872	Jun 27, 1872
ELDERT, Isaac	69y 5m 7d	27 Feb 1872	Feb 29, 1872

Name	Age	Date of death	Date of newspaper
ELDERT, Sarah	78y 2m 24d	5th inst	May 17, 1860
ELDERT, Sarah Amelia	26y 9m 9d	19 Jul 1871	Jul 20, 1871
ELDERT, Timothy N.	ca. 59	12 Jan 1870	Jan 27, 1870
ELDERT, Valentine	21	7 Sep 1862	Sep 11, 1862
ELDRED, Rebecca	77th y	12 Feb 1872	Feb 15, 1872
ELDRED, Sarah	85	22 Dec 1862	Dec 25, 1862
ELDRID, Mervin	10m	28 Aug 1878	Sep 5, 1878
ELDRIDGE, (Mrs. Richard)	no age	1st inst.	Nov 17, 1864
ELLINERS, --?--	no age	5th	Jul 15, 1875
ELLIOT, Jeremiah B.	no age	13 Jun 1858	Jun 17, 1858
ELLIOTT, Lydia	17	last Thur	Dec 8, 1864
ELLIS, (dau. of Mr. L.)	3	Tuesday	Aug 15, 1867
ELLIS, Charles W.	3y 6m 28d	19 Dec 1863	Dec 31, 1863
ELLIS, George	no age	Tues last w	Feb 10, 1870
ELLIS, Kate Louisa	7y 6m 6d	26 Nov 1863	Dec 3, 1863
ELLISON, Catherine J.	19	12 Mar 1865	Mar 30, 1865
ELLISON, Charity	no age	no date	Sep 1, 1870
ELLISON, Hewlett	24	7 Sep 1865	Sep 14, 1865
ELLISON, Thomas	ca. 32	28 Aug 1864	Sep 1, 1864
ELMORE, (Mrs. James H.)	no age	last Mon	Oct 10, 1872
ELMORE, Charley	20	26 Dec 1875	Dec 30, 1875
ELSESSER, John B.	no age	last Sun	Jan 29, 1863
ELTON, Robert	70	13 Sep 1871	Sep 21, 1871
ELTONS, Ann	56	no date	Oct 10, 1878
ELY, Samuel R.	70	11 May 1873	May 15, 1873
EMBERRY, Daniel	no age	10 Feb 1864	Feb 25, 1864
EMBREE, Sarah R.	65 or 66	6 Jan 1864	Jan 14, 1864
EMMS, Mary Gertrude	6m 7d	13 Jul 1872	Jul 18, 1872
ENKELSHARYER, Rutolf	48	26th inst	Jan 30, 1868
ENOS, Dewitt C.	no age	Monday	Dec 31, 1868
ERBER, (child of John F.)	5	Friday	Mar 22, 1877
ERICKSON, Clara Matilda	child	last Fri	Aug 22, 1872
ESEN, Matilda	5y 2m	2 May 1869	May 6, 1869
ESQUIROL, Melissa	76	25 Jun 1875	Jul 8, 1875
ESTRANGE, Patrick	no age	Sat	Jul 12, 1860
EVANS, John	65	27 Apr 1870	May 5, 1870
EVERETT, Sarah Elizabeth	32	8 Oct 1859	Oct 13, 1859
EVERITT, (wife of Edward)	no age	2 Jul 1859	Jul 7, 1859
EVERITT, Charles H.	42	26 Jun 1878	Jul 4, 1878
EVERITT, Edward	70	15 Jan 1865	Jan 19, 1865
EVERS, Catina	43	24 Jun 1864	Jun 30, 1864
EVERS, Emma	2y 3m	29 Oct 1876	Nov 2, 1876
EVERS, Francis	29y 8m 6d	no date	Mar 25, 1875
EVERS, Lizzie	5y 2m	9 Oct 1876	Oct 12, 1876
EVERSON, Mary	40	29 Aug 1873	Sep 4, 1873
EWELL, (Mrs.)	74	18th inst	Feb 10, 1859
EWELL, Charlotte	46	8 Aug 1874	Aug 13, 1874
F----R, (dau. of Capt. Benj)	2	no date	May 9, 1872
FAESAL, Mary Teresa	ca. 4m	1 Jul 1872	Jul 4, 1872
FAGAN, (son of Luke)	infant	14 Sep 1870	Sep 15, 1870
FAGAN, Edward B.	10m 21d	4 Sep 1872	Sep 5, 1872
FAGIN, Thomas	8m	23 May 1874	May 28, 1874
FAIR, James M.	15	28 Apr 1876	May 4, 1876
FALDRAC, Daniel A.	75y 1m 4d	26 Mar 1869	Apr 1, 1869
FANNING, Frances	no age	3 Mar 1864	Mar 10, 1864
FANNING, Hiram	70	22 Oct 1868	Oct 29, 1868
FANNING, William	81	25 Sep 1861	Sep 26, 1861
FARMER, August	no age	3rd inst	Oct 11, 1877

Name	Age	Date of death	Date of newspaper
FARMER, J. (Mrs.)	no age	6 Oct 1858	Oct 14, 1858
FARREL, James	no age	Monday	Sep 20, 1860
FARRINGTON, Dan	elderly	23 Jan 1874	Jan 29, 1874
FAY, Marcellus E.	35y 10m	18 Nov 1878	Nov 28, 1878
FEDERICO, Rocco	no age	no date	Sep 24, 1874
FEEKS, Daniel	87	28 Jan 1862	Feb 6, 1862
FEELY, Catharine	11m	7 Aug 1874	Aug 13, 1874
FEIST, Wilhelmina	36	24 Apr 1865	Apr 27, 1865
FERGUSON, Thomas	no age	12 Nov 1874	Nov 19, 1874
FERRELL, Mary	66	5 Nov 1865	Nov 16, 1865
FIELD, Mary	6	24 Jan 1859	Feb 3, 1859
FIELDS, W. F.	22	8 Apr 1876	May 4, 1876
FINCH, (Mr.)	no age	no date	Aug 28, 1873
FINCH, James Byron	1y 3m 7d	31 Dec 1872	Jan 9, 1873
FINN, (male)	no age	no date	Jul 15, 1875
FINN, James	no age	19th ult	Jun 11, 1863
FISCHER, Caroline	54	10 Jun 1878	Jun 13, 1878
FISH, Samuel, Jr.	11m 12d	18 Jul 1872	Jul 25, 1872
FITZGERALD, John	no age	Sat	Feb 5, 1863
FITZGERALD, Wm	12	27 Jun 1874	Jul 2, 1874
FLAGAN, James	50	20 Oct 1874	Oct 22, 1874
FLAHERTY, Edward	no age	last Thur	Sep 20, 1860
FLANAGAN, (child of Mr.)	9m	no date	Aug 22, 1867
FLANAGAN, (son of John)	14m	no date	Sep 1, 1870
FLANAGAN, Bridget	63	31 Aug 1870	Sep 8, 1870
FLANNERY, John	4	21 Dec 1878	Dec 26, 1878
FLANNIGAN, Ann	28	30 Sep 1873	Oct 2, 1873
FLEET, Alice Helena	7m	13 Apr 1863	Apr 16, 1863
FLEET, Ann	66	10 Feb 1862	Feb 13, 1862
FLEET, Caroline	1	31 Aug 1859	Sep 8, 1859
FLEET, Eugene F.	12	28 Dec 1870	Jan 5, 1871
FLEET, Jake	no age	19 Mar 1864	Apr 7, 1864
FLEET, John F.	8y 6d	30 Apr 1868	May 7, 1868
FLEET, Luke, Sr.	69	8 Feb 1862	Feb 13, 1862
FLEET, Mary	69	20 Feb 1859	Mar 3, 1859
FLEET, Rebecca Young	72	2 Jan 1874	Jan 8, 1874
FLEMING, William	62	15 May 1864	May 19, 1864
FLEMING, William	48	16 Jun 1877	Jun 21, 1877
FLEMMING, (Mrs.)	no age	last Tues	Jan 4, 1872
FLETCHER, Ruth M.	70th y	19 Nov 1869	Nov 25, 1869
FLEURY, James	infant	2 Aug 1865	Aug 10, 1865
FLOWER, Joseph	78y 3m	10 Dec 1877	Dec 13, 1877
FLOWER, Peggy	82	27 Sep 1861	Oct 3, 1861
FLOWERS, (son of William E.)	1m	23 Jan 1874	Feb 5, 1874
FLOWERS, Alonzo	2y 12d	29 Nov 1870	Dec 1, 1870
FLOWERS, Zebulon V.	17	no date	Jun 18, 1863
FLOYD, Peter	no age	no date	Sep 1, 1870
FLOYD-JONES, (widow of Henry)	ca. 85	18 Jul 1872	Aug 1, 1872
FLOYD-JONES, Mary S.	no age	23 May 1874	May 28, 1874
FLUHR, Anton	elderly	Thursday	Dec 30, 1875
FLYNN, Arthur	no age	last Thur	May 26, 1864
FOLK, John	no age	Monday	Dec 26, 1872
FOOTE, (child of John)	infant	3 Oct 1865	Oct 5, 1865
FORBES, Westcott	24	Thursday	Dec 20, 1877
FORDHAM, Hubbard	no age	last Mon	Aug 15, 1872
FOREMAN, Henrietta	71	1 May 1875	May 6, 1875
FORT, P. I. (Capt.)	37	20 Nov 1863	Nov 26, 1863
FOSDICK, Alexander S.	19y 1m 20d	1 Aug 1863	Aug 6, 1863
FOSDICK, Elbert E.	8m 10d	26th inst	Oct 5, 1865
FOSDICK, Margaret	65y 5m 21d	17th inst	Oct 20, 1864

Name	Age	Date of death	Date of newspaper
FOSDICK, Morris L.	8m	31 Oct 1861	Nov 7, 1861
FOSDICK, Seaman	75y 10d	26 Sep 1874	Oct 1, 1874
FOSDICK, Stephen M.	29y 6m 21d	8th inst	Jun 16, 1864
FOSTEL (or FOSTER), Joseph A.	26y 4m	3 Dec 1863	Dec 10, 1863
FOSTER (or FOSTEL), Joseph A.	26y 4m	3 Dec 1863	Dec 10, 1863
FOSTER, (child of William)	infant	no date	Aug 12, 1858
FOSTER, Amy	10d	10 Aug 1868	Aug 27, 1868
FOSTER, Eliza	52	no date	Jan 27, 1859
FOSTER, Herbert Ray Clarke	11m 22d	27 Aug 1865	Aug 31, 1865
FOSTER, Mariann	51y 8m	11th inst	May 26, 1864
FOSTER, Mary Jane	35	29 Oct 1874	Nov 5, 1874
FOSTER, Robert	4d	no date	Aug 16, 1860
FOSTER, Robert C.	36	9 Oct 1869	Oct 14, 1869
FOWLER, Adeline	56y 9m 17d	21 Mar 1876	Mar 30, 1876
FOWLER, Angeline	49	24 Feb 1876	Mar 2, 1876
FOWLER, Felix	32	1 Aug 1859	Aug 4, 1859
FOWLER, George	83y 2m 14d	11 Dec 1876	Dec 14, 1876
FOWLER, Gertrude	2m	2 Jan 1876	Jan 13, 1876
FOWLER, Joseph	40	11 Nov 1871	Nov 16, 1871
FOWLER, Mary	77y 11m 16d	25 Mar 1874	Apr 2, 1874
FOWLER, Phebe Ann	66y 1m 18d	28 Feb 1878	Mar 7, 1878
FOX, Catharine	no age	8 Jan 1870	Jan 13, 1870
FOX, Charles	80	22 Nov 1873	Dec 4, 1873
FOX, John	no age	20 Mar 1872	Apr 4, 1872
FOY, Charles A.	1y 9m	30 Oct 1875	Nov 4, 1875
FRANCIS, Emma	2	10 Aug 1868	Aug 20, 1868
FRANCIS, J. W.	71	Friday	Feb 14, 1861
FRANCIS, Jeanette	5y 1m 25d	5 Mar 1875	Mar 11, 1875
FRANCIS, John	27	5 Jun 1874	Jun 11, 1874
FRANK, Jacob B.	22	10 Dec 1858	Dec 16, 1858
FRANKLIN, Benjamin	no age	Monday	Feb 15, 1877
FRANKLIN, James J.	4y 3m	3 Mar 1876	Mar 9, 1876
FRAVEL, (child of John)	6m	2 Jul 1867	Aug 15, 1867
FREDERICKS, J. P. (Capt.)	45	8 Nov 1863	Nov 26, 1863
FREELY, Frank Joseph	7m 9d	7 Nov 1874	Nov 12, 1874
FREEMAN, Henry C.	no age	14 Jan 1871	Feb 9, 1871
FREYENHAGEN, Mary	77y 8m 12d	25 Oct 1868	Nov 5, 1868
FROST, (Mrs Marshall)	38	15 Nov 1870	Nov 24, 1870
FROST, Charles	24	5 Jan 1878	Jan 10, 1878
FROST, Edward L.	83rd y	31 Mar 1878	Apr 4, 1878
FROST, Ezekiel	28	5 Feb 1878	Feb 14, 1878
FROST, Fanny	80	3rd inst	Feb 13, 1868
FROST, Hannah	75	no date	Dec 23, 1858
FROST, Isaac	ca. 38	16th inst	Nov 15, 1860
FROST, Mary Ann	57	29 Sep 1877	Oct 4, 1877
FROST, Susan	70	26th inst	Mar 2, 1865
FULLER, Fannie E.	2y 8d	12 Aug 1876	Aug 17, 1876
FULTON, Margaret	78	23 Apr 1876	Apr 27, 1876
GAETONS, (son of late Patrick)	7	last Thurs	Oct 4, 1877
GALE, Addie Louise (nee POWELL)	30th y	21st inst	Aug 29, 1867
GALLAGHER, George	61	24 Oct 1868	Oct 29, 1868
GALLAGHER, James	16	Friday	Aug 16, 1877
GARDEN, (Mrs. J.)	no age	11 Jan 1875	Jan 28, 1875
GARDEN, J.	no age	2 Jan 1875	Jan 28, 1875
GARDENER, Margaret	25y 10m 27d	22 Feb 1870	Feb 24, 1870
GARDINER, Abigail	80	2 Mar 1861	Mar 21, 1861

Name	Age	Date of death	Date of newspaper
GARDINER, Lyon	94	24 May 1858	Jul 22, 1858
GARDINER, Mary L.	68	no date	Nov 29, 1860
GARDNER, Avis S.	60	27 Feb 1865	Mar 2, 1865
GARDNER, Camilla C.	2m 1d	25 Jul 1873	Jul 31, 1873
GARLAND, Thomas F.	no age	no date	Jul 19, 1877
GARNER, William T.	no age	20 Jul 1876	Dec 27, 1877
GARRETT, Frederick B.	2y 25d	13 Aug 1875	Aug 19, 1875
GARRISON, Thomas	77th y	30 Nov 1878	Dec 12, 1878
GARVIE, Helen	73	14 Feb 1859	Mar 3, 1859
GASTKE, August L.	4m	24 Aug 1878	Aug 29, 1878
GAULY, Roger	22	6 Aug 1865	Aug 10, 1865
GEARY, Isreal	84	30 Apr 1875	May 6, 1875
GEDNEY, Sylvester	28	1 Apr 1863	Apr 9, 1863
GENNITTY, (Mrs)	76	11 Feb 1877	Feb 22, 1877
GEORGEAN, (dau. of Michael)	4 1/2	no date	Jul 5, 1877
GERARD, Hiram E.	no age	last Sun	Oct 13, 1864
GERARD, Richmond	19	no date	Nov 4, 1858
GEROW, Andrew	55	25 May 1863	May 28, 1863
GERSTENBERG, (Mrs Frederick)	31	8 Dec 1867	Dec 12, 1867
GEWITCHE, Frank	no age	Sunday	May 4, 1876
GIBNEY, James	18y 4m	9 Jan 1877	Jan 11, 1877
GIBNEY, Patrick	76	22 Jan 1874	Feb 5, 1874
GIBSON, Patrick	92nd y	9 Nov 1874	Nov 12, 1874
GIBSON, William	ca. 60	13th inst	Sep 27, 1860
GILBERT, John C.	68	3 Nov 1873	Nov 6, 1873
GILDERSLEEVE, Cynthia	no age	no date	Sep 1, 1870
GILDERSLEEVE, Eliza	70	16 Feb 1861	Mar 21, 1861
GILDERSLEEVE, Ellen E.	23	27 Mar 1861	Apr 4, 1861
GILDERSLEEVE, George A.	29	25 Sep 1860	Oct 11, 1860
GILDERSLEEVE, James T.	73	15 Jul 1876	Jul 27, 1876
GILDERSLEEVE, Jane	59	18 Jun 1871	Jun 22, 1871
GILDERSLEEVE, Jesse L.	no age	26 Sep 1870	Sep 29, 1870
GILDERSLEEVE, John	46	23 Apr 1874	Apr 30, 1874
GILDERSLEEVE, Joseph	71	15 Mar 1865	Mar 16, 1865
GILDERSLEEVE, Josiah	79y 8m 12d	18 Apr 1876	Apr 20, 1876
GILDERSLEEVE, Martha	73y 7m	25 Nov 1863	Dec 3, 1863
GILDERSLEEVE, Martha	77y 4m 5d	15 Apr 1874	Apr 16, 1874
GILDERSLEEVE, Martha Ann	61	11 Aug 1863	Aug 13, 1863
GILDERSLEEVE, Mary H.	53	14 Oct 1862	Oct 16, 1862
GILDERSLEEVE, Rosetta	85th y	10 Jul 1878	Jul 11, 1878
GILDERSLEEVE, Van de Water Weekes	8y 6m 14d	20 Oct 1867	Nov 7, 1867
GILL, Elizabeth	27	6 Feb 1859	Feb 10, 1859
GILL, Helen E.	6	6 Feb 1859	Feb 10, 1859
GILL, Mary E.	2	6 Feb 1859	Feb 10, 1859
GILL, Thomas	no age	20 Jun 1858	Jun 24, 1858
GILLEN, Edward	41	22 Jul 1872	Jul 25, 1872
GILLEN, Edward	no age	22nd	Aug 8, 1872
GILLETTE, Daniel	18	last Sun	May 17, 1860
GILLIAN, Isaac	44	30 Jun 1878	Jul 4, 1878
GISSERMAN, (male)	ca. 25	last Sat	Jun 11, 1863
GLANDERS, Henry	7	9 Jun 1858	Jun 17, 1858
GLEASON, (female)	14	8 Nov 1861	Nov 14, 1861
GLOVER, Lewis N.	14	22 Nov 1876	Nov 30, 1876
GOCH, (Dr.)	ca. 72	no date	Jul 26, 1860
GOLD, Mary	78	no date	Aug 26, 1858
GOLDECK, (son of Lewis)	1m	7 Oct 1871	Oct 12, 1871
GOLDEN, (Mrs.) (nee BEDELL)	83rd y	Wed last w	Oct 22, 1874
GOLDEN, Alanson	60y 28d	5 Sep 1874	Sep 10, 1874
GOLDEN, Albert	4y 3m 20d	6 Nov 1870	Nov 10, 1870

Name	Age	Date of death	Date of newspaper
GOLDEN, Caroline	2	26 Sep 1872	Oct 3, 1872
GOLDEN, Charles S.	14y 9m 7d	30 Oct 1870	Nov 3, 1870
GOLDEN, Fannie	2y 6m	7 Aug 1875	Aug 12, 1875
GOLDEN, George W.	1y 6m	21 Jul 1875	Aug 5, 1875
GOLDEN, George W.	35y 11m	26 May 1877	May 31, 1877
GOLDEN, Mary C.	82y 7m 5d	16 Oct 1874	Oct 22, 1874
GOLDER, (son of Charles)	infant	24 Sep 1875	Oct 7, 1875
GOLDER, Betsey H.	63y 8m 21d	24 Nov 1872	Nov 28, 1872
GOLDER, Emma	4	25 Mar 1870	Mar 31, 1870
GOLDER, Frank	ca. 17	last Sun	Apr 18, 1872
GOLDER, Jane	96	26 Jul 1858	Aug 5, 1858
GOLDER, Jemima	2y 21d	23 Feb 1872	Feb 29, 1872
GOLDER, John	no age	11 Sep 1863	Oct 15, 1863
GOLDER, Lydia J.	26y 3m 18d	14 Jul 1878	Jul 18, 1878
GOLDER, Newman	26y 7m 5d	5 Jul 1872	Jul 18, 1872
GOLDER, Samuel	34y 2m	? inst	Jun 29, 1865
GOLDER, William	33	no date	May 28, 1863
GOODWIN, Cathrine T.	no age	18 Oct 1858	Nov 4, 1858
GORDON, Nathaniel P.	no age	21 Feb 1862	Feb 27, 1862
GORMAND, Margaret	79	27 Aug 1875	Sep 2, 1875
GORMERLY, James	no age	last week	Sep 27, 1877
GOSBERCER, Anna	36	21 Sep 1859	Sep 22, 1859
GOSLANE, P.	65	14 Dec 1858	Dec 23, 1858
GOTTERT, Charles	69	29 Apr 1873	May 1, 1873
GOULD, Conklin	86	3 Nov 1867	Nov 7, 1867
GOULD, Jane C.	75	4 Oct 1876	Oct 26, 1876
GOULD, Rosetta	30	no date	Sep 30, 1858
GOULD, William H.	30	5 Jul 1875	Jul 8, 1875
GOWAN, Angel	45	6 Nov 1859	Nov 10, 1859
GOWAN, Sarah	70	21 Feb 1878	Feb 28, 1878
GRAGE, John	no age	Sunday	Jul 25, 1878
GRAHAM, (female)	5	last Mon	Mar 7, 1872
GRAHAM, Ida Emma	4m	17 Nov 1867	Nov 21, 1867
GRAHAM, Patrick	29	Sunday	May 8, 1862
GRANDIN, Estella	2y 3m	6 Aug 1874	Aug 13, 1874
GRANDIN, Lucie	5y 5m 14d	25 Dec 1874	Dec 31, 1874
GRANGER, George	21y 4m	7 Nov 1871	Nov 9, 1871
GREEN, Ezekiel	65	17 Nov 1877	Nov 22, 1877
GREEN, Patrick James	4	no date	Nov 10, 1864
GREEN, William	no age	last Wed	Jul 24, 1862
GREENE, John S.	80	6 Dec 1859	Jan 12, 1860
GREENE, Zachariah	99th y	21 Jun 1858	Jun 24, 1858
GREENE, Zachariah	99th y	21 Jun 1858	Jul 8, 1858
GREGORY, Isabella	13	20 Dec 1870	Dec 22, 1870
GREGORY, Walter	no age	19 Feb 1874	Feb 26, 1874
GRICE, Walter	19	17 Jul 1858	Jul 22, 1858
GRIES, Frances Bernatta	2y 3m 9d	28 Jun 1858	Jul 1, 1858
GRIFFIN, (wife of Sidney L.)	no age	no date	Dec 13, 1860
GRIFFIN, Eliza D.	31y 10d	28 Jun 1873	Jun 26, 1873
GRIFFIN, Eliza D.	31y 10d	23 Jun 1873	Jul 3, 1873
GRIFFIN, John	2y 5m	7 Nov 1876	Nov 9, 1876
GRIFFIN, Joseph	no age	no date	Jul 23, 1874
GRIFFIN, Lillian Estelle	2	29 Dec 1860	Jan 3, 1861
GRIFFIN, M. (Capt)	25	12 May 1874	May 28, 1874
GRIFFIN, Patrick	ca. 60	Thursday	Nov 8, 1877
GRIFFIN, Sarah Emma	18y 8m 23d	27th ult	Jul 11, 1867
GRIFFIN, Sarah H.	58y 11m 15d	1 Sep 1867	Sep 5, 1867
GRIFFIN, Wareham G.	9m 11d	last Mon	Apr 28, 1864
GRIFFING, Absalom S.	ca. 47	Friday	Jul 6, 1876
GRIFFING, Sidney	no age	13 Dec 1867	Dec 26, 1867

Name	Age	Date of death	Date of newspaper
GRITMAN, Benjamin	70	21 Mar 1861	Mar 28, 1861
GRITMAN, Joseph	ca. 40	Saturday	Dec 7, 1871
GUIN, Agnes	4m	26 Aug 1870	Sep 1, 1870
GUMIEN, Adolph Hippolyte	ca. 4m	Monday	Sep 5, 1872
GUMIEN, Mary	ca. 19	Monday	Sep 5, 1872
GUNSER, John	no age	recently	Jul 19, 1877
HAAS, Mary	70	20 Sep 1871	Sep 21, 1871
HADWICK, James	46	28 Jan 1869	Feb 4, 1869
HAFF, (dau. of Lawrence)	no age	9 Feb 1877	Feb 15, 1877
HAFF, (son of Valentine)	4w	5 Apr 1874	Apr 9, 1874
HAFF, Abraham	20	15 Sep 1867	Sep 19, 1867
HAFF, Amy	62	17 Aug 1868	Aug 20, 1868
HAFF, Benjamin Anson	3y 15d	18 Jan 1865	Jan 19, 1865
HAFF, David	48	7 Mar 1869	Mar 11, 1869
HAFF, Ebenezer	81	24 Oct 1876	Oct 26, 1876
HAFF, Mary	87	14 Mar 1872	Mar 21, 1872
HAFF, Mary Ann	ca. 25	4 Apr 1872	Apr 11, 1872
HAFF, Matilda	74y 1m 4d	31 Mar 1872	Apr 4, 1872
HAFF, Rapelyea	19	8 Sep 1867	Sep 26, 1867
HAFF, Stephen	ca. 65	3 Sep 1860	Sep 6, 1860
HAFF, Stephen	38	14 Apr 1865	Apr 27, 1865
HAGNER, Adelaide	74	15 Jun 1872	Jun 27, 1872
HAINES, S. Halsey	no age	last week	Feb 8, 1877
HAINES, William M.	37y 9m 11d	16 Jun 1869	Jun 24, 1869
HAINS, George	89y 2m	2 Jul 1878	Jul 4, 1878
HALEY, Michael	50	26 Apr 1878	May 2, 1878
HALL, (Miss)	no age	Tuesday	Aug 2, 1877
HALL, Annie	14	18 Dec 1870	Dec 22, 1870
HALL, Ellen	8m	3rd inst	Sep 14, 1865
HALL, Foster N.	3y 8m	last Sat	Jul 20, 1865
HALL, George Edwin	11m 17d	29 Sep 1874	Oct 8, 1874
HALL, Henry C.	32	20 Jun 1876	Jun 22, 1876
HALL, James	21	18 Jan 1873	Jan 16, 1873
HALL, Joseph B.	61y 8m	15 Sep 1872	Sep 19, 1872
HALL, R. D. (Rev.)	83	28 Jul 1873	Aug 7, 1873
HALLEN, Emily	30y 11m	24 Apr 1865	Apr 27, 1865
HALLENBECK, Charles	35	3 Aug 1859	Aug 4, 1859
HALLOCK, Benj. F.	60th y	24 Nov 1864	Dec 15, 1864
HALLOCK, Elvin	ca. 7	5 Feb 1877	Feb 22, 1877
HALLOCK, Peter	73y 10m 22d	5 Oct 1877	Oct 18, 1877
HALLOCK, Survia	83	21st ult	Jun 2, 1859
HALSEY, Albert, Jr.	25	26 Dec 1873	Jan 1, 1874
HALSEY, Allen	no age	22 Aug 1870	Aug 25, 1870
HALSEY, Edward	69	13 Dec 1858	Dec 23, 1858
HALSEY, Hugh	64	28 May 1858	Jun 10, 1858
HALSEY, Jame	no age	Monday	Mar 14, 1872
HALSEY, Jame	no age	Monday	Mar 14, 1872
HALSEY, Phebe	no age	2 Mar 1878	Mar 7, 1878
HAM, George	7	12 Mar 1859	Mar 24, 1859
HAMBER, Sarah Rebecca	24y 1m	11 Jun 1878	Jun 13, 1878
HAMILTON, Mary Ann	5	21 Jan 1862	Feb 6, 1862
HAMLETT, (child of John)	16m	10 Jan 1862	Jan 16, 1862
HAMMEL, Frank	12	14 Jul 1878	Jul 25, 1878
HAMMOND, (Mrs Frank)	41	26 Oct 1869	Oct 28, 1869
HAMMOND, Frances B.	no age	no date	Jul 8, 1858
HAMMOND, Jonathon	no age	no date	Jan 10, 1878
HAMMOND, William	no age	no date	Sep 23, 1858
HAMMOND, William G.	no age	19 Jun 1858	Jun 24, 1858

Name	Age	Date of death	Date of newspaper
HANAN, Clorinda H.	1y 5m	22 Jan 1874	Feb 5, 1874
HAND, Theron	no age	12th ult	May 17, 1877
HANEY, Thomas	no age	Thursday	Sep 2, 1875
HANLEY, John	65	31 Dec 1864	Jan 5, 1865
HANNON, (Mrs. Patrick)	no age	14 Mar 1875	Mar 18, 1875
HANNON, Patrick	no age	12 Mar 1875	Mar 18, 1875
HANS (OR HAUS), Philip	no age	23 Dec 1875	Dec 30, 1875
HANS, Philip	10	last Sun	Dec 23, 1875
HANSCOM, Sarah	82	11 Apr 1876	Apr 13, 1876
HANSELL, Hannah	no age	29 May 1874	Jun 4, 1874
HANSON, Jane	no age	no date	Oct 18, 1877
HANTZ, Catharine	4	Sunday	Jun 7, 1877
HARBECK, (child of Charles)	7w	4 Feb 1874	Feb 12, 1874
HARDMAN, (Mr)	no age	Tuesday	Aug 23, 1877
HARMON, Mary	10m 9d	18 Aug 1874	Aug 20, 1874
HARNESS, John	no age	9 Apr 1875	Apr 15, 1875
HAROLD, Eliza	62nd y	28 Jan 1872	Feb 1, 1872
HAROLD, Howard P.	2y 9m 5d	17 Jul 1876	Jul 20, 1876
HAROLD, John	71	29 Oct 1876	Nov 2, 1876
HARPER, James	no age	last year	Feb 17, 1870
HARPER, John	78	22 Apr 1875	Apr 29, 1875
HARPER, Joseph Wesley	69th y	14 Feb 1870	Feb 17, 1870
HARRALL, (Mr.)	no age	Friday	Aug 18, 1870
HARRISON, (Capt.)	no age	31 Dec 1859	Feb 23, 1860
HARRY, Dean	no age	no date	Nov 24, 1870
HART, (dau. of John L.)	3	Saturday	Nov 25, 1869
HART, Benjamin H.	65	18 Nov 1875	Dec 9, 1875
HART, Israel	86	8 May 1873	May 15, 1873
HART, Samuel	75	27 Dec 1860	Jan 3, 1861
HART, Sarah	no age	17 Jun 1875	Jun 24, 1875
HARTFORD, Frederick	no age	23rd inst	Apr 2, 1874
HARTMAN, Philip	40	5 Jul 1875	Jul 8, 1875
HARTY, Julia	75	19 Jun 1874	Jul 9, 1874
HASKINS, Isabella A.	no age	24 Sep 1859	Sep 29, 1859
HATTEN, George	no age	7 Dec 1871	Dec 14, 1871
HAUS (OR HANS), Philip	no age	23 Dec 1875	Dec 30, 1875
HAUSCHER, John	71	23 Jul 1875	Jul 29, 1875
HAVEMEYER, Mayor	70y 10m	30 Nov 1874	Dec 3, 1874
HAVENS, (Mr.)	no age	22 Jan 1874	Jan 29, 1874
HAVENS, David A.	no age	20 Nov 1874	Dec 3, 1874
HAVENS, Nathan	no age	last year	Dec 3, 1874
HAVILAND, William	68y 5m 3d	22 Nov 1863	Nov 26, 1863
HAWES, Benjamin	no age	11 Feb 1859	Mar 3, 1859
HAWKINS, Charles W.	no age	Tues	Jun 14, 1860
HAWKS, Francis	15	1 Jan 1860	Jan 5, 1860
HAWKSHURST, Ephraim	69	12 Nov 1859	Nov 17, 1859
HAWLEY, Cornelia P.	34	6 Dec 1862	Dec 11, 1862
HAWXHURST, Charity	76	7 Nov 1877	Nov 8, 1877
HAWXHURST, James O.	67th y	23rd ult	Nov 11, 1869
HAYDEN, Henry	17	last Fri	Mar 15, 1860
HAYES, Adelaide Bedell	no age	19 Apr 1864	Apr 28, 1864
HAYNES, Elmira Powell	ca. 49	3 Aug 1858	Aug 12, 1858
HAZEN, Frederic	no age	24 Jul 1858	Aug 5, 1858
HEALEY, James	1y 10m	8 Feb 1872	Feb 15, 1872
HEARNE, Edward B.	no age	last Thurs	Feb 3, 1870
HEATH, Frederick S.	no age	Sunday	Apr 25, 1872
HEBARD, Aurell	no age	27 Jun 1858	Jul 1, 1858
HEDDEN, Elias B.	no age	5 Nov 1875	Nov 18, 1875
HEDGEMAN, Jane	56	13 Jan 1861	Feb 7, 1861
HEDGES, Joseph	93	11 Mar 1861	Mar 14, 1861

Name	Age	Date of death	Date of newspaper
HEDGES, Joseph	23	25 Jul 1864	May 11, 1865
HEDGES, Lavinia	83	no date	Jan 17, 1861
HEDGES, Timothy	no age	last Mon	Aug 16, 1860
HEGEMAN, (Mrs Jacob)	70	2 Dec 1877	Dec 13, 1877
HEGEMAN, Andrew James	ca. 47	5 Jan 1863	Jan 8, 1863
HEGEMAN, Catherine	78	4 Sep 1872	Sep 12, 1872
HEGEMAN, Catherine J.	36	23 Aug 1877	Aug 30, 1877
HEID, August	34	Thursday	Apr 26, 1877
HEITZ, Anna Maria Elizabeth	79y 3m	27 Dec 1863	Jan 7, 1864
HEMMERLE, Conrad	41	18 Jun 1875	Jun 17, 1875
HEMPSTEAD, Hanora	infant	4 Aug 1874	Aug 6, 1874
HENDERSON, Carrie	1	13 Aug 1875	Aug 19, 1875
HENDERSON, Jane	no age	7 Jun 1858	Jun 17, 1858
HENDERSON, John	no age	11 Dec 1870	Dec 29, 1870
HENDERSON, Phebe E.	54y 11m 18d	4 Dec 1865	Dec 7, 1865
HENDERSON, Thomas H.	48y 1m 19d	21 Mar 1869	Mar 25, 1869
HENDRICKSON, (ch. of Asa)	no age	no date	Nov 14, 1872
HENDRICKSON, (dau. of Oliver)	no age	no date	Jun 7, 1877
HENDRICKSON, (male)	ca. 7	last Thur	Jul 26, 1860
HENDRICKSON, Abram	56y 3m 5d	13 Apr 1878	Apr 25, 1878
HENDRICKSON, Ada P.	1m 22d	9 Sep 1874	Sep 17, 1874
HENDRICKSON, Addiette	11m 1m 21d	28 May 1877	May 31, 1877
HENDRICKSON, Anna	59	8 Jan 1859	Jan 20, 1859
HENDRICKSON, Asa	29	4 May 1868	May 7, 1868
HENDRICKSON, David	ca. 75	14 May 1864	May 19, 1864
HENDRICKSON, David	57	13 Apr 1872	Apr 18, 1872
HENDRICKSON, Elbert M.	22	26 Sep 1863	Nov 26, 1863
HENDRICKSON, Eliza	67	no date	Oct 6, 1870
HENDRICKSON, Eliza	ca. 80	31 Mar 1873	Apr 3, 1873
HENDRICKSON, Elizabeth	3	no date	Aug 6, 1868
HENDRICKSON, Elizabeth Adelia	22y 2m 15d	4th inst	Apr 9, 1863
HENDRICKSON, Ellen	48	15 Nov 1864	Nov 17, 1864
HENDRICKSON, Gilbert	26y 7m 27d	27 Dec 1863	Dec 31, 1863
HENDRICKSON, Harriett Augusta	4m 12d	5 Dec 1860	Dec 20, 1860
HENDRICKSON, Jacob	14y 4m 26d	12 Jun 1872	Jun 27, 1872
HENDRICKSON, John	ca. 49	22nd inst	Jan 26, 1860
HENDRICKSON, John	ca. 56	13 Sep 1878	Sep 26, 1878
HENDRICKSON, Joseph	78y 1m	28th ult	May 7, 1863
HENDRICKSON, Julia A.	40	25 Dec 1868	Feb 18, 1869
HENDRICKSON, Julia Ann	57th y	21 Mar 1864	Apr 7, 1864
HENDRICKSON, Lizzie	1y 7m 6d	6 Sep 1867	Sep 12, 1867
HENDRICKSON, Marta	63	14 Mar 1874	Mar 19, 1874
HENDRICKSON, Martha Elizabeth	52y 5m 20d	21 Aug 1873	Aug 28, 1873
HENDRICKSON, Mary	81	4 Mar 1869	Mar 11, 1869
HENDRICKSON, Nicholas	45d	16 Sep 1861	Sep 19, 1861
HENDRICKSON, Oldfield	64	16 Dec 1871	Dec 21, 1871
HENDRICKSON, Phebe Ann	71	2 Mar 1878	Mar 7, 1878
HENDRICKSON, Phoebe	29	19 Jul 1874	Sep 17, 1874
HENDRICKSON, Sadie	8m 21d	14 Aug 1874	Aug 20, 1874
HENDRICKSON, Samuel	38y 11m 24d	3 Sep 1874	Sep 10, 1874
HENDRICKSON, Samuel D.	62y 18d	6 Oct 1871	Oct 12, 1871
HENDRICKSON, Stephen	74y 11m 5d	6 Feb 1874	Feb 12, 1874
HENDRICKSON, Treadwell	94	Saturday	Aug 30, 1877
HENDRICKSON, Wellington Wilber	2y 2m	28 Sep 1865	Oct 19, 1865
HENGELER, (Mrs. Jacob)	ca. 80	24 Sep 1874	Oct 1, 1874
HENLEY, William	34	5 Nov 1869	Nov 11, 1869
HENTZ, Abbey	65	14 Jun 1874	Jun 18, 1874
HENTZ, Henry	83y 11m 12d	25 Mar 1873	Mar 27, 1873
HENTZ, Margaret A.	68y 9m 1d	24 Nov 1878	Nov 28, 1878

Name	Age	Date of death	Date of newspaper
HERBS, G. (Mr)	no age	Wednesday	Aug 9, 1877
HERBST, (ch. of Carl)	infant	17 Aug 1874	Aug 20, 1874
HERRIMAN, James	ca. 70	21st inst	Apr 23, 1863
HERSCHEL, (dau. of Sullivan)	4	1 Aug 1868	Aug 6, 1868
HERSCHEL, (son of Sullivan)	3	1 Aug 1868	Aug 6, 1868
HERZOG, Adrian I.	6	30 Aug 1871	Aug 31, 1871
HERZOG, Herman	16y 7m	25 Sep 1865	Sep 28, 1865
HESTON, Newton	41st y	13 Jul 1865	Jul 20, 1865
HEWLETT, (Miss)	no age	no date	Mar 15, 1860
HEWLETT, (wife of Samuel)	no age	no date	Mar 15, 1860
HEWLETT, A. V. W.	55	2 Apr 1865	Apr 27, 1865
HEWLETT, Alexander	ca. 33	12 Aug 1860	Aug 16, 1860
HEWLETT, Alexander	32y 7m 20d	12 Aug 1860	Aug 23, 1860
HEWLETT, Christopher	no age	25 Jan 1860	Jan 26, 1860
HEWLETT, Elizabeth	75	28 May 1874	Jun 4, 1874
HEWLETT, Elizabeth	80	29 Aug 1875	Sep 9, 1875
HEWLETT, Emma	39y 15d	10 Sep 1874	Sep 17, 1874
HEWLETT, George M.	88y 8m	17 May 1870	May 19, 1870
HEWLETT, George M.	no age	no date	Sep 1, 1870
HEWLETT, H. Elisa	14y 7m 24d	4 Aug 1870	Aug 11, 1870
HEWLETT, Harriet A.	30	23 Oct 1868	Oct 29, 1868
HEWLETT, James	73y 5m	31 Aug 1870	Sep 8, 1870
HEWLETT, James	no age	19 Mar 1872	Mar 21, 1872
HEWLETT, John D.	59th y	23 Nov 1863	Dec 3, 1863
HEWLETT, John J.	87	17 Sep 1862	Sep 25, 1862
HEWLETT, John J.	no age	27 Mar 1872	Mar 28, 1872
HEWLETT, John J.	29y 3m 20d	??	Apr 4, 1872
HEWLETT, Katie Jane	1y 3m 27d	5 Apr 1877	Apr 12, 1877
HEWLETT, Mary	81	3 Apr 1865	Apr 27, 1865
HEWLETT, Nancy	87	13th inst	Feb 16, 1860
HEWLETT, Oliver	65y 7m 14d	10 Nov 1867	Nov 21, 1867
HEWLETT, Oliver D.	70y 17d	26 Mar 1873	Mar 27, 1873
HEWLETT, Phebe	69	17 Apr 1862	Apr 24, 1862
HEWLETT, Richard	70	4 Jul 1863	Jul 9, 1863
HEWLETT, Samuel	68	15 Mar 1868	Apr 2, 1868
HEWLETT, Samuel L.	66	28 Feb 1868	Mar 5, 1868
HEWLETT, Sarah	66th y	11 Aug 1864	Aug 18, 1864
HEWLETT, Sarah Ann	56	17th	Apr 23, 1863
HEWLETT, Sarah Ann	58y 6m 19d	13 Aug 1878	Aug 15, 1878
HEWLETT, Sarah Jane	30	19 Oct 1865	Oct 26, 1865
HEWLETT, Stephen	72	9 Oct 1862	Oct 16, 1862
HEWLETT, Tredwell	40	30 Jan 1862	Feb 6, 1862
HEWLETT, William	63	28 Sep 1861	Oct 3, 1861
HEWLETT, Wm. M.	84y 14d	1 Jan 1864	Jan 28, 1864
HIBBARD, Jesse M.	30	5 Jul 1875	Jul 8, 1875
HIBBERD, (Mr.)	no age	5 Jul 1875	Sep 30, 1875
HICKS, (dau. of Valentine)	3	5 Mar 1864	Mar 10, 1864
HICKS, Adeline	no age	3rd inst	Sep 12, 1867
HICKS, Albert W.	no age	last Fri	Jul 19, 1860
HICKS, Albertson	47	12 Aug 1863	Aug 13, 1863
HICKS, Amelia	25	24 Dec 1874	Dec 31, 1874
HICKS, Carrie	4m 20d	18 Aug 1870	Aug 25, 1870
HICKS, Elias	83y 6m 11d	19 Aug 1863	Aug 27, 1863
HICKS, Eliza	95th y	5 Mar 1878	Mar 7, 1878
HICKS, Elizabeth	83rd y	14 May 1878	May 16, 1878
HICKS, Emily	3	22 Jan 1864	Jan 28, 1864
HICKS, Francis	17y 4d	1 Aug 1860	Aug 16, 1860
HICKS, Harmon	19	15 Jan 1865	Feb 9, 1865
HICKS, John, Jr.	22	28 Mar 1872	Apr 11, 1872
HICKS, Lavinia	15	Sunday	Aug 22, 1878

Name	Age	Date of death	Date of newspaper
HICKS, Lawrence	19	no date	May 13, 1875
HICKS, Maria	82	21 Sep 1877	Sep 27, 1877
HICKS, Mary	97	21st inst	Oct 28, 1858
HICKS, Mary	96	22 Oct 1858	Nov 4, 1858
HICKS, Mary	52y 5d	22nd inst	May 31, 1860
HICKS, Mary	78	9 Dec 1861	Dec 12, 1861
HICKS, Nellie	32	28 Dec 1877	Jan 3, 1878
HICKS, Phebe	79	23 Nov 1861	Nov 28, 1861
HICKS, Rachel	89	13 Aug 1878	Aug 15, 1878
HICKS, Silas	84	30 Mar 1861	Apr 4, 1861
HICKS, William	no age	Jul 1874	Jul 23, 1874
HIGBIE, Abby S.	73	5 May 1877	May 10, 1877
HIGBIE, Ann	53y 7m 15d	30 Jan 1868	Feb 6, 1868
HIGBIE, Eliza	70	5 Mar 1869	Mar 18, 1869
HIGBIE, Hannah A.	72	18 Dec 1875	Dec 23, 1875
HIGBIE, James W.	18	22 Jan 1877	Feb 1, 1877
HIGBIE, John U.	18y 1m 19d	22 Jan 1877	Feb 1, 1877
HIGBIE, Laura A.	11m	11 Nov 1862	Nov 20, 1862
HIGBIE, William	51	29 Aug 1877	Sep 6, 1877
HIGGINS, Mary	8	no date	May 9, 1872
HILDEN, Benedict	no age	9 Aug 1872	Aug 22, 1872
HILDRETH, Luther	47	no date	Aug 26, 1858
HILL, Charles	5y 5m	1 Aug 1873	Aug 7, 1873
HILL, George	9y 1m 7d	23 Aug 1863	Aug 27, 1863
HILL, Hanna	42	3 Sep 1858	Sep 16, 1858
HILL, Mary Jane	21y 7d	30 Apr 1874	May 7, 1874
HILL, Nicholas, Jr.	no age	1 May 1859	May 5, 1859
HILL, Samuel	51	13th inst	Sep 20, 1860
HILL, Sarah E. (nee PEARSALL)	29y 8m 17d	13 Feb 1871	Feb 23, 1871
HILL, Sarah V.	2y 5m 28d	8 Aug 1873	Aug 14, 1873
HILL, William R.	6m 6d	12 Oct 1877	Oct 18, 1877
HINCH, Margaret	no age	17 Feb 1864	Feb 25, 1864
HINCHMAN, Abraham	no age	no date	Aug 11, 1859
HINDS, Albert Irving	11m	31 Jan 1861	Feb 7, 1861
HINGLE, (dau. of Edward)	2y 6m	9 Nov 1876	Nov 16, 1876
HINMAN, Herman	79	17 Jun 1861	Jun 20, 1861
HINMAN, Sarah T.	56th y	24th of 6 m	Jun 29, 1865
HINMAN, Singleton Mitchell	21y 27d	25 Jan 1864	Jan 28, 1864
HIRTEN, Jacob	no age	13 Aug 1858	Aug 19, 1858
HOBBS, Hannah	88	10th of 3 m	Mar 23, 1865
HOCKS, Jane	5	26 Mar 1870	Mar 31, 1870
HOFF, Ezekiel Baldwin	4m 18d	27 Dec 1867	Jan 9, 1868
HOFFMAN, Frederick Jacob	1y 3m 24d	6 Feb 1864	Feb 11, 1864
HOGAN, Edmund	88	13 Dec 1867	Dec 19, 1867
HOGAN, John Sheridan	no age	no date	Apr 4, 1861
HOLBAN, Johnny	child	week Thur	Jul 6, 1876
HOLDEN, Horace H.	no age	26 Jan 1859	Feb 3, 1859
HOLEFONT, Patrick	7y	4 Aug 1873	Aug 14, 1873
HOLLAND, Michael P.	54	24 Jan 1859	Feb 3, 1859
HOLLINTEN, (Mr)	no age	last Thurs	Sep 13, 1877
HOLLISTER, Maria V. (nee LUSH)	no age	16 Dec 1868	Dec 24, 1868
HOLLY, (widow of Christopher)	no age	no date	May 5, 1859
HOLMES, Nathaniel	26y 10m 11d	31 May 1877	Jun 7, 1877
HOLMES, Rebecca	81y 3m 12d	13 Apr 1873	Apr 17, 1873
HOLMES, Thomas	no age	no date	Mar 19, 1863
HOLT, Margaret E.	61	8 Oct 1864	Oct 20, 1864
HOMAN, (child of Benjamin)	4	no date	Jun 23, 1859
HOMAN, Elizabeth	72	5 Nov 1869	Nov 25, 1869
HOMAN, Joseph	no age	no date	Mar 15, 1877

Name	Age	Date of death	Date of newspaper
HOOD, George	no age	no date	Jul 7, 1859
HOOFMAN, John	15	22 Oct 1861	Nov 14, 1861
HOOGLAND, Benjamin R.	46	7 Jul 1858	Jul 8, 1858
HOOGLAND, Catherine	86	21 Dec 1863	Jan 7, 1864
HOOK, Christian	62	14 Apr 1868	Apr 23, 1868
HOOPER, John	no age	Wednesday	Jul 4, 1872
HOOPLE, Mary Elizabeth	no age	3 May 1873	May 8, 1873
HOPKINS, Louisa	61	1 Sep 1873	Sep 4, 1873
HORNBLOWER, Joseph C.	88th y	11 Jun 1864	Jun 16, 1864
HORSFIELD, George Hewlett	66y 8m 15d	14 Jan 1878	Jan 17, 1878
HORSFIELD, George I.	6m 24d	4 Jun 1878	Jun 6, 1878
HORSFIELD, Isreal	19	22 Sep 1870	Sep 29, 1870
HORSFIELD, Richard T.	63	30 Oct 1871	Nov 2, 1871
HORSTMAN, George	6m	17 Sep 1871	Sep 21, 1871
HORTON, (male)	ca. 17	no date	Dec 29, 1864
HORTON, (son of Elijah)	3m	3 Aug 1872	Aug 15, 1872
HORTON, Eugene	33y 3m	17 Apr 1876	Apr 20, 1876
HORTON, Horace	21	8 Nov 1870	Nov 17, 1870
HORTON, Jannett	73	9 Oct 1877	Oct 18, 1877
HORTON, John	35	22 Jan 1875	Jan 28, 1875
HORTON, Mary	24	19 Oct 1876	Nov 2, 1876
HORTON, Minnie F.	1y 7m	5 Mar 1876	Mar 16, 1876
HORTON, Townsend	19	19 Oct 1863	Nov 5, 1863
HOUSE, O. A. (Mr.)	no age	no date	Jul 6, 1876
HOUSEN, Jacob	no age	Sunday	Apr 11, 1872
HOVER, Henry S.	58	24th ult	Mar 9, 1865
HOWARD, Annie	no age	no date	Jul 5, 1860
HOWARD, Susan	91	15 May 1859	May 19, 1859
HOWE, Elias, Jr.	48th y	4 Oct 1867	Oct 10, 1867
HOWELL, (son of Mortimer D.)	9	15 Jul 1874	Jul 23, 1874
HOWELL, Charles	67	5 Nov 1878	Nov 7, 1878
HOWELL, Daniel	41	31 Jan 1859	Feb 10, 1859
HOWELL, G. Henry	27	26 Aug 1858	Sep 2, 1858
HOWELL, Nancy	19	30 Jul 1858	Aug 19, 1858
HOWELL, Phebe	90th y	7th inst	Apr 19, 1860
HOWELL, Rachel Graham	10m 16d	2 Jul 1876	Jul 6, 1876
HOWIE, James	no age	Sunday	Apr 19, 1877
HOXIE, Joseph	75	18 Aug 1870	Sep 8, 1870
HOYT, Elizabeth	41	17 Sep 1865	Sep 21, 1865
HUBBARD, Maria L.	no age	no date	Aug 22, 1878
HUBBS, (male, adult)	no age	10 May 1864	May 19, 1864
HUBBS, Catherine J.	31	4 Nov 1878	Nov 7, 1878
HUBBS, Luther	2m 6d	7 Aug 1868	Aug 13, 1868
HUBBS, Mary	55y 8m	23 Oct 1876	Oct 26, 1876
HUBBS, Mercy	90	4 Mar 1868	Mar 12, 1868
HUDSON, (Capt)	no age	20 Mar 1872	Apr 25, 1872
HUDSON, Walter	no age	20 Mar 1872	Apr 4, 1872
HUGHES, Patrick	no age	3 Mar 1875	Mar 4, 1875
HULL, John R.	49	1 Sep 1859	Sep 8, 1859
HULSE (or HULST), David	61y 1m 28d	16th inst	Sep 21, 1865
HULSE, (wife of Daniel)	no age	31 Jan 1860	Feb 9, 1860
HULSE, Charles L.	no age	21st inst	Sep 29, 1864
HULSE, John D.	30	last Thurs	Aug 15, 1867
HULSE, Lorenzo	49y 8m 5d	25 Dec 1876	Jan 4, 1877
HULSE, Melia	65	no date	Jan 10, 1878
HULST (or HULSE), David	61y 1m 28d	16th inst	Sep 21, 1865
HULST, Andrew S.	1y 4m 12d	22nd inst	Aug 31, 1865
HULTS, Alice Ann	4y 12d	18th inst	Aug 3, 1865
HULTS, Amelia	65	19 Nov 1877	Nov 22, 1877
HULTS, Anna	40	9 Aug 1870	Aug 18, 1870

                                  DEATHS
Name   Age   Date of   Date of
                                               death   newspaper
----

HULTS, Phebe Jane   38   17 Feb 1877   Feb 22, 1877
HULTZ, (child of B.)   infant   11 Nov 1864   Nov 17, 1864
HULTZ, (child of Benjamin)   infant   6 Aug 1867   Aug 8, 1867
HULTZ, (wife of Patrick)   70   19 Jul 1871   Jul 20, 1871
HULTZ, Flower   96   Saturday   Sep 6, 1877
HUMBER, Agnes   73y 6d   13 Nov 1875   Dec 2, 1875
HUMBER, Edgar   9m   2 Jul 1878   Jul 4, 1878
HUNT, Benjamin   53   6 Oct 1878   Oct 10, 1878
HUNT, Elizabeth   1y 10m 15d   3 Aug 1864   Aug 11, 1864
HUNT, Georgianna (nee KELLUM)   24   13th inst   Jun 15, 1876
HUNTER, (Lieut.)   no age   last winter   Jun 9, 1864
HUNTLEY, Lydia   32   22 Dec 1858   Dec 30, 1858
HURST, Joseph   no age   no date   Apr 25, 1872
HUSSON, James   no age   4 Nov 1878   Nov 7, 1878
HUTCHINGS, (child of John)   15m   no date   Sep 12, 1867
HUTCHINGSON, George   ca. 45   Saturday   Aug 23, 1860
HUTCHINSON, (Mr)   no age   few wks ago   Nov 8, 1877
HUTTON, (Mrs J. W.)   no age   last Sat   Jan 28, 1875
HYER, Tom   45   Sunday   Jul 7, 1864

IKELEY, (Mrs. Adam)   no age   6 May 1874   May 7, 1874
IRELAND, Catharine Colter   77   23 Apr 1876   Apr 27, 1876
IRELAND, Eara S.   66   23 Dec 1878   Dec 26, 1878
IRELAND, Mary E.   no age   last Thurs   Jul 6, 1876
IRISH, Maggie   23   26 Dec 1874   Dec 31, 1874
IRISH, Tillinghast   72   10 Jul 1867   Jul 11, 1867
IRWIN, Edwin   no age   Sat/Sun   Feb 19, 1863

JACKSON, (child of Maria)   2   no date   Dec 29, 1864
JACKSON, (child of Maria)   4   no date   Dec 29, 1864
JACKSON, (child of Maria)   12   no date   Dec 29, 1864
JACKSON, (dau. of Benjamin)   no age   6 Aug 1870   Aug 11, 1870
JACKSON, Aaron   71   22 Aug 1868   Sep 3, 1868
JACKSON, Abby   75   25 Jul 1867   Aug 1, 1867
JACKSON, Albert   28   18 Jan 1871   Jan 26, 1871
JACKSON, Alfred M.   4y 2m   11 Mar 1878   Mar 14, 1878
JACKSON, Anna   6m   21 Jul 1872   Jul 25, 1872
JACKSON, Ansel   6m   28 Sep 1875   Oct 7, 1875
JACKSON, Augustus W.   ca. 22   29th ult   Jan 12, 1860
JACKSON, Charity A.   15   9 Apr 1877   Apr 12, 1877
JACKSON, Edgar   28   10 Apr 1864   Apr 14, 1864
JACKSON, Edgar   28   no date   Jun 2, 1864
JACKSON, Elbert   no age   last Fri   Jan 21, 1875
JACKSON, George R.   5   23 Apr 1875   Apr 29, 1875
JACKSON, Henrietta   21y 1m 8d 24 Jun 1874   Jul 9, 1874
JACKSON, Henry   ca. 10   Wed last w   Oct 31, 1867
JACKSON, Henry   80   31 Mar 1878   Apr 4, 1878
JACKSON, Isaac   19   15 Aug 1874   Aug 20, 1874
JACKSON, Jacob   78   3 Dec 1867   Jan 9, 1868
JACKSON, Jacob   78   2nd inst   Jan 23, 1868
JACKSON, James   65   10 Sep 1865   Sep 21, 1865
JACKSON, James   71   5 Apr 1874   Apr 9, 1874
JACKSON, Jane   78   10 Feb 1863   Feb 12, 1863
JACKSON, Jarvis   89y 6m   20 Sep 1870   Sep 29, 1870
JACKSON, John   85   5 Mar 1861   Mar 7, 1861
JACKSON, John   13y 8m 15d 3 Oct 1873   Oct 9, 1873
JACKSON, John   50y 12d   3 May 1874   Jun 18, 1874
JACKSON, John   83   2 Jun 1874   Jun 25, 1874

Name	Age	Date of death	Date of newspaper
JACKSON, Joseph	ca. 54	14 Sep 1877	Sep 20, 1877
JACKSON, Maria Louisa	32	24 Aug 1874	Aug 27, 1874
JACKSON, Martha	19	24 Feb 1877	Mar 1, 1877
JACKSON, Martha E.	7m	20 Aug 1877	Aug 30, 1877
JACKSON, Mary Elizabeth	34	20 Apr 1859	Apr 28, 1859
JACKSON, Mary Emma	3	5 Dec 1876	Dec 7, 1876
JACKSON, Moses	60	4 May 1859	May 19, 1859
JACKSON, Reba S.	1y 5m 17d	3 Jan 1873	Jan 9, 1873
JACKSON, Richard	30	16 Jul 1877	Jul 19, 1877
JACKSON, Samuel W.	25y 8m	18 Sep 1865	Sep 21, 1865
JACKSON, Townsand	11	26 Aug 1876	Aug 31, 1876
JACKSON, Townsend W.	4th y	27 Mar 1872	Apr 4, 1872
JACKSON, William S.	34y 4m	7 Jan 1870	Jan 20, 1870
JAGGER, Harriet	51	18 Nov 1861	Nov 21, 1861
JAGGER, William	ca. 85	16 Jan 1877	Feb 1, 1877
JAMES, (child of Stephen)	1	8 Jul 1867	Jul 11, 1867
JAMES, Asa	80y 7m 7d	9 Feb 1871	Feb 16, 1871
JAMES, George	16	13 Nov 1864	Nov 17, 1864
JAMES, Warren T.	22	16 Nov 1858	Dec 2, 1858
JAMISON, (son of Mrs Jamison)	6	no date	Mar 28, 1861
JARVIS, Carlton	73y 3m 29d	7 Jul 1878	Jul 18, 1878
JARVIS, Caroline	22	17 Jun 1876	Jun 22, 1876
JARVIS, Lewis	no age	last Fri	Jan 21, 1875
JARVIS, Mary	40	10 Mar 1869	Mar 18, 1869
JARVIS, Thomas W.	24	8 Jan 1864	Jan 14, 1864
JAYNE, George	55	1 Mar 1876	Mar 2, 1876
JAYNE, William	75	25 Oct 1868	Oct 29, 1868
JEFFREYS, (Mrs.)	no age	no date	Mar 12, 1874
JENCH, John	36	Tues/Wed	Dec 7, 1871
JENKINS, Frank W.	no age	last Tues	Dec 30, 1875
JENKINS, Susan	75	21 Dec 1875	Dec 23, 1875
JENNINGS, (ch. of Sidney)	6m	17 Jul 1872	Jul 25, 1872
JENNINGS, Ida	23	21 Feb 1870	Feb 24, 1870
JEPSON, Anna Dorothea	51	29 Dec 1873	Jan 1, 1874
JEROME, (dau. of Edward)	infant	1 Aug 1858	Aug 5, 1858
JEROME, Harriet G.	44y 5m 15d	4 Sep 1872	Sep 19, 1872
JEROME, Phebe Ann	60	27 May 1862	May 29, 1862
JERVIS, Maria	22	no date	Jul 8, 1858
JESSUP, Edward	no age	13 Mar 1874	Apr 9, 1874
JEWETT, George W.	no age	Thursday	Apr 12, 1877
JEWETT, Orville D.	no age	Thursday	Apr 12, 1877
JOCHER, John	no age	no date	Sep 1, 1870
JOEKEL, (child of Anthony)	3m	19 Aug 1877	Aug 23, 1877
JOHNSON, (Mrs. J. Wesley)	no age	25 Jul 1875	Jul 29, 1875
JOHNSON, (dau. of Charles)	11d	6 Jan 1873	Jan 9, 1873
JOHNSON, Abraham	75	16 Oct 1878	Oct 24, 1878
JOHNSON, Addie	10m	23 May 1874	May 28, 1874
JOHNSON, Annie	26y 6m 1d	9 Mar 1877	Mar 22, 1877
JOHNSON, Annie Louise	1y 26d	18th inst	Aug 22, 1867
JOHNSON, Arthur	1	16 Dec 1858	Jan 6, 1859
JOHNSON, Charles	2d	26 Nov 1873	Nov 27, 1873
JOHNSON, Charles A.	1y 8m	10 Feb 1872	Feb 15, 1872
JOHNSON, Cornelia H. (male)	no age	31 Dec 1859	Jan 5, 1860
JOHNSON, Ditmars	22y 7m 7d	1st inst	May 17, 1860
JOHNSON, Edward	1y 5m	21 Oct 1865	Oct 26, 1865
JOHNSON, Edward Seymour	25	25 Dec 1861	Jan 2, 1862
JOHNSON, Eliza M.	75	20 Jan 1869	Jan 28, 1869
JOHNSON, Elizabeth	62	12 Dec 1876	Dec 21, 1876
JOHNSON, Emeline	22	9 Jun 1875	Jun 24, 1875
JOHNSON, F. Asbury	51	21 May 1876	May 25, 1876

Name	Age	Date of death	Date of newspaper
JOHNSON, George	74	13 May 1865	May 18, 1865
JOHNSON, Gilbert	80	5 Sep 1859	Sep 8, 1859
JOHNSON, Henry	44y 11m 27d	last Sun	May 3, 1860
JOHNSON, Henry	34	11 Nov 1865	Nov 16, 1865
JOHNSON, Henry W.	33	20 Dec 1863	Dec 24, 1863
JOHNSON, Isaac	80	18 Apr 1872	Apr 25, 1872
JOHNSON, James Francis	3y 9m 6d	15 Jul 1872	Jul 18, 1872
JOHNSON, Jane	no age	no date	Mar 11, 1875
JOHNSON, Jeremiah	40	14 Apr 1865	Apr 27, 1865
JOHNSON, John	73	14 Apr 1874	Apr 16, 1874
JOHNSON, John	77	12 Jan 1877	Jan 25, 1877
JOHNSON, John M.	46y 10m 8d	19 Aug 1863	Aug 27, 1863
JOHNSON, John W.	36	6 Feb 1876	Feb 10, 1876
JOHNSON, Leander	6m	9 Oct 1869	Oct 14, 1869
JOHNSON, Margaret	4	23 Feb 1865	Mar 2, 1865
JOHNSON, Maria	70	24th inst	Jul 29, 1869
JOHNSON, Mary A.	35	2 Feb 1864	Feb 4, 1864
JOHNSON, Mary Louisa Adams	no age	16th inst	Jul 21, 1859
JOHNSON, Nancy	29y 4m	18 Jan 1875	Jan 21, 1875
JOHNSON, Ramenia	11	31 Aug 1863	Sep 17, 1863
JOHNSON, Samuel E.	53	3rd inst	Feb 10, 1870
JOHNSON, Sarah	no age	30 Mar 1862	Apr 3, 1862
JOHNSON, Sarah Ann	2y 6m	10 Nov 1871	Nov 16, 1871
JOHNSON, Stephen	30	26 Apr 1859	May 5, 1859
JOHNSON, Stephen	86y 8m	2 Mar 1875	Mar 4, 1875
JOHNSON, Stephen	1y 11m 17d	1 Jan 1877	Jan 4, 1877
JOHNSON, Tiney	17	21 Jul 1876	Jul 27, 1876
JOHNSON, William	59y 7m 11d	last Sun	Jun 27, 1867
JOHNSON, William	59y 7m 11d	23 Jun 1867	Jul 11, 1867
JOHNSON, William H.	61	2 Jan 1865	Jan 12, 1865
JOHNSON, William S.	23	6 Dec 1865	Dec 14, 1865
JOHNSON, William Townsend	6m	Sunday	Sep 22, 1864
JOHNSON, Wm. L.	70	4 Aug 1870	Aug 11, 1870
JOISLE, Christianna	3	3 Mar 1864	Mar 17, 1864
JOISLE, John	19m	5 Mar 1864	Mar 17, 1864
JOLINE, Mary	55	9 Dec 1872	Dec 19, 1872
JONES, (child of Daniel)	6d	24 Oct 1867	Nov 7, 1867
JONES, Alice	23	18 Oct 1875	Nov 4, 1875
JONES, Ann	62	1 Oct 1858	Oct 7, 1858
JONES, Charles H.	56y 3m 20d	5 Jan 1876	Jan 13, 1876
JONES, Elbert Harris	34	2 Nov 1862	Nov 20, 1862
JONES, Elizabeth	73	19 Nov 1868	Dec 3, 1868
JONES, Henry Floyd	71	20 Dec 1862	Dec 25, 1862
JONES, Isaac	23	Sat	Sep 5, 1872
JONES, J. B. (Mr)	no age	23 Jun 1877	Jul 19, 1877
JONES, Jacob P.	64	no date	Sep 30, 1858
JONES, James	50	12 Aug 1875	Aug 19, 1875
JONES, John	52	9 Aug 1874	Aug 13, 1874
JONES, Maria L.	4y 6m	10 Feb 1876	Feb 24, 1876
JONES, Mary T.	68	no date	Oct 21, 1858
JONES, Phebe H.	84y 2m 1d	24 Jun 1863	Jul 2, 1863
JONES, Rebecca	73	7th inst	Jul 12, 1860
JONES, S.J. (Mr.)	no age	Jun 1873	Oct 29, 1874
JONES, Sabina	80	17 Oct 1873	Oct 23, 1873
JONES, Samuel	no age	a month ago	Dec 27, 1877
JONES, Samuel I.	70	27 Jun 1873	Jul 3, 1873
JONES, Samuel J.	no age	Jun 1873	Dec 3, 1874
JONES, Samuel Y.	25	22 Jun 1858	Jul 8, 1858
JONES, Sarah	84	26 Jul 1871	Aug 3, 1871
JONES, Susannah	21y 2m 3d	11 Aug 1872	Aug 15, 1872

Name	Age	Date of death	Date of newspaper
JONES, Thomas Langley	2	30 Aug 1861	Sep 5, 1861
JONES, Vincent P.	20	18 Aug 1862	Aug 28, 1862
JONES, William	4	14 Mar 1872	Apr 11, 1872
JONES, William	no age	last Wed	Nov 18, 1875
JONES, William H.	46y 11m	10th inst	Feb 13, 1868
JORDAN, Daniel	no age	Sat/Sun	Feb 19, 1863
JORDON, Maggie	no age	15 Sep 1877	Sep 27, 1877
JORNS, Mary Ann	1y 7m	28 Sep 1863	Oct 15, 1863
JUDD, (son of Orange)	young	9 Jul 1877	Jul 19, 1877
JUDGE, Robert	20y 2m	1 Jul 1858	Jul 8, 1858
JUENGST, Georgenia	1y 11m 7d	9 Dec 1878	Dec 12, 1878
JUNG, (Mrs.)	no age	20 May 1875	May 27, 1875
JUNG, John George	no age	Friday	May 27, 1875
KANE, Thomas	no age	25 Oct 1868	Nov 4, 1869
KARKHECK, Matta C.	53rd y	21 Jul 1878	Jul 25, 1878
KARST, (child of Valentine)	infant	7th inst	Sep 13, 1860
KARST, Mary Elizabeth	69	28 Apr 1878	May 2, 1878
KARST, Rose	7y 9m 28d	7 May 1875	May 13, 1875
KARST, Sophia F.	1y 2m 24d	29 Jul 1867	Aug 1, 1867
KASSON, Elvira	49	1 Sep 1858	Sep 2, 1858
KAUFMAN, Fred	9	last week	Jul 12, 1877
KAY, George	30	21 May 1873	May 29, 1873
KAYSER, Henry	no age	last Fri	Jun 10, 1858
KEARNAN, (Mrs. Owen)	no age	no date	Jul 25, 1878
KEATING, (ch. of John)	1y 2m	14 Nov 1874	Nov 26, 1874
KEATING, (ch. of John)	2y 2m	14 Nov 1874	Nov 26, 1874
KEATOR, Elizabeth	47	30 Mar 1862	Apr 10, 1862
KEAVER, Caroline	3y 2m 5d	5 Oct 1875	Oct 14, 1875
KEELER, Phebe S.	60y 2m 22d	11th inst	Jun 16, 1864
KEENAR, Catherine	67	12 Apr 1878	Apr 18, 1878
KEHRWEIDER, (male)	a lad	no date	Jul 13, 1876
KEIGHT, Matthies	60	1 Apr 1874	Apr 9, 1874
KEILLER, (Mr.)	no age	last Tues	Aug 28, 1873
KEIST, (Mr.)	no age	no date	Mar 1, 1860
KELLER, Christian	3m	no date	Aug 10, 1871
KELLER, Joseph	23	30 Oct 1875	Nov 4, 1875
KELLER, Matthew P.	53y 3m 1d	7 Sep 1870	Sep 22, 1870
KELLEY, (dau. of James Q.)	3	14 Aug 1861	Aug 22, 1861
KELLEY, Rose Ann	69	25 Nov 1878	Nov 28, 1878
KELLUM, (wife of John)	30	27 Sep 1858	Sep 30, 1858
KELLUM, Annie E.	no age	30 May 1876	Jun 1, 1876
KELLUM, Benjamin	30	31 May 1862	Jun 5, 1862
KELLUM, Eliza	68y 12d	26 Sep 1874	Oct 1, 1874
KELLUM, Hannah	66	10 Jun 1877	Jun 14, 1877
KELLUM, John	61y 10m 27d	24 Jul 1871	Jul 27, 1871
KELLUM, John H.	7y 11m	10 Aug 1875	Aug 12, 1875
KELLUM, Phinehas	86	22 Sep 1870	Sep 29, 1870
KELLUM, William H.	25y 3m 17d	2 Apr 1868	Apr 9, 1868
KELLY, Ann	27y 8m 10d	11 Nov 1871	Nov 16, 1871
KELLY, Bernard	32y 8d	22 Apr 1870	Apr 28, 1870
KELLY, David	86y 7m 9d	3 Jan 1872	Jan 4, 1872
KELLY, Eddie	4m	29 Jul 1870	Aug 11, 1870
KELLY, Lawrance	95	29th ult	Feb 9, 1871
KELLY, Mary	71	30 Jul 1876	Aug 3, 1876
KELLY, Mary Ellen	3y 19d	13 Nov 1867	Nov 21, 1867
KELLY, Patrick	no age	last Thur	Dec 6, 1860
KELLY, Rose	no age	15 Apr 1858	Jun 17, 1858
KELLY, Timothy	no age	Thurs	Feb 1, 1872

Name	Age	Date of death	Date of newspaper
KELLY, William	23	8 Aug 1875	Aug 12, 1875
KELSEY, George W.	no age	11 Jul 1865	Sep 21, 1865
KEMP, Richard	11m	2 Jan 1875	Jan 7, 1875
KENDRICK, Lucy	88	16 Aug 1859	Aug 18, 1859
KENNIFF, Maggie	10	18 Sep 1877	Sep 27, 1877
KERNELL, Charles	17	20 Sep 1870	Sep 22, 1870
KERRIGAN, (Mrs. Michael)	no age	no date	Oct 24, 1872
KESTEEN, Josephine	68y 4m	2 May 1870	May 12, 1870
KETCHAM, (dau. of Joshua)	no age	Nov 1862	Dec 4, 1862
KETCHAM, Andrew	no age	3 Jun 1859	Jun 9, 1859
KETCHAM, Augustus	ca. 19	8 Apr 1865	Apr 13, 1865
KETCHAM, Catherine A.	35y 7m 13d	20 Jan 1875	Jan 28, 1875
KETCHAM, Ella Augusta	1y 7m 27d	25 Jul 1858	Aug 19, 1858
KETCHAM, Emma	2y 6m	14th inst	Aug 3, 1865
KETCHAM, Hannah	80	1 May 1872	May 9, 1872
KETCHAM, Jarvis	70	31 Jan 1861	Feb 7, 1861
KETCHAM, John	84	last Wed	Aug 31, 1865
KETCHAM, Joshua	no age	Dec 1874	Feb 25, 1875
KETCHAM, Leroy L.	2y 9m 21d	23 Nov 1873	Nov 27, 1873
KETCHAM, Martha	62	1 Apr 1868	Apr 9, 1868
KETCHAM, Mary	44	12 Mar 1865	Mar 30, 1865
KETCHAM, Philip	85y 6m	18 Dec 1870	Dec 22, 1870
KETCHAM, Sarah E.	24y 10m 10d	15 Sep 1871	Sep 21, 1871
KETCHAM, Smith	84	14 Jan 1869	Jan 21, 1869
KETCHAM, Susanna S.	47	5 Jan 1864	Jan 14, 1864
KETCHAM, Townsend	12	19 Feb 1862	Feb 27, 1862
KETCHAM, William	27	9 Jan 1864	Jan 14, 1864
KETCHAM, William Post	6m	8 Aug 1872	Aug 15, 1872
KETCHUM, Amelia G.	9	no date	Feb 17, 1876
KETCHUM, Catharine	3	no date	Feb 17, 1876
KETCHUM, Joel	5	no date	Feb 17, 1876
KETTELTAS, Rebecca	72	6 Sep 1859	Sep 15, 1859
KEY, Philip Barton	no age	26 Feb 1859	Mar 3, 1859
KIERSTEAD, Mary Eva	1y 2m	22 Mar 1872	Mar 28, 1872
KIERSTED, George W., Sr.	63	16 Oct 1869	Oct 21, 1869
KIESAL, Nicholas	1y 8m 10d	13 Mar 1869	Mar 18, 1869
KILDUFFEE, Ellen	24	27 Jun 1858	Jul 1, 1858
KILLS, Oliver	no age	27 Feb 1877	Mar 15, 1877
KIMMEY, Louise	27y 2m 10d	16 Jan 1872	Jan 25, 1872
KING, Charles	78	no date	Oct 10, 1867
KING, Cornelia Ray	no age	27 Oct 1860	Nov 22, 1860
KING, Mary	83	no date	Aug 21, 1873
KING, Phebe	87	8 Apr 1861	Apr 18, 1861
KING, Richard	70	10 Apr 1861	Apr 18, 1861
KINGSLAND, Ambrose C.	74	Sunday	Oct 17, 1878
KINGSLEY, Wilhelmina	2	6 Jan 1864	Jan 14, 1864
KINSEY, John	no age	2 Aug 1861	Aug 8, 1861
KIPP, Louis	15	21 Jun 1858	Jun 24, 1858
KIRBY, Hannah	88	29 Nov 1863	Dec 10, 1863
KIRBY, Mary Anil	77	24 Oct 1875	Oct 28, 1875
KIRK, (Mr.)	no age	Friday	Jul 25, 1872
KIRK, George	ca. 12	last Wed	Oct 27, 1864
KIRK, Mis Frances (Mrs.)	30	26 Nov 1864	Dec 1, 1864
KIRNER, John Oscar	7m	12 Dec 1872	Dec 19, 1872
KIRWAN, Mary	65	2 May 1874	May 14, 1874
KIRWAN, Sebastian	no age	4 Jan 1875	Jan 7, 1875
KISSAM, (Dr.)	no age	last Mon	Nov 18, 1875
KISSAM, (Mrs. George C.)	no age	2 Sep 1875	Sep 9, 1875
KISSAM, Benjamin T.	no age	no date	Sep 1, 1870
KISSAM, George T.	2y 11m 21d	26 Mar 1865	Mar 30, 1865

Name	Age	Date of death	Date of newspaper
KISSAM, Mary A.	50y 28d	6 Aug 1864	Aug 11, 1864
KISSAM, Mary Louisa	11m 10d	27 Jul 1863	Aug 6, 1863
KISSAM, Phebe	83	2 May 1862	May 8, 1862
KISSIM, Mary Cornelia	1y 3m 20d	18th inst	Sep 19, 1867
KIVLIN, William	1	7 Sep 1875	Sep 9, 1875
KLEIN, Peter	no age	14 Aug 1874	Aug 20, 1874
KLEIN, Simon	no age	20 Jan 1875	Jan 28, 1875
KLIMPEKE, John	a boy	Sunday	Jun 7, 1877
KNALLY, (dau. of John)	infant	3 Sep 1875	Sep 9, 1875
KNEELAND, Arthur Cheever	14m 16d	30 Jul 1870	Aug 11, 1870
KNOWLES, Charles	ca. 50	15 Dec 1877	Dec 27, 1877
KOELLER, John	no age	Tuesday	May 10, 1877
KOLYER, (male)	no age	12th inst	Nov 29, 1860
KONRAD, Anna Magdalena	64y 1m	17 Dec 1868	Dec 24, 1868
KOSEL, Charles Henry	8y 4m	30 Jul 1871	Aug 10, 1871
KOSEL, Gustavus Christopher	8d	29 Jul 1868	Aug 6, 1868
KOSEL, Ludwig	1y 1m	18 Sep 1873	Sep 25, 1873
KRAMER, William	60y 1m	Tuesday	Aug 2, 1877
KRATZ, Michael	75	30 Sep 1858	Oct 7, 1858
KREBE, Sopha	57	Tuesday	Oct 18, 1877
KREIGER, William	3	Monday	Aug 22, 1878
KREISCHER, Loisa	54	14 Jun 1878	Jun 20, 1878
KRUG, John	8m 9d	9 Sep 1873	Sep 11, 1873
KRUMANOCKER, (male)	a lad	last Thurs	Aug 15, 1867
KUENSTNER, Charles	27th y	27 Nov 1863	Dec 3, 1863
KUHL, George G.	31y 4m 4d	20 Nov 1871	Nov 23, 1871
LA FARGE, John	73	25 Jun 1858	Jul 1, 1858
LA ROSA, Charles C.	48y 1m 18d	30 Apr 1878	May 9, 1878
LAING, Stuart Fitz Randolph	26th y	7 Mar 1864	Mar 10, 1864
LAING, William L.	71	Saturday	Jun 7, 1877
LAMBERT, John	2	29 Oct 1865	Nov 2, 1865
LAND, James M.	no age	30 Mar 1861	Apr 4, 1861
LANDER, Catherine	no age	1 Dec 1870	Dec 15, 1870
LANDON, Dillon Stevens	51	20 Apr 1873	Apr 24, 1873
LANE, Benjamin	49y 10m 10d	11 Aug 1863	Aug 13, 1863
LANE, Carman D.	no age	22 Dec 1872	Dec 26, 1872
LANE, Emma	7	no date	May 19, 1859
LANE, Freddy A.	2m	8 Mar 1872	Mar 28, 1872
LANE, Katie	no age	22nd ult	Mar 19, 1874
LANE, Maria Louisa	43y 3m 23d	15 Aug 1863	Aug 20, 1863
LANE, Mary Emma	23	2 Dec 1875	Dec 9, 1875
LANG, Edgar	76	21 Nov 1858	Nov 25, 1858
LANG, Mary L.	25y 11m 5d	15 Dec 1865	Dec 21, 1865
LANGDON, Hollet	84	Tuesday	Jul 25, 1878
LANGDON, Israel	no age	7 Aug 1859	Aug 11, 1859
LANGDON, Israel			Aug 18, 1859
LANGDON, Pearsall	80	9 Mar 1861	Mar 14, 1861
LANGE, Mary	no age	16 Jul 1874	Jul 30, 1874
LANGGUTH, John	57	17 Nov 1877	Nov 22, 1877
LANGGUTH, John	54	no date	Jan 10, 1878
LANZ, Edward C.	7m	17 Jul 1876	Aug 17, 1876
LARKIN, Mary	104	25 Jul 1875	Jul 29, 1875
LARKINS, Margaret Jane (nee NOLAN)	32y 2m 1d	1 Mar 1877	Mar 15, 1877
LARRABEE, Gamallee	88	5 Sep 1878	Sep 26, 1878
LARRISON, James	no age	30 Jul 1863	Aug 6, 1863
LATHAM, Jonathon	elderly	14 Sep 1875	Sep 16, 1875
LATON, David	94	24 Nov 1862	Dec 4, 1862

Name	Age	Date of death	Date of newspaper
LATON, William	71y 10m 20d	15 Nov 1872	Nov 21, 1872
LATTING, Elizabeth	72	6 Feb 1859	Feb 17, 1859
LAWLER, Patrick	35	23 Nov 1874	Nov 26, 1874
LAWRENCE, (Capt)	ca. 60	no date	Sep 2, 1875
LAWRENCE, Abraham	63	5 Jan 1874	Jan 22, 1874
LAWRENCE, Cornelius Van Wyck	70	20 Feb 1861	Feb 28, 1861
LAWRENCE, Eva Adelia	3m 13d	3 Oct 1867	Nov 7, 1867
LAWRENCE, Gilbert	95	23 Sep 1870	Sep 29, 1870
LAWRENCE, Henry	7m	26 Sep 1858	Oct 7, 1858
LAWRENCE, Joseph E.	no age	last Mon	Jul 18, 1878
LAWRENCE, L. (Capt)	no age	27 Aug 1875	Sep 16, 1875
LAWRENCE, Maria	61	16 Feb 1861	Feb 21, 1861
LAWRENCE, Watson Effingham	81st y	no date	Sep 26, 1872
LAWRENCE, William P.	no age	no date	Aug 18, 1859
LAWSON, John	80y 10m	20 Nov 1870	Nov 24, 1870
LAYTON, Charles Augustus	24	1 Mar 1863	Mar 12, 1863
LAYTON, Harriet	56	3 Dec 1877	Dec 6, 1877
LAYTON, Thomas J.	24th y	31st ult	Sep 15, 1864
LAYTON, William	no age	last Fri	Nov 21, 1872
LEE, Hattie	7m 11d	22 Dec 1878	Dec 26, 1878
LEE, James	no age	22 Nov 1875	Dec 16, 1875
LEE, John D.	no age	last Fri	Mar 29, 1877
LEE, Priscilla	31	19 Apr 1861	Apr 25, 1861
LEE, Sarah A.	21y 7m 16d	18 Aug 1870	Aug 25, 1870
LEE, Willie	3m	27 Apr 1870	May 5, 1870
LEECH, Susan	80	17th inst	Jan 23, 1868
LEEK, Benjamin	54	2nd inst	Apr 9, 1863
LEEK, Libbie	23y 8m 4d	14 Jun 1867	Jun 27, 1867
LEGGETT, Eva A. (nee THORP)	23y 2m 18d	5 Feb 1876	Feb 10, 1876
LEGGETT, Frances V.	80	15 Jun 1876	Jun 22, 1876
LEGGETT, Isabel	28y 6m	23 Dec 1873	Dec 25, 1873
LEGGETT, Isabel	1m	17 Sep 1874	Sep 24, 1874
L'HOMMEDIEU, Samuel	77	Mon last wk	Apr 3, 1862
LEIDINGER, Katie	10	last Fri	Dec 19, 1872
LEITCH, Robert	no age	recently	Sep 6, 1877
LEONARD, (male)	ca. 45	5 Mar 1859	Mar 10, 1859
LEONARD, John	no age	no date	Sep 1, 1870
LEONARD, Michael	ca. 5	Saturday	Apr 12, 1877
LEONARD, Sarah	61y 1m 24d	26 Feb 1876	Mar 2, 1876
LEONARD, Stephen	72	22 May 1865	Jun 1, 1865
LEONARD, William F.	62y 6m	no date	Jan 10, 1878
LESEY, Richard	62	no date	Jan 20, 1859
LESLER, (ch. of Mary)	infant	16 Jan 1872	Jan 25, 1872
LESTER, Harriet	41	11 Oct 1858	Oct 21, 1858
LESTER, John T.	95	Saturday	Dec 23, 1875
LEUPP, Charles M.	52	no date	Oct 13, 1859
LEVALLEY, Frank W.	7	no date	Aug 16, 1877
LEVALLEY, Thomas G.	10	no date	Aug 16, 1877
LEVI, (son of John)	2	12 Mar 1865	Mar 30, 1865
LEVINA, Mary	13	14 Dec 1874	Dec 24, 1874
LEVY, Joseph	25	27 Oct 1875	Oct 28, 1875
LEWIN, (dau. of George)	4y 3m	22 Mar 1875	Apr 1, 1875
LEWIS, (child of Charles)	2	19 Nov 1878	Nov 21, 1878
LEWIS, (son of Wright F.)	1y 4m	6 Sep 1865	Sep 14, 1865
LEWIS, Charles	1y 7m 4d	16 Sep 1863	Sep 24, 1863
LEWIS, Charles Edgar	16m 12d	no date	Dec 10, 1868
LEWIS, Elias	82y 6m 23d	16 Apr 1864	Apr 28, 1864
LEWIS, Ezra F.	32	17 Sep 1864	Sep 22, 1864
LEWIS, George R.	3m	8 Dec 1868	Dec 17, 1868
LEWIS, Helen	4m	8 Aug 1877	Aug 16, 1877

Name	Age	Date of death	Date of newspaper
LEWIS, Isaiah, Jr.	42y 6m	4 Oct 1864	Oct 6, 1864
LEWIS, Jacob	11	5 May 1865	May 25, 1865
LEWIS, Jordan	73y 2m 18d	15 Jun 1878	Jun 20, 1878
LEWIS, Junius S.	74	25 Oct 1868	Nov 5, 1868
LEWLER, Mary Ann	1y 2m 7d	22 Oct 1867	Oct 24, 1867
LINCOLN, (Mrs E. M.)	no age	6th inst	Aug 18, 1870
LINCOLN, Charles R.	65th y	no date	Dec 30, 1869
LISTER, Clarissa E.	37	last Sat	Apr 3, 1862
LITTLE, James	no age	1 Aug 1871	Aug 10, 1871
LITTLE, Robert E.	no age	no date	Feb 25, 1864
LIVINGSTONE, Mabel	4y 1m 15d	3 Mar 1872	Mar 14, 1872
LLOYD, Thomas	68	11 Mar 1872	Mar 21, 1872
LOBETZ, William	58	5 Jun 1874	Jun 11, 1874
LOCKE, N. C.	no age	21 Jul 1862	Jul 24, 1862
LOCKHART, (male)	no age	last Mon	Feb 26, 1863
LOCKIE, John	no age	17 Dec 1874	Mar 25, 1875
LODGE, William	23	8 Sep 1863	Sep 10, 1863
LONG, (wife of David)	40	no date	Jul 29, 1858
LONG, Frank A.	7m	19 Jul 1876	Jul 27, 1876
LONG, Julia	20	24 Jul 1865	Jul 27, 1865
LONGBOTHAM, Pamelia	75	3rd inst	Sep 15, 1870
LONGBOTHAM, William H.	no age	Monday	May 17, 1877
LONGFELLOW, (wife of Prof.)	no age	10 Jul 1861	Jul 25, 1861
LOOP, Melinda McKinstry	70th y	8 Jan 1864	Jan 14, 1864
LOPER, Erastus	47y 5m 22d	5th inst	Aug 9, 1860
LOPER, Francis Edgar	24	7 Sep 1865	Oct 5, 1865
LOPER, Sarah	83y 1m 27d	6th inst	Jan 20, 1870
LORD, Daniel M.	62	26th ult	Sep 5, 1861
LORD, Frederick W.	no age	no date	May 31, 1860
LORENZ, (male)	4	Sunday	Aug 9, 1877
LOSEA, Carrie Amelia	3m 7d	26 Jul 1875	Aug 5, 1875
LOSEA, Eddie	13y 4m	13 Jun 1877	Jun 21, 1877
LOSEA, Edward B.	3m 6d	28 Jun 1878	Jul 4, 1878
LOSEA, Mary Julia	28y 4m	3 Sep 1863	Sep 10, 1863
LOSEA, Phebe D.	56th y	14 Oct 1869	Oct 21, 1869
LOSEA, Richard	no age	no date	Sep 1, 1870
LOSEE, Anna Elizabeth	2y 6m	1st inst	Apr 5, 1860
LOSEE, Carrie W.	4y 7m 26d	22 Jul 1873	Jul 24, 1873
LOSEE, Elizabeth	68y 6m	19 Jul 1864	Jul 28, 1864
LOSEE, Hannah	59y 8m	21 Mar 1875	Mar 25, 1875
LOSEE, Irene Georgene	ca. 8m	27 Jul 1867	Aug 1, 1867
LOSEE, Jennie E.	no age	13 Jan 1877	Jan 18, 1877
LOSEE, John Wright	62	10 Nov 1865	Dec 14, 1865
LOSEE, Johnnie C.	5y 14d	18 Jun 1873	Jun 26, 1873
LOSEE, Mary E.	18	1 Mar 1861	Mar 7, 1861
LOSEE, Mary E.	2y 6m 28d	12 Jul 1873	Jul 17, 1873
LOSEE, Mordecai	80	15th inst	Jan 20, 1870
LOSEE, Oliver	72y 9d	19 Feb 1873	Feb 27, 1873
LOSEE, Stephen	81	18 Aug 1874	Aug 20, 1874
LOTT, (child of Hendrick)	infant	31st ult	Sep 9, 1858
LOTT, Catalina	40	31st ult	Nov 16, 1865
LOTT, Cornelia	55	31 Mar 1861	Apr 11, 1861
LOTT, Elizabeth A.	63	22 Apr 1861	Apr 25, 1861
LOTT, George L.	83	6 Feb 1861	Feb 14, 1861
LOTT, Henry	40y 11m 5d	2nd inst	Nov 16, 1865
LOTT, Jeremiah	85	17 Aug 1861	Aug 22, 1861
LOTT, John A.	74th y	20 Jul 1878	Jul 25, 1878
LOTT, John Denton	19	23rd ult	Mar 9, 1865
LOTT, John S.	78th y	24 Mar 1872	Apr 4, 1872
LOTT, Marvin	87	22 Jan 1875	Jan 28, 1875

| | | DEATHS | |
Name	Age	Date of death	Date of newspaper
LOTT, Sarah J.	22	17th inst	Jan 23, 1868
LOTT, Stephen G.	39	2 Sep 1858	Sep 9, 1858
LOTT, Stephen H.	70	20 Jan 1859	Feb 3, 1859
LOTT, Stephen N.	41	15 Jan 1862	Jan 23, 1862
LOUCH, Lawrence	47	last Sun	Feb 8, 1872
LOUNDERS, Wm.	no age	last Mon	May 9, 1872
LOVELL, Eliza	20	3 Aug 1863	Aug 6, 1863
LOWDEN, (child of William)	1	28 Jun 1858	Jul 1, 1858
LOWDEN, Carrie S.	7m 26d	26 Mar 1869	Apr 1, 1869
LOWDEN, Elizabeth	79th y	26 Mar 1872	Mar 28, 1872
LOWDEN, Floyd Southard	10m 3d	20 Aug 1872	Aug 22, 1872
LOWDEN, George	76	30 May 1871	Jun 1, 1871
LOWELL, Sarah Jane	no age	2 Jun 1858	Jun 17, 1858
LOWERRE, David M.	no age	last Mon	Nov 18, 1858
LOWERRE, Henrietta Frazer	24	23rd ult	Mar 9, 1865
LOWLER, William	3y 8m 3d	2 Nov 1867	Nov 7, 1867
LOWTHER, John	75y 10m 22d	12 Oct 1876	Oct 19, 1876
LOZIER, George W.	no age	26 Apr 1859	Apr 28, 1859
LUDLAM, Jesse	no age	Monday	May 28, 1874
LUDLAM, Joseph	10m 9d	24th inst	Aug 29, 1867
LUDLAM, Lottie	2y 9m 16d	21st inst	Aug 29, 1867
LUDLOW, James	ca. 18	Sunday	Mar 15, 1860
LUDLOW, Newton Perkins	13	15 Nov 1858	Nov 18, 1858
LUDLUM, Elizabeth	71y 8m	5th inst	Sep 13, 1860
LUDLUM, Nicholas	69y 6m 11d	26 Dec 1868	Dec 31, 1868
LUSH, Carman	58y 6m 11d	11 Apr 1872	Apr 18, 1872
LUSH, Carman	no age	last Thur	Apr 18, 1872
LUSH, James	3y 11m 27d	6 Oct 1873	Oct 9, 1873
LUSH, Maggie May	4y 6m	14 Mar 1876	Mar 16, 1876
LUSH, Stephen B.	ca. 7	23rd inst	Feb 24, 1870
LUSH, William	8y 6m	28 Feb 1870	Mar 3, 1870
LUTHER, Frank	60	24 Sep 1878	Oct 3, 1878
LUYSTER, Adrian	no age	23 Dec 1861	Dec 26, 1861
LYDEN, Isabella	no age	3 Jan 1878	Jan 17, 1878
LYDEN, William	no age	11 Jan 1878	Jan 17, 1878
LYMAN, Joseph H.	47	Sunday	Feb 1, 1872
LYNCH, (ch. of John)	1	16 Jul 1872	Jul 25, 1872
LYNCH, Barney	no age	19 Jan 1861	Jan 24, 1861
LYNCH, James	no age	3rd inst	Aug 9, 1860
LYON, Stephen	88	no date	Jun 9, 1859
LYONS, Cornelius	no age	Sunday	Aug 15, 1867
LYONS, Francis	no age	29 Oct 1865	Nov 2, 1865
LYONS, Mary	no age	no date	Nov 2, 1865
MAARS, Adolph	no age	last Mon	Feb 1, 1872
MCALLEN, James	no age	Monday	Sep 20, 1877
MCBRAND, Mary	no age	no date	Feb 26, 1874
MCCABE, Lawrence E.	no age	21 Mar 1872	Apr 25, 1872
MCCARTHY, Joseph	7	Monday	Dec 16, 1875
MCCARTY, Katie	38	7 Apr 1877	Apr 12, 1877
MCCLELLAND, Thos.	ca. 14	20 Jan 1872	Feb 1, 1872
MCCLELLAND, William	30	27 Sep 1861	Oct 3, 1861
MCCLOSKEY, (Mr)	no age	Monday	Jun 7, 1877
MCCLURG, (female)	no age	Friday	Jul 15, 1875
MCCOMB, John S.	38y 1m 26d	1 Jun 1875	Jun 3, 1875
MCCOMBS, Lottie Imogene	2y 1m 7d	16 Feb 1876	Feb 24, 1876
MCCOON, Samuel	68	30th ult	Apr 8, 1869
MCCOON, Thomas	40	11 Jul 1872	Jul 18, 1872
MCCORMACK, John A.	31	17 Jul 1861	Aug 1, 1861

Name	Age	Date of death	Date of newspaper
MCCORMICK, Patrick	45	1 Jan 1873	Jan 9, 1873
MCCORMICK, Sarah M.	66y 1m	11 Jan 1878	Jan 17, 1878
M'COSKER, Bradshaw	22	last Sat	Oct 21, 1869
MCCOUN, Daniel	37y 4m	23 May 1875	May 27, 1875
MCCOUN, Georgianna	32y 4m	8 Aug 1877	Aug 16, 1877
MCCOUN, Jane	21	Thurs	May 9, 1872
MCCOUN, Mary	32y 22d	20 Feb 1870	Feb 24, 1870
MCCOUN, William T.	92	18 Jul 1878	Jul 25, 1878
MCCOUN, William T.	92nd y	18 Jul 1878	Jul 25, 1878
MCCOY, (child of John)	infant	1 Oct 1870	Oct 6, 1870
MCCOY, Alexander	3m 17d	17 Aug 1874	Aug 27, 1874
MCCOY, Janie	12y 6m	23 Jul 1878	Jul 25, 1878
MCCOY, Janie	12	23 Jul 1878	Oct 10, 1878
MCCOY, John G.	35	28 Dec 1876	Jan 4, 1877
MCCOY, Winnifred	38	11 Feb 1877	Feb 15, 1877
MCCRUMB, Jennie	26y 1m 14d	2nd inst	Mar 9, 1865
MCCUSKER, John	35	Friday	May 31, 1877
MACDONALD, Allen	67	no date	Jan 23, 1862
MACDONALD, John M.	73	15 Nov 1863	Nov 19, 1863
MCDONALD, Mary Ann	7	no date	Apr 16, 1863
MCDONALD, Michael	no age	28 Apr 1859	May 5, 1859
MCDONALD, Michael W.	no age	27 Jan 1863	Feb 12, 1863
MACDONALD, Robert C.	no age	no date	May 17, 1860
MCDONALD, Winfield	10m	no date	Apr 16, 1863
MCDOUGALL, Hugh	89	22 Jul 1858	Jul 29, 1858
MCGANN, Michael	no age	last Tue	Dec 15, 1864
MCGEE, John	no age	last Fri	Aug 28, 1873
MCGEE, Phebe Ann	44	21 Feb 1868	Feb 20, 1868
MCGLYNN, William	40	yesterday	Dec 20, 1860
MCGOWEN, Terence	no age	Sunday	Aug 15, 1867
MCGUIRE, Johanna	90	16 Jun 1877	Jun 21, 1877
MCGUNNIGLE, Mary	37	31 Jan 1874	Feb 5, 1874
MCHUGH, Frank	no age	last Tues	Jul 23, 1874
MCHUGH, William	no age	no date	Dec 31, 1874
MACK, John	no age	last week	Jun 25, 1874
MACK, Valentine	no age	25th ult	Jul 6, 1876
MCKAY, Elizabeth Waters	4m 25d	7 May 1865	May 11, 1865
MCKEE, Margaret E.	5y 2m 25d	24th inst	Apr 2, 1863
MCKENNA, James	no age	no date	Aug 25, 1870
MACKENZIE, Ellen	11y 5m	1 Jul 1876	Jul 6, 1876
MACKERELL, Willian H.	55	11 Aug 1858	Aug 19, 1858
MACKEY, Charles	1	8 Jul 1872	Jul 18, 1872
MACKEY, John	ca. 80	last Sat	Oct 17, 1872
MACKIVER, Daniel	9	30 May 1876	Jun 1, 1876
MACKIVER, Thomas	12	31 May 1876	Jun 1, 1876
MACKLE, Wm.	75	no date	Nov 11, 1869
MCLAREN, David	no age	no date	Sep 1, 1870
MCLEOD, Flora	no age	13 Aug 1872	Aug 15, 1872
MCLINDON, Mary	31y 23d	18 Oct 1868	Oct 29, 1868
MCLINDON, Susan J.	20y 9m 17d	24 Oct 1868	Oct 29, 1868
MCLOUGHIN, Robert	no age	Thursday	Aug 26, 1875
MCMANNUS, (son of Sgt.)	no age	Tuesday	Jun 27, 1872
MCMANUS, Margaret	21	5 Sep 1871	Sep 14, 1871
MCNALLY, Jane	no age	Sunday	Apr 5, 1860
MCNAMEE, John	no age	28 Sep 1878	Oct 3, 1878
MCPHAIL, William L.	no age	no date	Nov 3, 1859
MCQUEEN, Catharine L.	18y 5m 23d	3 Jun 1876	Jun 8, 1876
MCQUEEN, David	no age	9 Apr 1872	Apr 11, 1872
MCQUEEN, David	no age	no date	May 16, 1872
MCQUIRE, (son of Patrick)	no age	25 Aug 1877	Sep 13, 1877

Name	Age	Date of death	Date of newspaper
MCVEIGH, Joseph	67	30 Aug 1875	Sep 9, 1875
MADDEN, Catherine	3	last Wed	Oct 25, 1860
MAGRATH, John P.	33	22 Jun 1858	Jun 24, 1858
MAGUIRE, Elmira A.	8y 2m	13 Dec 1873	Dec 18, 1873
MAGUIRE, Rose	40	12 Feb 1874	Feb 19, 1874
MAGWIRE, John B.	33	17 Sep 1870	Sep 22, 1870
MAHAN, Michael	no age	24 Oct 1874	Nov 19, 1874
MAHAR, Thomas	no age	no date	Aug 22, 1872
MAHER, (Mr.)	no age	Monday	Jan 18, 1872
MAHER, James	63	8 Apr 1872	Apr 11, 1872
MAHEW, (Mr)	40	12 Aug 1867	Aug 22, 1867
MAHEW, Ellen	40	19 May 1877	May 24, 1877
MALIN, William	no age	21st inst	Jul 25, 1867
MALISON, Charles	58y 8m 25d	no date	Sep 8, 1870
MALLOY, Edward	no age	17 Sep 1878	Sep 19, 1878
MALONE, Thomas	no age	last Tues	Jul 15, 1875
MALONEY, (ch. of Patrick)	4m	15 Jul 1872	Jul 25, 1872
MALONY, Margaret	65	17 Sep 1876	Sep 21, 1876
MANEY, James	14	last week	Feb 2, 1860
MANICE, DeForest	63	18th inst	Apr 24, 1862
MANICE, Edith	13m 22d	22 Jul 1878	Jul 25, 1878
MANICE, Edward A.	no age	last Tues	Dec 13, 1877
MANN, (male)	4	11 Mar 1865	Mar 30, 1865
MANN, Charles A.	no age	no date	Jan 26, 1860
MANN, Sarah Maria	30	30 Dec 1864	Jan 5, 1865
MANNING, Ann	76	30 Aug 1877	Sep 6, 1877
MANWARING, Mary L.	9m	no date	Aug 31, 1865
MAPES, Jason	74	18 Jan 1865	Jan 26, 1865
MARGOT, Elizabeth Maria Louise	6w 4d	12 Sep 1876	Sep 14, 1876
MARSH, William	no age	6 Oct 1870	Oct 13, 1870
MARSHALL, Geo. W.	38	26 Jul 1864	Aug 4, 1864
MARSHALL, Samuel	30	Sunday	Apr 26, 1877
MARTIN, David	no age	6 Aug 1861	Aug 8, 1861
MARTIN, Eliza	23	10 Nov 1874	Nov 12, 1874
MARTIN, John	no age	Saturday	Sep 27, 1877
MARTIN, Joseph	3y 2m	18 Jun 1873	Jul 3, 1873
MARTIN, Mary Elma	1m	17 Sep 1874	Sep 24, 1874
MARTIN, Silas	no age	no date	Sep 17, 1874
MARTIN, Stephen	25	22 Jun 1863	Jun 25, 1863
MARVIN, Benjamin Franklin	11	28 Dec 1858	Jan 6, 1859
MARVIN, Sally	78	18 Apr 1876	Apr 20, 1876
MASON, John T.	no age	3 Oct 1859	Oct 20, 1859
MASON, William	2m 11d	10 Sep 1870	Sep 15, 1870
MATHEWBAKER, Christian	42	20 Aug 1858	Aug 26, 1858
MATHEWS, Deborah	79	19 Apr 1862	Apr 24, 1862
MATHEWS, Elizabeth	ca. 60	13th inst	Apr 19, 1860
MATHEWS, Emma	24	7 Jan 1868	Jan 9, 1868
MATHEWS, Margaret	no age	17th inst	Jan 23, 1868
MATHEWS, Mary D.	61y 2m 17d	2 Sep 1874	Sep 10, 1874
MATHEWS, Oliver	60	31 May 1862	Jun 5, 1862
MATHEWS, Rebecca	no age	no date	Sep 1, 1870
MATHEWS, Sarah	ca. 61	15 Jan 1864	Jan 21, 1864
MATHEWS, Wallace	31y 5m 11d	17 Mar 1870	Apr 7, 1870
MATHEWS, William	9m 6d	24 Jun 1863	Jul 2, 1863
MATTHEWS, (child of Henry)	16m	4th inst	Sep 6, 1860
MATTHEWS, (dau. of Alexander)	9	no date	Nov 2, 1865
MATTHEWS, (dau. of Whitman)	3y 10m	27 Jan 1861	Jan 31, 1861
MATTHEWS, (son of John)	infant	8 Nov 1877	Nov 15, 1877
MATTHEWS, James J.	44y 10m 4d	Thursday	Oct 25, 1877

Name	Age	Date of death	Date of newspaper
MATTHEWS, James J.	44y 10m	no date	Jan 10, 1878
MATTHEWS, John W.	no age	last Sat(?)	Jul 5, 1860
MATTHEWS, Mary Ann	8d	29 Jul 1871	Aug 10, 1871
MATTHEWS, Mary D.	2y 10m 11d	no date	Apr 9, 1868
MATTHEWS, Mary Ellen	12	18 Sep 1862	Sep 25, 1862
MATTHIAS, Pamelia	38	5 Aug 1858	Aug 19, 1858
MAURER, Edward	no age	last Wed	Jul 18, 1878
MAVERICK, Lydia	19	4 Dec 1863	Dec 10, 1863
MAY, Horace	59	28 Jan 1868	Feb 6, 1868
MAY, Martin	55	26 Feb 1875	Mar 4, 1875
MAYHER, Ann Amelia	26y 11m 28d	28 Feb 1863	Mar 5, 1863
MAYHER, George W.	6m 3d	26 Oct 1862	Oct 30, 1862
MAYHER, George W.	43	14 Apr 1874	Apr 23, 1874
MAYHEW, (child of John)	ca. 4	20 Dec 1864	Dec 29, 1864
MAYHEW, Althea	1y 5m	30 Jul 1876	Aug 3, 1876
MAYHEW, Martin	21	22 Aug 1877	Aug 30, 1877
MAYHEW, Mary Elizabeth	4m 27d	7 Aug 1877	Aug 16, 1877
MAYHEW, Sylvester W.	28	21 Mar 1877	Mar 29, 1877
MAYHEW, Thomas	no age	4 Aug 1877	Aug 9, 1877
MEACHAM, (wife of Henry)	no age	6 Jan 1860	Jan 12, 1860
MEACHAM, Henry	no age	6 Jan 1860	Jan 12, 1860
MEAD, Lucretia	69y 1m 18d	16 May 1877	May 24, 1877
MEAD, Sidney M.	22nd y	no date	Oct 27, 1864
MEDAD, George	no age	last Wed	Aug 11, 1864
MEEKER, Stephen H.	87	2 Feb 1876	Feb 10, 1876
MEEKS, Robert	no age	6th inst	Nov 8, 1860
MEGINN, Jacob G.	15	26 Dec 1869	Dec 30, 1869
MEIGS, John	80	20th inst	Aug 25, 1864
MEINELL, James	79th y	2 Jul 1865	Jul 6, 1865
MEIR, (ch. of Barney)	infant	17 Mar 1872	Mar 21, 1872
MERCEREAU, George Hurst	6m 19d	21st inst	Jul 29, 1869
MERCEREAU, Willie	16	11 Mar 1874	Mar 12, 1874
MERITT, Willet	no age	no date	Feb 5, 1874
MERRALL, Wm. O.	boy	no date	Jul 24, 1862
MERRITT, (Mrs Coles)	22	9 Oct 1867	Oct 24, 1867
MERRITT, Jackson	22	14 Jun 1869	Jun 17, 1869
MERRITT, John	no age	no date	Feb 5, 1874
MERSEREAU, Charlotte E.	no age	5 Sep 1862	Sep 11, 1862
MERSEREAU, George Hurst	9m 23d	29 Aug 1868	Sep 3, 1868
MERSEREAU, Helen	79	23 Jan 1876	Jan 27, 1876
MERSHON, Stephen	no age	19 Apr 1874	Apr 23, 1874
MERWIN, Anna M.	4m	29 Sep 1874	Oct 1, 1874
MESSENGER, John F.	no age	2 Jul 1861	Jul 25, 1861
METTLER, Arthur R. C.	1y 8m 2d	10 Jan 1863	Jan 15, 1863
METZ, (dau. of Wm.)	2	14 Aug 1875	Aug 19, 1875
MEYER, (son of Gotlieb)	9	9 Sep 1864	Sep 15, 1864
MEYER, Dora	no age	Thursday	Sep 6, 1877
MEYER, Henry	56y 9m	19 Dec 1874	Dec 24, 1874
MEYER, Veronika	51y 8m 12d	28 Dec 1874	Dec 31, 1874
MEYERS, John	no age	last Sat	Dec 9, 1869
MEYERS, John, Jr.	no age	last Sept	Jan 27, 1870
MIER, Frank	2y 9m	no date	Mar 26, 1874
MIERS, (son of James Scott)	no age	last Mon	Apr 18, 1872
MILLER, (Mrs. Adam)	no age	no date	Jan 20, 1870
MILLER, (dau. of Henry)	14m	last Thur	Feb 6, 1862
MILLER, (son of Hugh)	8	Saturday	Apr 18, 1872
MILLER, (son of Judy)	infant	10 Sep 1864	Sep 15, 1864
MILLER, Annie	32y 6m	4 Nov 1877	Nov 8, 1877
MILLER, Benjamin	1y 8m 5d	13 Apr 1874	Apr 16, 1874
MILLER, Bessie	4y 3m 21d	10 Jul 1875	Jul 22, 1875

Name	Age	Date of death	Date of newspaper
MILLER, Elizabeth	76y 6m 24d	12 Oct 1877	Oct 18, 1877
MILLER, Emma C.	6y 11m 16d	14 Oct 1873	Oct 16, 1873
MILLER, Frederick	2m	29 Jul 1873	Jul 31, 1873
MILLER, George	no age	17 Feb 1859	Feb 24, 1859
MILLER, Harry	60y 7m	4 Mar 1877	Mar 8, 1877
MILLER, Hattie Mae	4y 12d	20 Jun 1875	Jul 22, 1875
MILLER, Henry	no age	30 Jun 1874	Jul 16, 1874
MILLER, Henry Anthony	11	16 Jan 1874	Jan 22, 1874
MILLER, Henry S.	39	21st inst	Jun 27, 1867
MILLER, Henry S.	39	21st ult	Jul 11, 1867
MILLER, John	ca. 50	24 Aug 1872	Aug 29, 1872
MILLER, Judah H.	58	4 Aug 1873	Aug 7, 1873
MILLER, Liance	75	3 May 1878	May 9, 1878
MILLER, Minnie	3y 8m	6 Aug 1873	Aug 7, 1873
MILLER, Nellie	1m 8d	22 Sep 1876	Oct 5, 1876
MILLER, Sophia	37	27 Nov 1867	Dec 5, 1867
MILLER, William	53	17 Aug 1863	Aug 20, 1863
MILLER, William G.	3y 3m	9 Apr 1864	Apr 14, 1864
MILLER, William H.	1y 1m 16d	7 Sep 1876	Sep 21, 1876
MILLINGTON, Edwin	31	26 Aug 1864	Aug 10, 1865
MILLINGTON, Eliza	46	11 Sep 1877	Sep 13, 1877
MILLINGTON, Matthew	75	26 Dec 1874	Dec 31, 1874
MILLS, (Mr.)	no age	last Thurs	Jan 4, 1872
MILLS, (Mr.)	no age	no date	May 11, 1876
MILLS, Abner	no age	no date	Jan 25, 1872
MILLS, Eliza A.	63	16 Jul 1865	Jul 20, 1865
MILLS, Mary Hester	2y 3m	8th inst	Jun 16, 1864
MILLS, Ruth	82	no date	Mar 12, 1868
MILLS, Samuel, Sr.	75	29 Jan 1861	Feb 7, 1861
MILLS, Willet S.	5m 24d	2 Nov 1874	Nov 5, 1874
MILLS, William Henry	29y 10m 12d	2 Aug 1863	Aug 6, 1863
MINGO, John	53	27 Oct 1873	Oct 30, 1873
MINOCKS, (son of Officer)	no age	last week	Jul 11, 1878
MISSNER, Catherine	25y 4m	17 Dec 1874	Dec 24, 1874
MITCHELL, (son of George)	infant	2 Oct 1875	Oct 7, 1875
MITCHELL, Bertha	2y 9m	10 Apr 1875	Apr 15, 1875
MITCHELL, Bertha	2y 9m	21 Apr 1875	Apr 29, 1875
MITCHELL, Erastus	42	3rd inst	Sep 12, 1867
MITCHELL, Jacob	no age	19 Mar 1864	Apr 7, 1864
MITCHELL, Margaret	33	17 Feb 1873	Feb 20, 1873
MITCHELL, Margaret Eliza	80th y	26 Mar 1865	Mar 30, 1865
MITCHELL, Singleton	83	9 Dec 1861	Dec 12, 1861
MITCHELL, William L.	55th y	last Sun	Dec 1, 1864
MOGER, Micah M.	no age	Wednesday	Apr 5, 1877
MOLE, Henry	67	no date	Jan 10, 1878
MOLLE, Laura	11m 16d	12 Mar 1876	Mar 16, 1876
MOLLINEAUX, (dau. of John)	6m	19 Aug 1877	Aug 23, 1877
MOLLINEAUX, Willie Hendrickson	4m	24 Jul 1878	Aug 1, 1878
MOLLINEUX, Lidia L.	32y 5m 10d	28 Dec 1870	Jan 5, 1871
MOLLINEUX, Mary P.	59y 6m 8d	11 Sep 1875	Sep 16, 1875
MONAHAN, Luke	58	18 Mar 1876	Mar 23, 1876
MONAHAN, Maggie	1y 4m	28 Jul 1876	Aug 3, 1876
MONFORT, George W.	no age	6 Jan 1878	Jan 17, 1878
MONROE, Charles S.	55	27 Mar 1870	Mar 31, 1870
MONTFORT, Mary Ann	19	2 Oct 1864	Oct 13, 1864
MONTFORT, Peter	80	last Tue	Jul 19, 1860
MONTGOMERY, David	42	23 Apr 1878	Apr 25, 1878
MOODE, Henry	96	19 Jan 1877	Jan 25, 1877
MOODE, Henry	96	19 Jan 1877	Jan 25, 1877

Name	Age	Date of death	Date of newspaper
MOORE, (wife of Joseph)	60	26th ult	Aug 3, 1865
MOORE, Ann Eloisa	81y 3m 11d	5 Dec 1869	Dec 16, 1869
MOORE, Annie	39	8 Aug 1872	Aug 15, 1872
MOORE, Charles C.	37	4 Oct 1878	Oct 10, 1878
MOORE, Cynthia	72	20 May 1859	Jun 2, 1859
MOORE, Eliza Jane	8-9	Tues week	May 10, 1877
MOORE, Jane M.	29y 3m	25 May 1877	May 31, 1877
MOORE, Nathaniel F.	90	no date	May 9, 1872
MOORE, Rebecca	1y 7m	28 Aug 1871	Aug 31, 1871
MOORE, S. T. (Capt.)	98	no date	Jan 25, 1872
MOORE, Samuel	38	14 Apr 1864	Apr 21, 1864
MOORE, Sarah Ann	49y 5m	13 Jun 1878	Jun 20, 1878
MORDENTHAU, Henrietta	no age	no date	Sep 20, 1877
MORGAN, Anne	65th y	23rd ult	Mar 12, 1863
MORGAN, Patrick	no age	Sunday	Aug 26, 1875
MORLAND, Eliza	8m	22 Aug 1865	Aug 31, 1865
MORRELL, Richard	no age	7 Jun 1858	Jun 17, 1858
MORRIS, (Mrs. James)	84	no date	Aug 1, 1872
MORRISON, (female)	no age	no date	Apr 11, 1872
MORRISON, Winie Way	2m	18 Sep 1871	Sep 21, 1871
MORSE, Carman	20	30 Mar 1865	Apr 6, 1865
MOSHER, William	no age	Monday	Dec 17, 1874
MOTE, (ch. of Charles)	infant	last Sun	Aug 8, 1872
MOTLEY, John Lothrap	no age	Tuesday	Jun 7, 1877
MOTT, (Mr.)	no age	5 Jul 1875	Sep 2, 1875
MOTT, (child of George)	6w	30 Dec 1860	Jan 3, 1861
MOTT, (child of Samuel B.)	ca. 8m	9 Jul 1864	Jul 21, 1864
MOTT, (son of Hamilton)	1m 21d	1 Sep 1868	Sep 3, 1868
MOTT, Alfred A.	56th y	18 Jun 1867	Jun 27, 1867
MOTT, Catharine M.	35	11 Aug 1876	Aug 17, 1876
MOTT, Charles	1	17 Sep 1872	Sep 19, 1872
MOTT, Chauncey	39y 4m 24d	3 Aug 1864	Aug 11, 1864
MOTT, Dandridge B. P.	no age	15 Jun 1864	Jul 7, 1864
MOTT, Elizabeth	73rd y	18 Oct 1869	Oct 21, 1869
MOTT, Elizabeth	70	19 Oct 1874	Oct 22, 1874
MOTT, Emily	35	12 Dec 1876	Dec 14, 1876
MOTT, Emma Jane	27y 2m	10 Feb 1877	Feb 15, 1877
MOTT, George	15	21 Oct 1878	Oct 24, 1878
MOTT, Henry	no age	2 Nov 1875	Nov 4, 1875
MOTT, Henry M.	51	4 Jan 1878	Jan 10, 1878
MOTT, John	18	no date	Dec 4, 1862
MOTT, John	1	2 Jan 1865	Jan 5, 1865
MOTT, John L.	57	24 Jan 1876	Jan 27, 1876
MOTT, Joseph	no age	Oct	Apr 6, 1865
MOTT, Josephine	38	28 Feb 1860	Mar 8, 1860
MOTT, Martha	76	16 Jun 1872	Jun 20, 1872
MOTT, Mary	70y 9d	24 Jan 1864	Jan 28, 1864
MOTT, Mary	4	28 Nov 1865	Nov 30, 1865
MOTT, Mary	81y 2m 13d	8 Oct 1875	Oct 14, 1875
MOTT, Milton	50	25 May 1863	May 28, 1863
MOTT, Orlando B.	5	5 Feb 1861	Feb 7, 1861
MOTT, Robert	59	5 Jul 1863	Jul 9, 1863
MOTT, S. Elizabeth	42nd y	26th inst	Aug 1, 1867
MOTT, Samuel	85	19 Oct 1859	Oct 20, 1859
MOTT, Samuel W.	5	28 Dec 1860	Jan 3, 1861
MOTT, Sarah	71st y	20 Jan 1864	Jan 28, 1864
MOTT, Smith	90	23 Nov 1863	Dec 3, 1863
MOTT, William B.	no age	last Sat	Feb 5, 1874
MOTT, William B.	30	5 Jul 1875	Jul 8, 1875
MOTT, Willie H.	5y 5m 17d	11th inst	Feb 19, 1863

Name	Age	Date of death	Date of newspaper
MOULTON, Joseph W.	86	23 Apr 1875	May 6, 1875
MOUNT, Elizabeth H.	44	no date	Aug 26, 1858
MOZLER, John	16	last Tues	Apr 26, 1877
MUDGE, Elizabeth	64	10th inst	Apr 19, 1860
MUGER, Minnie	5m 5d	11 Aug 1875	Aug 19, 1875
MUGNUG, Louisa	1y	11 Sep 1873	Sep 18, 1873
MUHLENBURG, William A.	82nd y	8th inst	Apr 12, 1877
MULHEARN, Thomas	no age	28 Apr 1870	May 5, 1870
MULLEN, (Mr)	no age	22 Dec 1877	Dec 27, 1877
MULLER, Andrew	no age	Sunday	Mar 19, 1874
MULLER, Catherine	no age	30 Aug 1875	Sep 2, 1875
MULLER, George C.	9	5 Feb 1874	Feb 12, 1874
MULLER, Josephine	no age	30 Aug 1875	Sep 2, 1875
MULLIGAN, (male)	11	Saturday	Dec 20, 1860
MULLIGAN, (son of Patrick)	5-6	15 Jul 1874	Jul 23, 1874
MULLIGAN, Henry	no age	last Tues	Oct 25, 1877
MULLIGAN, Maggie	no age	24 Jun 1876	Jun 29, 1876
MULLINER, Emeline	40	24 Jan 1872	Feb 1, 1872
MULLINER, Hamilton Voorhies	9m 18d	7 Aug 1875	Aug 12, 1875
MUNCEY, Silas	ca. 81	no date	Jul 29, 1869
MUNEY, Sarah	82	18th ult	Feb 2, 1860
MUNEY, Silas	85	18th ult	Feb 2, 1860
MUNSELL, Abby T.	82	3 Jul 1858	Jul 15, 1858
MURDOCK, (Mrs. Rubin)	no age	20 Jan 1874	Jan 22, 1874
MURPHY, (son of Ed.)	3	7 Sep 1875	Sep 9, 1875
MURRAY, (son of John)	infant	21st inst	Oct 5, 1865
MURRAY, Cornelius	35	13 Apr 1876	Apr 20, 1876
MURRAY, Ellen Amelia	27	16 Sep 1867	Sep 26, 1867
MURRAY, Mary	62	8 Aug 1873	Aug 14, 1873
MURRAY, Mary	75	5 Jun 1874	Jun 11, 1874
MURRAY, Thomas	no age	12th inst	Oct 1, 1874
MUSGNUG, Jacob	74	13 Feb 1877	Feb 22, 1877
MYERS, (son of Martin)	no age	1 Mar 1876	Mar 9, 1876
MYERS, Charles Edward	10y 11m 11d	11 Oct 1863	Oct 15, 1863
MYERS, Edith Amelia	no age	15 Jul 1878	Jul 25, 1878
MYERS, Emma Kirtland	9m 9d	29 Dec 1876	Jan 4, 1877
MYERS, Irving P.	15y 5m	14 Nov 1870	Nov 24, 1870
MYERS, Isabel Read	3y 7m 18d	20 Dec 1876	Dec 28, 1876
MYERS, Martha B.	12	29 Nov 1876	Dec 7, 1876
MYERS, William	65	8th inst	Feb 16, 1865
NAFIE, Emma	25y 3m 4d	25 Sep 1875	Oct 7, 1875
NAPIER, Catherine B.	83rd y	1 Jan 1864	Jan 7, 1864
NASH, Hattie F.	20	last Sat	Jul 20, 1865
NASH, Richard Henry	4y 2m	29 Feb 1860	Mar 8, 1860
NATHO, Catherine	no age	18 Nov 1874	Dec 3, 1874
NAUMANN, Emile	no age	Tuesday	Jun 14, 1877
NEAL, Anna Maria	1y 3m	6 Dec 1863	Dec 10, 1863
NEARY, Thomas	65	18 Nov 1875	Dec 2, 1875
NEBE, Charles	12y 8m	6 Sep 1873	Sep 11, 1873
NEILSON, Henry L.	1y 3m 7d	2 Jan 1864	Jan 14, 1864
NEITZKA, Frederick	9m 22d	2 Oct 1874	Oct 8, 1874
NELSON, Annie	75	8 Oct 1877	Oct 18, 1877
NELSON, Thomas	74	28 Jul 1860	Aug 2, 1860
NESBITT, Margaret Ann	4y 5m	9 Mar 1875	Mar 11, 1875
NEWBURY, (Mrs. James)	no age	no date	Oct 14, 1869
NEWCOMB, (Mrs.)	85	24 May 1865	Jun 8, 1865
NEWTON, Isaac	no age	26th ult	Jul 4, 1867
NEWTON, Libbie Hendrickson	no age	16 Jul 1875	Jul 22, 1875

DEATHS

Name	Age	Date of death	Date of newspaper
NEWTON, Libbie Hendrickson	no age	16 Jul 1875	Jul 29, 1875
NICHOLLS, Henry	75th y	19 Apr 1860	Apr 26, 1860
NICHOLS, (male)	no age	20 Sep 1860	Dec 6, 1860
NICHOLS, Charles Forster	5m 19d	23 Aug 1867	Aug 29, 1867
NICHOLS, Edwin C.	59	6 Sep 1873	Sep 11, 1873
NICHOLS, Elizabeth	78	22 Oct 1858	Nov 4, 1858
NICHOLS, Elizabeth	78	22 Oct 1858	Nov 11, 1858
NICHOLS, Ellen	8w	7 Mar 1875	Mar 11, 1875
NICHOLS, Henry M.	65y 11m 19d	4 Mar 1874	Mar 5, 1874
NICHOLS, Jackson	67	24 Dec 1867	Jan 2, 1868
NICHOLS, Jane	36	21st ult	Mar 9, 1865
NICHOLS, John	79	27 Feb 1870	Mar 3, 1870
NICHOLS, Merrivelle H.	22y 6m	22 Oct 1867	Oct 24, 1867
NICHOLS, Merrivill	16	no date	Jun 8, 1865
NICHOLS, Merriville H.	23	21 Oct 1867	Nov 7, 1867
NICHOLS, Minnie	4m	27 Oct 1874	Nov 5, 1874
NICHOLS, Phebe	77th y	15 Sep 1878	Sep 19, 1878
NICHOLS, Wilbur	10m	21 Sep 1873	Sep 25, 1873
NIMMO, Joseph	63	19th inst	Apr 27, 1865
NIX, Ann Eliza	19y 9m 9d	27 May 1871	Jun 1, 1871
NIX, Eliza M.	41y 11m	30 Apr 1868	May 7, 1868
NIX, Harry W.	14y 7m 23d	25 Aug 1873	Aug 28, 1873
NOBLE, Kate Paulina	5y 6m	23 Jan 1878	Jan 24, 1878
NOLAN, (Miss)	28	29 Jun 1861	Jul 4, 1861
NOLAN, Mary	60	17 Oct 1876	Oct 19, 1876
NOLL, Charles Frederick	29	no date	Apr 16, 1863
NOLL, John	no age	9th inst	Aug 18, 1864
NOON, Catherine	70	7 Feb 1872	Feb 15, 1872
NOON, Henry	35	26 Jun 1872	Jun 27, 1872
NOON, Henry	72	24 Jun 1876	Jun 29, 1876
NOON, John	70	1 Sep 1868	Sep 3, 1868
NOON, John	28	13 Oct 1873	Oct 16, 1873
NOON, Lydia Ann	4	20 Oct 1861	Nov 14, 1861
NOON, Martha	no age	18 May 1875	May 20, 1875
NOON, Sarah E.	2	22 Aug 1870	Aug 25, 1870
NOON, William	no age	17 Jun 1863	Jun 25, 1863
NORRIS, Emily Lucinda	10m	1 Sep 1873	Sep 4, 1873
NORRIS, William H.	77	19 Oct 1878	Oct 24, 1878
NORTON, (Mr.)	no age	4 Jul 1872	Jul 18, 1872
NORTON, (Mrs.)	no age	4 Jul 1872	Jul 18, 1872
NORTON, (two ch.)	no age	4 Jul 1872	Jul 18, 1872
NORTON, Lambert	70y 9m 24d	4 May 1864	May 12, 1864
NORTON, Samuel	no age	Sunday	Mar 15, 1877
NORTON, William	52y 9m 14d	28 Sep 1870	Oct 6, 1870
NOSTRAND, Caroline	3y 10m	3 Nov 1865	Nov 16, 1865
NOSTRAND, Catharine	84	13th inst	Feb 16, 1860
NOSTRAND, Catherine	41	31 Aug 1858	Sep 9, 1858
NOSTRAND, Catherine	no age	14 Sep 1862	Sep 25, 1862
NOSTRAND, Charlotte	33y 4m 25d	29 Jan 1877	Feb 1, 1877
NOSTRAND, Chrisitana	82	10 Aug 1874	Aug 13, 1874
NOSTRAND, Ella Louise	3y 7m	15 Apr 1865	May 4, 1865
NOSTRAND, Foster	72	20 Jun 1861	Jun 27, 1861
NOSTRAND, Garret Wort	no age	21 Jan 1871	Jan 26, 1871
NOSTRAND, George	93	9th inst	Jun 21, 1860
NOSTRAND, Isaac	no age	2nd inst	Mar 15, 1860
NOSTRAND, Isaac	68y 2m 6d	13 Jun 1867	Jun 27, 1867
NOSTRAND, Isaac	no age	14 Nov 1878	Nov 21, 1878
NOSTRAND, James S.	17m 13d	13 Mar 1865	Mar 30, 1865
NOSTRAND, Jane	73	7 Nov 1869	Nov 11, 1869
NOSTRAND, Jesse	7d	15 Jun 1872	Jun 20, 1872

DEATHS

Name	Age	Date of death	Date of newspaper
NOSTRAND, John	105	24 Feb 1865	Mar 23, 1865
NOSTRAND, John S.	7y 4m 23d	27th inst	Oct 5, 1865
NOSTRAND, John Wilber	10m 26d	28th ult	Aug 3, 1865
NOSTRAND, Martha	92	28 Jan 1861	Feb 7, 1861
NOSTRAND, Mary Emma	5y 4m 23d	19 Apr 1865	May 4, 1865
NOSTRAND, Nancy	ca. 70	29 Dec 1870	Jan 5, 1871
NOSTRAND, Nathaniel	58y 7m 3d	20th inst	Jan 30, 1868
NOSTRAND, Robert	24	1 Dec 1874	Dec 3, 1874
NOSTRAND, Robert H.	57y 2m	2 Nov 1869	Nov 18, 1869
NOSTRAND, Smith	34	20th ult	Mar 9, 1865
NOSTRAND, Stephen	29y 2m	20th inst	Aug 24, 1865
NOYES, Wm. Curtis	60	31 Dec 1864	Jan 5, 1865
NUGENT, G. W. P.	no age	last week	Mar 27, 1862
NULET, Joseph	no age	Monday	Nov 10, 1864
O'BRIEN, Catherine	11m	30 Sep 1870	Oct 6, 1870
O'BRIEN, Catherine	no age	4 Feb 1874	Feb 12, 1874
O'BRIEN, David	1	11 Sep 1877	Sep 13, 1877
O'BRIEN, Jerry	25	Friday	Aug 15, 1867
O'BRIEN, Mary	45y 11d	5 Sep 1875	Sep 9, 1875
O'BRIEN, William	young	recently	Aug 29, 1867
O'BRYAN, James	2y 8m	23 Aug 1865	Sep 7, 1865
O'CONNOR, Harriet	29	31 Mar 1878	Apr 4, 1878
O'CONNOR, Patrick	45	1 Oct 1865	Oct 5, 1865
O'DONNELL, Eva J.	22nd y	14 Sep 1878	Sep 26, 1878
O'DONNELL, James	56	2 Aug 1874	Aug 13, 1874
O'DONNELL, John, Sr.	86th y	28 Oct 1872	Oct 31, 1872
O'DONNELL, Margaret	79	11 May 1874	May 21, 1874
O'GORMAN, Florence Mary	no age	22nd inst	Aug 31, 1865
O'NEIL, Joseph	76	12 Sep 1875	Sep 16, 1875
OAKES, (Miss)	no age	no date	Sep 2, 1875
OAKLEY, John	88y 1m 27d	27 Jul 1863	Jul 30, 1863
OAKLEY, Miles	71y 9m 16d	13 Feb 1871	Feb 16, 1871
OAKLEY, Solomon	87y 3m 11d	6 Oct 1877	Oct 18, 1877
OAKLEY, William M.	no age	15 Jul 1871	Jul 20, 1871
OCKSHOTT, Pearl M.	8m	22 Jul 1878	Jul 25, 1878
ODELL, Jonathan W.	69	30 Jul 1858	Aug 5, 1858
ODEN, Manuel	22y 4d	2 Apr 1877	Apr 5, 1877
OEFINGER, Elias	13m 1d	13 Jan 1878	Jan 17, 1878
OFFINGER, Jacob	6y 3m	25 May 1874	May 28, 1874
OGDEN, Benjamin	70	18 Jun 1867	Jun 27, 1867
OGSBURY, Francis	ca. 9	last Sun	Dec 2, 1869
OLDENBURG, William	36	no date	Jul 22, 1858
OLDRIN, Edward	72	20 Feb 1874	Feb 26, 1874
OLDRIN, Nettie B.	31y 3m 24d	3 Feb 1869	Feb 4, 1869
OLIVER, Anthony	65	7 Apr 1876	Apr 13, 1876
OLIVER, Elizabeth Ann	57	19th inst	Dec 27, 1860
OLIVER, Maria	10y 3m 25d	17 Jun 1874	Jun 18, 1874
OLIVER, Martha	32y 4m	11 Mar 1873	Mar 13, 1873
OLIVER, Smith Saunders	5m	25 Jul 1873	Jul 31, 1873
OLIVER, W. F.	7m	24 Aug 1873	Aug 28, 1873
OLIVER, William	65	18 Aug 1870	Aug 25, 1870
OLIVER, William	no age	no date	Sep 1, 1870
ONDERDONK, Abraham	68	24 Jan 1870	Jan 27, 1870
ONDERDONK, Benjamin Treadwell	70	30 Apr 1861	May 2, 1861
ONDERDONK, Eliza	71	30 Jul 1876	Aug 3, 1876
ONDERDONK, Elizabeth F.	no age	20 May 1878	May 23, 1878
ONDERDONK, Maria	70	15 Jul 1859	Jul 21, 1859
ONDERDONK, Maria M.	no age	27 Jan 1875	Jan 28, 1875

Name	Age	Date of death	Date of newspaper
OPPER, Katherine	26	8 Nov 1877	Nov 15, 1877
ORCHARD, Nicholas	no age	2 Jun 1874	Jun 4, 1874
ORNELL, John R.	no age	Thurs	Sep 19, 1872
ORR, John H.	64	5 Aug 1870	Aug 11, 1870
ORR, John H.	no age	no date	Sep 1, 1870
ORREN, Frederick	40	9 Jun 1875	Jun 17, 1875
OSBORN, Alexander	25	25 Dec 1873	Jan 1, 1874
OSBORN, Harvey	69	17 Jul 1858	Jul 29, 1858
OSBORN, J. Nicholas	no age	Saturday	Oct 11, 1877
OSBORNE, David	no age	Friday	Oct 18, 1877
OSTERMAN, William	24	11 Sep 1875	Sep 16, 1875
OSWALD, Mark	no age	28 Oct 1874	Nov 5, 1874
OUTERBRIDGE, Jennie P.	30	23 Apr 1875	May 6, 1875
OVERTON, Elizabeth	b. 1786	22nd inst	Apr 5, 1877
OVERTON, Verona Vesta	no age	15 Dec 1876	Dec 21, 1876
OVINGTON, Charles H.	6	4 Dec 1875	Dec 23, 1875
OVINGTON, Hattie	8	4 Dec 1875	Dec 23, 1875
OWENS, Amanda	38	30 Nov 1871	Dec 7, 1871
OWENS, Thomas	no age	19th inst	Sep 30, 1875
PADGETT, Catherine	82	6 Apr 1874	Apr 9, 1874
PAFF, Andrew	7y 10m 12d	14 Oct 1874	Oct 22, 1874
PAFF, Charlotte	33y 4m 22d	9 Dec 1875	Dec 16, 1875
PAFF, Charlotte Levinia	7y 2m	27 Dec 1871	Jan 4, 1872
PAFF, Susannah	78	13 May 1874	May 14, 1874
PAFF, Townsend D.	34y 5m	24 Sep 1878	Sep 26, 1878
PAGETT, Charles	no age	12 Nov 1859	Nov 17, 1859
PAIGE, Eldridge F.	no age	1 Jan 1860	Jan 5, 1860
PAINE, George M.	3m 6d	14 Feb 1876	Feb 24, 1876
PAINTER, David	21y 11m 15d	25 Feb 1872	Feb 29, 1872
PAINTER, William S.	17y 2m	8 Sep 1864	Sep 15, 1864
PALMER, Phebe Ann	18	no date	Jul 29, 1858
PALMER, William	no age	25 Dec 1874	Dec 31, 1874
PAPE, (Mr.)	ca. 60	Wednesday	Jul 4, 1872
PARKER, Susan	45y 7m	4 Jun 1877	Jun 7, 1877
PARKER, Theodore	no age	the 10th	May 31, 1860
PARKER, William M.	ca. 68	14th inst	Sep 20, 1860
PARKS, Charles, II	2y 7m 12d	26 Jun 1858	Jul 15, 1858
PARSELS, Mary	77	11 May 1878	May 16, 1878
PARSONS, (son of Charles)	ca. 6	Wednesday	May 28, 1874
PARSONS, Eva Minerva	2	25 Aug 1874	Aug 27, 1874
PARSONS, Robert Clarence	no age	11th inst	Jan 19, 1865
PARSONS, W. B.	63y 3m 15d	24 Oct 1870	Oct 27, 1870
PARSONS, Wm. H.	26	last week	Feb 2, 1860
PATTERSON, (Mr)	no age	Sunday	Mar 1, 1877
PATTERSON, Henry	2y 4m 23d	4th inst	Nov 14, 1867
PAUL, George S.	1y 24d	24 Aug 1877	Aug 30, 1877
PAULDING, Hiram	81	20 Oct 1878	Oct 24, 1878
PAYNE, Anna	76	18 Dec 1873	Dec 25, 1873
PAYNE, George W.	35	3 Feb 1861	Apr 18, 1861
PAYNE, Hannibal	80	25 Mar 1869	Apr 1, 1869
PAYNE, Joseph R.	32	4 Apr 1861	Apr 18, 1861
PAYNE, Nancy	53y 10m 21d	31 Aug 1877	Sep 6, 1877
PAYNE, Steven H.	19	27 Mar 1861	Mar 28, 1861
PEARSALL, (son of Sellick)	5w	11 Mar 1865	Mar 16, 1865
PEARSALL, (wife of James)	80	30 Oct 1859	Nov 3, 1859
PEARSALL, Andrew	80	29 Feb 1864	Mar 17, 1864
PEARSALL, Anthony	no age	no date	Jul 5, 1860
PEARSALL, Eliza	60y 4m 1d	22 Dec 1876	Jan 4, 1877

Name	Age	Date of death	Date of newspaper
PEARSALL, Elizabeth L.	60	23 Apr 1869	May 6, 1869
PEARSALL, Epenctus(?) W.	50th y	19 Feb 1872	Feb 22, 1872
PEARSALL, Georgia	no age	10 Aug 1870	Aug 18, 1870
PEARSALL, Gideon	55	18 Sep 1870	Sep 29, 1870
PEARSALL, Hannah	85	28 Oct 1867	Nov 7, 1867
PEARSALL, Hattie	1y 2m	26 Feb 1869	Mar 11, 1869
PEARSALL, Henrietta	25	19th inst	Aug 3, 1865
PEARSALL, Henrietta	8m 7d	18 Aug 1867	Aug 22, 1867
PEARSALL, Henrietta	16y 9m	9 Mar 1877	Mar 22, 1877
PEARSALL, Henry B.	61	10 Jul 1861	Jul 18, 1861
PEARSALL, Jonas	65th y	13 Sep 1878	Sep 19, 1878
PEARSALL, Jonas	64y 3m 15d	13 Aug 1878	Sep 26, 1878
PEARSALL, Margaret	35	9 Mar 1865	Mar 16, 1865
PEARSALL, Oliver D.	no age	no date	Sep 1, 1870
PEARSALL, Phebe	94	9 Dec 1875	Dec 16, 1875
PEARSALL, Ruth Augusta	no age	4 Aug 1873	Aug 7, 1873
PEARSALL, Sarah	69th y	23 Jul 1860	Aug 16, 1860
PEARSALL, Susan	63	19 Jun 1878	Jun 27, 1878
PEARSALL, Thomas	60y 6m	14 Aug 1869	Sep 2, 1869
PEARSALL, Thomas Cornell	no age	18 May 1878	May 23, 1878
PEARSALL, Uriah	67th y	17 Jun 1878	Jun 27, 1878
PEASE, George	23	2 Nov 1871	Nov 9, 1871
PECK, Clarissa	38	31 Aug 1858	Sep 23, 1858
PECK, Emily Jane	26	10 Nov 1862	Nov 13, 1862
PECK, James P.	65y 6d	1 Mar 1876	Mar 9, 1876
PECKAM, William H.	34	6th inst	Aug 24, 1871
PECKNER, Danl. G.	19th y	no date	Mar 21, 1861
PEDRICK, Samuel	no age	Wednesday	May 17, 1877
PEIRCE, Mary	45y 2m 13d	19 Mar 1877	Mar 29, 1877
PELL, Nancy	63	15 Oct 1878	Oct 24, 1878
PELT, Charles	40	12 Nov 1870	Nov 17, 1870
PENNY, Edeliza	1	1 Jan 1859	Jan 13, 1859
PENNY, Sarah R.	28	12 Aug 1858	Aug 19, 1858
PENTECOST, Laura	25	4 Dec 1877	Dec 13, 1877
PERRIN, Albert	2y 9m	8 Apr 1864	Apr 14, 1864
PERRIN, Charles	4m	24 Jul 1858	Jul 29, 1858
PERRY, (dau. of Joshua)	11	17 Dec 1870	Dec 29, 1870
PETERS, Joshua	25-30	1 Mar 1870	Mar 3, 1870
PETERS, Mary	50	16 May 1875	May 20, 1875
PETERSEN, (male)	no age	no date	May 28, 1874
PETERSON, Charlotte	38	26 Apr 1865	May 4, 1865
PETERSON, Henry	no age	17 Sep 1869	Nov 11, 1869
PETRIE, Catherine	47	19 Jun 1863	Jun 25, 1863
PETRIE, James S.	54	17 Jun 1863	Jun 25, 1863
PETTIT, Adelaide	ca. 7m	3 Apr 1864	Apr 7, 1864
PETTIT, Ann	65	14 Oct 1874	Oct 22, 1874
PETTIT, Anna L.	3y 9m 4d	2 May 1865	May 4, 1865
PETTIT, Barney	ca. 82	21 Nov 1864	Nov 24, 1864
PETTIT, C. Floyd	31y 25d	31 Dec 1877	Jan 3, 1878
PETTIT, Cornell V.	42y 3m 18d	23 Mar 1874	Mar 26, 1874
PETTIT, Elizabeth	80	15 Sep 1863	Sep 17, 1863
PETTIT, Elizabeth	87th y	14 Jul 1867	Jul 18, 1867
PETTIT, Elizabeth	70	28 May 1874	Jun 4, 1874
PETTIT, Ella	75y 5m 22d	16 Dec 1875	Dec 23, 1875
PETTIT, Elsy	65	28 Nov 1871	Nov 30, 1871
PETTIT, Fanny Augusta	3y 9m 10d	25 Apr 1877	May 3, 1877
PETTIT, Frances	6m	23 Feb 1876	Mar 2, 1876
PETTIT, Freddy S.	1y 2m 24d	16 Aug 1868	Aug 20, 1868
PETTIT, George	84	last Thur	May 17, 1860
PETTIT, George C.	17y 4m	7 Aug 1865	Aug 10, 1865

| | DEATHS | | |
Name	Age	Date of death	Date of newspaper
PETTIT, Hiram	22	25 Aug 1868	Aug 27, 1868
PETTIT, J. Harvey	56	24 Mar 1874	Apr 2, 1874
PETTIT, Jannet A.	43	14 Nov 1861	Nov 21, 1861
PETTIT, Jessie	69y 2m 20d	9 Apr 1877	Apr 12, 1877
PETTIT, Joel	no age	10 Jul 1876	Jul 13, 1876
PETTIT, John	59	16 Feb 1877	Feb 22, 1877
PETTIT, John S.	57	22nd inst	Jun 28, 1860
PETTIT, Lewis	64y 5m	5 Apr 1875	Apr 8, 1875
PETTIT, Martha J.	22	8 Mar 1862	Mar 13, 1862
PETTIT, Sarah	70	2 Oct 1869	Oct 14, 1869
PETTIT, Timothy	68	27 Dec 1860	Jan 3, 1861
PETTIT, Townsend H.	28y 4m	18 Jan 1871	Jan 26, 1871
PETTIT, Warren	4m 2d	27 Jan 1874	Feb 5, 1874
PETTIT, Wellington D.	ca. 22	31 Mar 1872	Apr 4, 1872
PETTIT, William	73	13th inst	Sep 20, 1860
PETTIT, William Clinton	19y 7m	5 Feb 1878	Feb 14, 1878
PETTIT, Willie S.	17	19 May 1872	May 23, 1872
PETTY, Elizabeth	84	25 Nov 1874	Dec 3, 1874
PETTY, George S. P.	no age	no date	Sep 16, 1858
PETTY, John	no age	17 Sep 1869	Nov 11, 1869
PETTY, Luther	69	23 Jul 1858	Aug 5, 1858
PFINDER, Jeremiah	no age	31 Mar 1874	Apr 16, 1874
PHELPS, James Alexander	7m 15d	20 Aug 1867	Aug 22, 1867
PHIFER, P. C.	45	5 Jul 1875	Jul 8, 1875
PHILEY, Thomas	70	23 Jul 1863	Jul 30, 1863
PHILLIPS, John	74	24 Nov 1868	Nov 26, 1868
PHILLIPS, Maria	58y 8m 28d	10 Jan 1876	Jan 13, 1876
PHILLIPS, Samuel	66	26 Aug 1858	Sep 2, 1858
PHRANER, Anna I. (T?)	14y 5m 22d	10th inst	Aug 18, 1864
PHRANER, Charles	infant	5th inst	Nov 14, 1867
PICKENS, Mary Elizabeth	6y 2m	22 Jul 1875	Aug 5, 1875
PIERSON, Samuel	no age	no date	Jan 26, 1860
PINDER, (female)	ca. 100	4 Feb 1870	Feb 10, 1870
PINE, (Mrs)	no age	21st inst	Dec 23, 1875
PINE, Abram S.	71	17 Jan 1861	Jan 24, 1861
PINE, Amelia	83	19 Apr 1874	Apr 23, 1874
PINE, Anna	39	30 Jun 1874	Jul 9, 1874
PINE, Benjamin Franklin	3y 7m	11 May 1877	May 17, 1877
PINE, Carrie	4m 21d	15 Oct 1878	Oct 24, 1878
PINE, Catharine	59y 3m 15d	22 Mar 1868	Mar 26, 1868
PINE, Edward	5y 8m	28 Jun 1877	Jul 5, 1877
PINE, Emma A.	65y 2m 10d	16 Nov 1875	Nov 18, 1875
PINE, Jerusha	51y 8m	31 Aug 1860	Sep 6, 1860
PINE, Mary Frances	7m	2 Feb 1869	Feb 4, 1869
PINE, Reuben	68	26th inst	Jan 30, 1868
PINE, Rhoda	72	26 Sep 1859	Sep 29, 1859
PINKHAM, Charlie P.	6m 2w	14 Aug 1877	Aug 16, 1877
PISHON, Jane	24y 4m 11d	30 Jun 1864	Aug 4, 1864
PITKIN, John R.	80	2 Sep 1874	Sep 10, 1874
PLACE, Daniel	no age	29 Mar 1868	Apr 2, 1868
PLACE, Frankie	11m 8d	30 Jan 1871	Feb 9, 1871
PLACE, Henrietta H.	2m	8 Oct 1868	Oct 15, 1868
PLACE, Phebe	82y 5m	5th inst	Mar 8, 1860
PLACE, Sadie	1y 13d	23 Oct 1878	Oct 31, 1878
PLACE, Samuel S.	87y 7m 12d	28 Oct 1873	Oct 30, 1873
PLACIDE, Henry	ca. 70	23 Jan 1870	Jan 27, 1870
PLACY, Thomas, Jr.	no age	25 Dec 1858	Dec 30, 1858
PLANEL, Henry	no age	no date	Feb 22, 1872
PLUMMER, John	82	17 Apr 1865	Apr 27, 1865
PLUMPTON, William	no age	14 Nov 1871	Nov 23, 1871

Name	Age	Date of death	Date of newspaper
PLYER, William	68	22 Mar 1874	Mar 26, 1874
POOLE, Fanny Maria	17y 7m 5d	18 Feb 1864	Mar 10, 1864
POOLE, James Horatio	60y 3d	14 Jun 1871	Jun 22, 1871
POOLE, Samuel C.	52y 3m 14d	22nd inst	Jun 27, 1867
POOLE, Sarah	79	9 Oct 1863	Oct 15, 1863
POOR, William	15	recently	Apr 26, 1877
POPE, Annie	no age	Friday	Nov 15, 1877
PORTEUS, (Rev. Dr.)	no age	28 Sep 1875	Oct 7, 1875
PORTLAND, Hannah	70	21 Jan 1877	Jan 25, 1877
POST, (Dr)	no age	recently	Aug 9, 1877
POST, (son of John)	1	3 Sep 1865	Sep 7, 1865
POST, Clara E.	7w	6 Jun 1876	Jun 15, 1876
POST, Edmund	no age	26 Apr 1875	May 6, 1875
POST, Henry T.	6m 14d	20 Sep 1875	Oct 21, 1875
POST, Isaac	89y 9m	8 Nov 1869	Nov 25, 1869
POST, Jackson	51y 5m 6d	14 Mar 1878	May 16, 1878
POST, James	86	7 Sep 1870	Sep 15, 1870
POST, Jepthea	50	no date	Jan 10, 1878
POST, Jepthes (or Jepthea)	50	3 Nov 1877	Nov 8, 1877
POST, Jerehmiah	74	29 Jul 1872	Aug 1, 1872
POST, Jeremiah	45	25 Dec 1874	Dec 31, 1874
POST, Jotham	no age	23 Nov 1870	Dec 15, 1870
POST, Jotham	86	27 Oct 1874	Oct 29, 1874
POST, Lydia T.	no age	21 Apr 1875	Apr 29, 1875
POST, Mary	80	17 May 1875	May 20, 1875
POST, Richard	60	last Wed	Dec 14, 1865
POST, Samuel	73	21 Dec 1867	Jan 2, 1868
POST, Samuel	2	30 Jun 1871	Jul 6, 1871
POST, Willis	5m	16 Aug 1874	Aug 20, 1874
POTTER, Thaddeus	19y 6m 2d	23 Dec 1863	Dec 31, 1863
POTTER, William	62	24 May 1877	May 31, 1877
POWELL, Abigail	87	26th ult	Oct 7, 1858
POWELL, Ann	72y 10m	22 Jan 1872	Feb 1, 1872
POWELL, Anna	69y 9m	5 Apr 1875	Apr 8, 1875
POWELL, Anna Maria	28	11 Dec 1872	Dec 19, 1872
POWELL, Charles	no age	no date	Sep 1, 1870
POWELL, Charles A.	38y 3m	4 Dec 1876	Dec 7, 1876
POWELL, Charles S.	38	17 Jul 1871	Jul 27, 1871
POWELL, Cordelia	17	4 May 1859	May 19, 1859
POWELL, Eddie	12	25 Jul 1878	Aug 1, 1878
POWELL, Elizabeth	75	14 Jul 1873	Jul 17, 1873
POWELL, Esther H.	22	2 Nov 1862	Dec 4, 1862
POWELL, Franklin	32	22 Nov 1871	Nov 23, 1871
POWELL, Frederick W.	3	1 Mar 1862	Mar 6, 1862
POWELL, Hermann	6m 19d	25 Apr 1875	Apr 29, 1875
POWELL, Joel	59	9 Mar 1862	Mar 13, 1862
POWELL, John B.	68y 7m 7d	10 Jan 1875	Jan 14, 1875
POWELL, Joshua	76th y	7 Jan 1861	Feb 7, 1861
POWELL, Kate M.	5m 26d	30th ult	Aug 3, 1865
POWELL, Lana L. (nee REMSEN)	26y 6m 20d	9 Mar 1873	Mar 13, 1873
POWELL, Mary	14	25 Jan 1863	Feb 5, 1863
POWELL, Mary	88y 8m 22d	26 Jun 1864	Jun 30, 1864
POWELL, Mary A.	28	18th inst	Jun 1, 1865
POWELL, Mary Emma	23y 7m 14d	1 Nov 1870	Nov 3, 1870
POWELL, Oliver	61y 3m 28d	25 Aug 1869	Sep 2, 1869
POWELL, Prudence	83	26 Aug 1869	Sep 2, 1869
POWELL, Richard	88	2 Sep 1860	Nov 8, 1860
POWELL, Sands, Jr.	33y 3m	29 Apr 1872	May 2, 1872
POWELL, Sarah	78	10 Dec 1865	Dec 28, 1865
POWELL, Sarah	36	3 Oct 1870	Oct 6, 1870

Name	Age	Date of death	Date of newspaper
POWELL, Sarah Parmlia	3y 6m 26d	13 Jun 1864	Jun 23, 1864
POWELL, Solomon	76y 6m 4d	19 Sep 1870	Sep 22, 1870
POWELL, Willet	44	23 Jul 1863	Jul 30, 1863
POWER, Rachel	85	21 Jan 1865	Jan 26, 1865
POWERS, Emma Jane	16y 7m 2d	17 Feb 1876	Feb 24, 1876
POWERS, Joseph B.	1m	11 Mar 1872	Mar 14, 1872
POWERS, Katie	9m 15d	23 Oct 1873	Nov 6, 1873
POWERS, Maria A.	59	19 Dec 1873	Jan 1, 1874
POWERS, Mary	21	5 Dec 1864	Dec 8, 1864
POWERS, Mary	80	23 Feb 1877	Mar 1, 1877
POWERS, William	5y 9m	29 Feb 1876	Mar 9, 1876
POYNTZ, Thomas J.	no age	Sat 4th	Feb 8, 1877
PRATT, John	ca. 35	30th ult	Sep 8, 1864
PRATT, Sarah	76y 9m	26 Aug 1870	Sep 1, 1870
PRAY, John H.	23y 9m	3 Feb 1864	Feb 11, 1864
PRAY, John H.	23y 9m	3 Feb 1864	Feb 18, 1864
PRAY, John M.	no age	Monday	Nov 11, 1869
PRAY, Margaret L.	28	11 Jan 1870	Jan 20, 1870
PRAY, Matilda R.	50	23 Apr 1869	Apr 29, 1869
PRAY, Orestes M.	27	23 Apr 1869	Apr 29, 1869
PRENDERGAST, J. Martin	62	14 Sep 1865	Sep 21, 1865
PRESTON, Mary	103	recently	Jul 25, 1867
PRICE, Charles W.	no age	no date	Jan 10, 1878
PRICE, James H.	no age	27th ult	Jan 5, 1871
PRICE, Mary E.	no age	19 Nov 1878	Nov 21, 1878
PRIME, Claudius	60	3 Jul 1878	Jul 11, 1878
PRINCE, Alfred	53	29 Sep 1858	Oct 7, 1858
PRINCE, Ann	2y 4m	15 May 1864	May 19, 1864
PRIOR, James	78y 8m 26d	16 Sep 1874	Sep 17, 1874
PRIOR, Selina Gertrude	21y 9m	7 Aug 1867	Aug 22, 1867
PROARDMAN, (3 ch. of J. L.)	no age	no date	Dec 30, 1875
PRYOR, P. F. (Dr.)	46	17 Dec 1867	Dec 26, 1867
PULLIS, William M.	55	28 Apr 1868	Apr 30, 1868
PURCELL, Thomas	68	17 Dec 1875	Dec 23, 1875
PURDY, George B.	73	15th inst	Jan 26, 1865
PURDY, George S.	9m	20 Aug 1869	Sep 2, 1869
PYE, Catherine E.	11m	25 Feb 1865	Mar 2, 1865
QUARTERMAN, George H.	50	2 Oct 1877	Oct 11, 1877
QUIGLEY, (son of John)	5	31 Jul 1875	Aug 5, 1875
QUIGLEY, John	35	31 Jul 1875	Aug 5, 1875
QUIGLEY, Lorett	10m	no date	Jan 5, 1871
QUINLAN, (male)	no age	Sunday	Jul 15, 1875
QUINN, James	no age	26 Nov 1859	Jan 12, 1860
QUINN, Michael E.	no age	16 Nov 1871	Nov 23, 1871
QUINN, Patrick	19	Wed. last	Jul 15, 1875
QUIRK, Andrew	no age	1871	Feb 25, 1875
RACKETT, Nevelle	59	7 Jul 1858	Jul 22, 1858
RADFORD, Samuel	26	14 Oct 1863	Oct 15, 1863
RAMSEY, William	48	7th inst	Oct 13, 1864
RANDALL, Augustus	3y 4m 6d	17 Sep 1871	Sep 21, 1871
RANDALL, Wallace Harold	5m	5th inst	Feb 9, 1860
RANDOLPH, Caroline	27y 6m	1 Feb 1865	Feb 9, 1865
RANKINS, Marie Elizabeth	116	28 Aug 1875	Sep 2, 1875
RANTAS, James	106	1 Feb 1871	Feb 9, 1871
RAPALJE, Ann	64y 2m 14d	25th inst	Jan 30, 1868
RAPALJE, Cornelius M.	57	4 Jun 1859	Jun 9, 1859

Name	Age	Date of death	Date of newspaper
RAPALJE, Sarah	81st y	30 Jul 1864	Aug 18, 1864
RAPELJE, Margaret	58	27 Mar 1861	Apr 4, 1861
RAPELYE, Mary Elizabeth	50y 7m 20d	2nd inst	Nov 16, 1865
RAPELYE, Phebe	88y 8m 17d	6th inst	Nov 16, 1865
RAPELYEA, Rebecca	72	14 Dec 1868	Dec 17, 1868
RATH, Caroline	31y 8m 11d	30 Sep 1875	Oct 7, 1875
RATHYON, John H.	no age	no date	Sep 1, 1870
RATZ, Gustavus	27	yesterday	Aug 16, 1860
RAYNOR, (dau. of John C.)	ca. 8	9 Dec 1864	Dec 15, 1864
RAYNOR, (son of Charles)	12y 4d	3 May 1862	May 8, 1862
RAYNOR, (widow of Benjamin)	86	8 Aug 1858	Aug 12, 1858
RAYNOR, Alice Ann	35	23 Mar 1876	Mar 30, 1876
RAYNOR, Allen	65	26 Aug 1862	Aug 28, 1862
RAYNOR, Alongo	18y 11m 28d	2 Feb 1872	Feb 8, 1872
RAYNOR, Charles	3y 7m	2 Sep 1871	Sep 7, 1871
RAYNOR, Cornelia G. A.	2y 6m	12 Jun 1864	Jun 16, 1864
RAYNOR, Dallas B.	23y 8m 15d	20 Jan 1869	Jan 28, 1869
RAYNOR, Daniel	77	27 Dec 1867	Jan 9, 1868
RAYNOR, David M.	18	17 Sep 1858	Sep 23, 1858
RAYNOR, Elijah	17y 5m 29d	11 Jun 1864	Jun 30, 1864
RAYNOR, Elijah	8m 21d	14 Jul 1877	Jul 19, 1877
RAYNOR, Eliza	22	17 Feb 1874	Feb 19, 1874
RAYNOR, George	1y 6m	3 Mar 1876	Mar 9, 1876
RAYNOR, Hannah	77	10 Feb 1859	Mar 3, 1859
RAYNOR, Jacob	65	16 Jun 1872	Jul 4, 1872
RAYNOR, Joanna	97	12 Dec 1858	Jan 20, 1859
RAYNOR, John	no age	27 Apr 1860	May 10, 1860
RAYNOR, John	68y 7m	19 Apr 1869	Apr 22, 1869
RAYNOR, John S.	9y 1m 25d	27 Dec 1870	Dec 29, 1870
RAYNOR, John Thomas	4	20 Oct 1865	Oct 26, 1865
RAYNOR, Marion Gray	5y 7m 21d	16 Feb 1876	Feb 24, 1876
RAYNOR, Mary	78	26 Dec 1875	Dec 30, 1875
RAYNOR, Mary Ann	73y 5m	15 Mar 1872	Mar 21, 1872
RAYNOR, Mary Ann	66	17 Feb 1873	Feb 20, 1873
RAYNOR, Melcie S.	20y 9m 29d	13 Sep 1876	Sep 14, 1876
RAYNOR, Micajah	70y 8d	26 Apr 1870	Apr 28, 1870
RAYNOR, Oliver	ca. 23	25 Jan 1864	Feb 4, 1864
RAYNOR, Rachael	88	21 Sep 1861	Sep 26, 1861
RAYNOR, Rebecca	70y 1m 5d	6 Jul 1871	Jul 20, 1871
RAYNOR, Ruby	15m	15 Jul 1877	Jul 19, 1877
RAYNOR, Thomas	60	16 Oct 1871	Oct 19, 1871
RAYNOR, William	64	7 May 1874	May 14, 1874
RAYNOR, William B.	66y 3m 4d	14 Jul 1867	Jul 18, 1867
REAGAN, (Mrs)	no age	last Thur	Sep 20, 1860
REDFIELD, (Rev.)	no age	24 Oct 1861	Oct 31, 1861
REDMOND, Mary	18	28 Sep 1878	Oct 3, 1878
REED, Abigail	74y 9m 18d	16 Feb 1878	Feb 28, 1878
REED, Caroline	25	14 Jul 1865	Jul 20, 1865
REED, John	66y 2m 12d	28 Jul 1876	Aug 10, 1876
REEVES, Henry J.	35	14th inst	Jan 5, 1871
REEVES, Jerehmiah	no age	Sat	Mar 7, 1872
REEVES, Olevia	no age	last Sun	Aug 25, 1870
REGAN, James	no age	recently	Sep 5, 1867
REILLY, (Mrs)	no age	Tuesday	Oct 25, 1877
REMMET, William	8	14 Mar 1876	Mar 16, 1876
REMSEM, Richard	76	20 Mar 1874	Mar 26, 1874
REMSEN, (child of James)	3m	9 Sep 1862	Sep 11, 1862
REMSEN, (or BEMSEN), Jeremiah	ca. 70	6th inst	Jul 20, 1865
REMSEN, (widow of Nathaniel)	no age	11th inst	Nov 16, 1865
REMSEN, Ann	46y 4m 5d	22nd inst	Nov 24, 1864

Name	Age	Date of death	Date of newspaper
REMSEN, Charles	1y 11m 24d	no date	Oct 27, 1864
REMSEN, Deborah	83	19 May 1877	May 24, 1877
REMSEN, Elizabeth	67th y	no date	Dec 24, 1863
REMSEN, George	1	1 Sep 1858	Sep 9, 1858
REMSEN, Jacob	86y 1m 16d	6 Feb 1872	Feb 8, 1872
REMSEN, Jordon Seaman	no age	31 Oct 1868	Nov 5, 1868
REMSEN, Letitia	76y 4m 10d	12 Aug 1861	Aug 15, 1861
REMSEN, Marietta	42y 9m 20d	23 Dec 1862	Jan 8, 1863
REMSEN, Rem	87	18th inst	Jul 24, 1862
REMSEN, Rem	70y 3m	5 Jan 1864	Jan 14, 1864
REMSEN, Richard	18	Jan 1871	Sep 19, 1872
REMSEN, Samuel H.	5y 9m 28d	15th inst	Aug 24, 1865
REMSEN, Susan L.	56y 9m	2 Jul 1878	Jul 4, 1878
REMSEN, Thomas B.	38y 3m 21d	11 Dec 1868	Dec 17, 1868
REYNOLDS, Alonzo	69	11 Jan 1877	Jan 18, 1877
REYNOLDS, Julia A.	no age	29 Oct 1865	Nov 2, 1865
RHODES, (ch. of Gilbert H. & Ann Eliza)	ca. 3m	18 Aug 1868	Aug 27, 1868
RHODES, (child of Andrew)	7	7 Jun 1858	Jun 10, 1858
RHODES, (child of Andrew)	10m	11 Jan 1861	Jan 17, 1861
RHODES, (dau. of Alexander)	14m	24 Aug 1865	Aug 31, 1865
RHODES, Adaline Moore	21	9 Jan 1878	Jan 17, 1878
RHODES, Albert C.	19y 3m 9d	25 Nov 1877	Nov 29, 1877
RHODES, Ann	70	25 Dec 1859	Dec 29, 1859
RHODES, Ann	73y 7m 3d	21 Mar 1865	Mar 30, 1865
RHODES, Ann	83y 1m	16 Apr 1873	Apr 24, 1873
RHODES, Benjamin	92y 9m 22d	26th inst	May 3, 1860
RHODES, Daniel	76	11 Feb 1876	Feb 24, 1876
RHODES, Daniel	71y 4m 28d	31 Aug 1877	Sep 6, 1877
RHODES, David W.	7	21 Apr 1865	Apr 27, 1865
RHODES, Eleanor Irene	no age	5 Sep 1875	Sep 9, 1875
RHODES, Elena Irene	no age	no date	Jan 10, 1878
RHODES, George	80	24 Jan 1877	Feb 1, 1877
RHODES, George Washington	6m 1d	3 Jul 1875	Aug 5, 1875
RHODES, Henry P.	3	16 Jun 1869	Jun 24, 1869
RHODES, John J.	17	11 Oct 1858	Oct 21, 1858
RHODES, Louise	3y 10m	30 Apr 1876	May 4, 1876
RHODES, Mary	49	15 Sep 1861	Sep 19, 1861
RHODES, Mary Ann	24y 10m	10 Aug 1878	Aug 15, 1878
RHODES, Mary Emma	26y 4m 14d	14 Jun 1877	Jul 5, 1877
RHODES, Mary S.	no age	no date	Jan 10, 1878
RHODES, Phoebe	79	8 Aug 1874	Aug 13, 1874
RHODES, Reuben	24y 10m 15d	25 Jul 1869	Jul 29, 1869
RHODES, Richard	80	12 Apr 1872	Apr 18, 1872
RHODES, Robert	81st y	20 Jun 1865	Jun 22, 1865
RHODES, Robert	60	1 Nov 1878	Nov 7, 1878
RHODES, Ruth	81y 10m 9d	17 Feb 1874	Feb 19, 1874
RHODES, Samuel	39y 11m 20d	2 Feb 1875	Feb 4, 1875
RHODES, Sarah	35	23 Oct 1862	Nov 6, 1862
RHODES, Solomon S.	4w	13 Aug 1870	Aug 18, 1870
RHODES, Susan	1	no date	Sep 19, 1867
RHODES, Timothy	50y 3m	29 Jul 1868	Aug 6, 1868
RHODES, William	85y 6m 28d	8 Nov 1867	Nov 14, 1867
RHODES, William	no age	17 Dec 1878	Dec 19, 1878
RICE, Oliver	37	no date	Nov 25, 1869
RICE, Phineas	76	5 Dec 1861	Dec 12, 1861
RICE, Robert C.	no age	10 Feb 1861	Feb 14, 1861
RICH, Dorotha	58y 4m 13d	15 May 1878	May 23, 1878
RICHARDSON, (Mr)	no age	Sunday	Apr 12, 1877
RICHARDSON, Henry C.	53	7 Aug 1878	Aug 15, 1878

Name	Age	Date of death	Date of newspaper
RICHEE, Adelia	40	22 Apr 1859	Apr 28, 1859
RICHEE, Henry	70	3 Mar 1865	Apr 27, 1865
RICHELHOF, Mary L.	56	9 Mar 1876	Mar 16, 1876
RICHIE, (dau. of Joseph)	6m	8 Aug 1870	Aug 11, 1870
RICHIE, Charles	1y 6m	10 Jul 1872	Jul 18, 1872
RICHMOND, George D.	56y 9m 19d	5 Apr 1875	Apr 15, 1875
RIDD, Edward	67	10 Dec 1875	Dec 23, 1875
RIDER, Alice	7	23 Feb 1865	Mar 16, 1865
RIDER, Bradley	27	5 Sep 1861	Sep 12, 1861
RIDER, Charles Franklin	4th y	8 Jun 1865	Jun 15, 1865
RIDER, Daniel	82y 1m 9d	15 Sep 1870	Sep 22, 1870
RIDER, Eliza	32y 1m	28 Mar 1878	Apr 4, 1878
RIDER, Ella	1y 7m	10 Mar 1865	Mar 16, 1865
RIDER, Hannah Jane	50	20 Sep 1870	Sep 29, 1870
RIDER, James	79y 1m 26d	30 Apr 1876	May 4, 1876
RIDER, James	87th y	last Sun	May 4, 1876
RIDER, John Hubbard	13y 5m	19 Sep 1870	Sep 29, 1870
RIDER, Marcia L.	30y 4m 4d	23 Feb 1870	Mar 3, 1870
RIDER, Margaret	77	10 Oct 1877	Oct 18, 1877
RIDER, Mary C.	43y 5m 29d	20 Jul 1877	Aug 2, 1877
RIDER, Monroe H.	4	13th inst	Jan 23, 1868
RIDER, Nathaniel	23	8 Sep 1865	Sep 21, 1865
RIDER, Nicholas	no age	no date	Feb 18, 1875
RIDER, Sanford	35	Sunday	Jul 20, 1865
RIDER, William	45	6 Aug 1863	Aug 13, 1863
RIKER, Henry	21	last Sat	Oct 21, 1869
RIKER, John L.	75	11 May 1861	May 16, 1861
RILEY, (child of Samuel)	5m	last week	Oct 21, 1858
RILEY, (dau of Owen)	2y 3m	23 Aug 1872	Aug 29, 1872
RILEY, (son of Peter)	1	23 Feb 1869	Feb 25, 1869
RILEY, James	50	no date	Dec 2, 1869
RILEY, Julia	21	15 Mar 1877	Mar 22, 1877
RILEY, Samuel	57y 5m 1d	6 May 1873	May 15, 1873
RILEY, William	16y 3m	8 Feb 1877	Feb 15, 1877
RILEY, William	12d	20 Mar 1877	Mar 22, 1877
RITCHIE, (son of William H.)	17d	9 Jan 1875	Jan 14, 1875
RITCHIE, --?--	child	12 Apr 1869	Apr 15, 1869
RITCHIE, Alice Lydia	1y 8m	12 Apr 1869	Apr 22, 1869
RITCHIE, John	41y 2m 14d	31 Dec 1873	Jan 15, 1874
RITCHIE, William	69	23 Apr 1875	Apr 29, 1875
ROACH, Mary	9y 2m	30 Sep 1875	Oct 7, 1875
ROANE, J. B.	ca. 35	11 Feb 1859	Mar 3, 1859
ROBBINS, Ann T.	72y 4m	22 Oct 1869	Oct 28, 1869
ROBBINS, Ann W.	30	16 Oct 1868	Oct 22, 1868
ROBBINS, Esther	85	30 Nov 1863	Dec 10, 1863
ROBBINS, Phebe	18	13 Sep 1874	Sep 17, 1874
ROBBINS, Phebe	18	16 Sep 1874	Sep 24, 1874
ROBBINS, Stephen	81	26 Jan 1870	Feb 3, 1870
ROBBINS, Valentine	71	7 May 1873	May 15, 1873
ROBBINS, Willet	80	11 Apr 1861	Apr 25, 1861
ROBBINS, William B.	no age	17 Apr 1869	May 6, 1869
ROBIN, William	75	22 Sep 1877	Oct 18, 1877
ROBINS, Ann W.	30	16 Oct 1868	Oct 29, 1868
ROBINS, John	18	4 May 1863	May 14, 1863
ROBINS, Rebecca J.	13	3 Feb 1869	Feb 18, 1869
ROBINSON, (ch. of Wells)	16m	15 Jul 1872	Jul 25, 1872
ROBINSON, Elizabeth	no age	30th inst	Jan 9, 1862
ROBINSON, Richard	77	24 Aug 1858	Sep 2, 1858
ROBSON, Adelia	no age	Thursday	Aug 29, 1867
ROBY, Willie J.	1y 6m 20d	18 Jun 1863	Jun 25, 1863

DEATHS

Name	Age	Date of death	Date of newspaper
ROCHE, Edward	no age	19th ult	Jun 11, 1863
ROE, Isabel H. Tuttle	41y 5m	10 Oct 1867	Oct 17, 1867
ROE, Martha	79	27 Apr 1874	Apr 30, 1874
ROE, Mary	8m	21 Nov 1876	Nov 30, 1876
ROE, Temperance Ann	67	15 Oct 1878	Oct 24, 1878
ROFF, John	no age	24 Dec 1870	Dec 29, 1870
ROGERS, Epenetus	ca. 35	28 Aug 1877	Sep 13, 1877
ROGERS, Hawley B.	no age	last Thurs	Dec 16, 1869
ROGERS, John	78	no date	Feb 22, 1877
ROGERS, Morgan Z.	18	no date	Sep 16, 1858
ROGERS, Rachael	85	31 Jan 1861	Feb 7, 1861
ROGERS, Sarah Hicks	no age	12 Dec 1878	Dec 19, 1878
ROGERS, Sarah W.	89	12 Jun 1871	Jun 22, 1871
ROHRBACH, Martha C.	no age	22 Jun 1864	Jul 14, 1864
ROOT, Hannah E.	59	25 Jan 1877	Feb 1, 1877
ROOT, Hannah S.	no age	24 Nov 1876	Nov 30, 1876
ROSANRU, Mary	10m	8 Aug 1875	Aug 12, 1875
ROSE, Edwin	57	12 Jan 1864	Jan 21, 1864
ROSE, Jackson	37y 4m	26 Dec 1869	Dec 30, 1869
ROSE, John	no age	13 Jun 1858	Jun 17, 1858
ROSEMAN, Joseph	no age	no date	Jul 23, 1874
ROSEMARRN, Mary	26	11 Oct 1874	Oct 22, 1874
ROW, Frank	no age	5 Jul 1872	Jul 18, 1872
ROW, Kate	no age	6 Jul 1872	Jul 18, 1872
ROWE, (Mrs. Nelson)	no age	no date	Aug 1, 1872
ROWE, (son of Nelson)	no age	no date	Aug 1, 1872
ROWE, David	27	yesterday	Oct 4, 1860
ROWE, George	no age	last Tues	Aug 28, 1873
ROWLAND, Harry F.	5m 4d	16 Oct 1877	Nov 1, 1877
ROWLAND, Jonathon	90y 2m 14d	13 Jul 1875	Jul 22, 1875
ROWLAND, Lewis D.	3m 19d	31 Aug 1877	Sep 6, 1877
RUBENSTEIN, (Mr.)	no age	Tuesday	May 11, 1876
RUDGARD, Elizabeth	72	15 Feb 1878	Feb 21, 1878
RUDYARD, Charles	22	20 Oct 1865	Oct 26, 1865
RUDYARD, George W.	no age	15 Jun 1864	Jul 7, 1864
RUDYARD, Lydia B.	3y 7m	10 Apr 1868	Apr 16, 1868
RUGG, John M.	50	24 Dec 1875	Dec 30, 1875
RULAND, (dau. of Horace)	20	20 Dec 1878	Dec 26, 1878
RULAND, Pichard	no age	17th inst	Sep 29, 1870
RUSHMORE, (Mrs. Elbert)	no age	9 Dec 1878	Dec 12, 1878
RUSHMORE, (dau. of William)	2y 7m	10th inst	Nov 15, 1860
RUSHMORE, Adelia	ca. 29	26 Feb 1870	Mar 3, 1870
RUSHMORE, Ann	58	24 Nov 1858	Nov 25, 1858
RUSHMORE, Annie	37	16 Jan 1874	Jan 22, 1874
RUSHMORE, Carman	no age	no date	Jan 10, 1878
RUSHMORE, Charles Wallace	7	7th inst	Dec 21, 1865
RUSHMORE, Eliza J.	no age	no date	Jan 10, 1878
RUSHMORE, Eliza Jane	45	12th inst	Oct 18, 1860
RUSHMORE, Fannie A.	28	5 Jul 1871	Jul 13, 1871
RUSHMORE, Frances	61y 3m	10 Dec 1878	Dec 12, 1878
RUSHMORE, Hannah	no age	no date	Jan 10, 1878
RUSHMORE, Harriet	53	29 Jan 1870	Feb 3, 1870
RUSHMORE, Henrietta	49	15 Dec 1871	Dec 21, 1871
RUSHMORE, James	87	7 Mar 1875	Mar 11, 1875
RUSHMORE, Jane	92y 21d	6 Nov 1871	Nov 9, 1871
RUSHMORE, John	71	no date	May 8, 1873
RUSHMORE, Margaretta	ca. 14	27 Nov 1871	Dec 7, 1871
RUSHMORE, Mary	no age	no date	Jan 10, 1878
RUSHMORE, Ruth	no age	no date	Jan 10, 1878
RUSHMORE, Willett Edward	11	2 Jan 1875	Jan 7, 1875

Name	Age	Date of death	Date of newspaper
RUSHMORE, William	75	16 Sep 1876	Sep 21, 1876
RUSHMORE, William C.	51	23 Apr 1869	Apr 29, 1869
RUSHMORE, William T.	35	21 May 1862	May 29, 1862
RUSSEL, A. D.	no age	Monday	Apr 28, 1870
RUSSEL, Ida	13m	22 Jun 1858	Jun 24, 1858
RUSSELL, Jane Kingsland	68	4 Dec 1870	Dec 8, 1870
RUSSELL, Letitia	60	19 May 1874	May 28, 1874
RUSSELL, Michael J.	no age	last Fri	Aug 22, 1878
RYAN, (Mrs.)	60	13 Sep 1874	Sep 17, 1874
RYAN, Michael	no age	Saturday	Aug 9, 1877
RYDER, Albert	9	20 Oct 1877	Nov 29, 1877
RYDER, Aletta B.	53y 9m	30 Oct 1863	Nov 5, 1863
RYDER, Stephen	no age	last Thur	Jul 21, 1864
RYDER, Williamson	91	21 Mar 1870	Mar 31, 1870
RYERSON, Martin, Jr.	22	7th inst	Apr 12, 1877
RYERSON, Phebe C.	4y 2m 1d	21 Nov 1867	Nov 28, 1867
SALMONDS, Carlotta C. A.	3m 16d	3 Dec 1869	Dec 9, 1869
SAMMIS, (son of Hiram)	1	17 Apr 1859	Apr 21, 1859
SAMMIS, Albert T.	11m 9d	19 Aug 1870	Aug 25, 1870
SAMMIS, Alexander	80	no date	Oct 18, 1877
SAMMIS, Anna Maria	22y 6m 16d	2 Nov 1867	Nov 14, 1867
SAMMIS, Edgar Roe	2m 19d	19 Oct 1867	Oct 24, 1867
SAMMIS, Edwin W.	17y 6m 17d	13 Jan 1863	Jan 22, 1863
SAMMIS, Franklin D.	33y 5m 20d	17 Feb 1864	Feb 25, 1864
SAMMIS, Harriet	34y 8m	29 Mar 1875	Apr 1, 1875
SAMMIS, Henry	9m	17 Mar 1859	Mar 24, 1859
SAMMIS, Mary E.	35y 5m 29d	7 Dec 1862	Dec 11, 1862
SAMMIS, Nehemiah	67y 10m 21d	5 Sep 1863	Sep 10, 1863
SAMMIS, Nelson G.	23y 10m 13d	8th inst	Oct 11, 1860
SAMMIS, Phebe	64	30 May 1859	Jun 2, 1859
SAMMIS, Samuel C.	64	19 Jan 1871	Jan 26, 1871
SAMMIS, Sarah	71y 5m 21d	18 Oct 1873	Oct 23, 1873
SAMMIS, Sarah F.	no age	17 Jan 1874	Jan 22, 1874
SAMMIS, Silvenus	18y 5m	no date	Oct 10, 1867
SAMMIS, William	43	15 Mar 1863	Mar 26, 1863
SAMMONS, (son of Hiram T.)	2m	22 Jan 1864	Jan 28, 1864
SAMMONS, Serena G.	5m 18d	2 Aug 1867	Aug 8, 1867
SANDERS, (Mr.)	no age	no date	Feb 1, 1872
SANDS, Abraham B.	46	6 Jul 1861	Jul 11, 1861
SANDS, Frank	no age	29th ult	Jul 13, 1876
SANDS, Gideon	63	8 May 1864	May 19, 1864
SANDS, Martha	76	24 Aug 1859	Sep 1, 1859
SANDS, Mary	94y 5m 10d	26 Aug 1878	Aug 29, 1878
SANDS, Nancy	90	17 Nov 1862	Dec 4, 1862
SANDS, Sophia	55y 9m	27 Jan 1865	Feb 23, 1865
SATTERLEY, John R.	75	1 Apr 1865	Apr 27, 1865
SAUNDERS, (son of widow Saunders)	10 or 11	no date	Jul 5, 1860
SAVAGE, Jane	69	19 May 1873	May 29, 1873
SAWYER, (male)	no age	ca. 1857	Dec 13, 1860
SAWYER, John	no age	15 Jun 1864	Jul 7, 1864
SAXTON, Richard C.	1	19 May 1859	May 26, 1859
SAXTON, Susan	42	14 Sep 1867	Sep 26, 1867
SAYRE, Julius	no age	no date	Dec 6, 1877
SAYRES, Abigail	no age	5 Sep 1873	Sep 11, 1873
SAYRES, Clarence Hunting	1y 21d	9th inst	Feb 13, 1868
SAYRES, Mary Regina	18	29 Nov 1871	Dec 7, 1871
SCALLEY, Patrick	40	21 Aug 1873	Aug 28, 1873

Name	Age	Date of death	Date of newspaper
SCHAFENBERGER, Mary Ann	no age	15 Feb 1874	Feb 19, 1874
SCHAFER, Christian G.	18	Sunday	Dec 7, 1871
SCHAFER, Martha Elizabeth	49y 8m 17d	14 Oct 1873	Oct 16, 1873
SCHANK, John Henry	3w	15 Jan 1878	Jan 17, 1878
SCHEGAL, Eva Barbara	1m 10d	23 Mar 1876	Mar 30, 1876
SCHENCK, Elizabeth	55y 6m 7d	18 Aug 1874	Aug 20, 1874
SCHENCK, Elizabeth	no age	21 Aug 1874	Aug 27, 1874
SCHENCK, George	82	23 Aug 1874	Aug 27, 1874
SCHENCK, Hannah	23	30 Aug 1874	Sep 3, 1874
SCHENCK, John R.	52	19th inst	Aug 23, 1860
SCHENCK, Samuel	no age	last Fri	May 4, 1876
SCHENCK, William	40	18th inst	Jan 26, 1865
SCHENK, Jacob	no age	26th inst	Apr 2, 1863
SCHLAGEL, (son of Charles)	2m	14 Jul 1878	Jul 18, 1878
SCHLEIDER, John	no age	Thursday	Feb 8, 1877
SCHLISMAN, Emily A.	41	28 May 1875	Jun 3, 1875
SCHLUY, William	no age	Wednesday	Nov 18, 1875
SCHMALENBERGER, J. Adam	44	23 Nov 1878	Nov 28, 1878
SCHMIDITLING, George	no age	recently	Aug 9, 1877
SCHMIT, Frank	16	8 Apr 1872	Apr 11, 1872
SCHMOLL, E. Theodore	55y 11m	27 Aug 1877	Aug 30, 1877
SCHRAPF (?), Carrie	no age	Tues	Aug 15, 1872
SCHRODER, Katie	10y 4m	4 Mar 1872	Mar 7, 1872
SCHRODER, Louis	2y 10m	7 Mar 1872	Mar 14, 1872
SCHROEDER, Frederick	53	10 Apr 1876	Apr 13, 1876
SCHROEDER, Susan	7	28 Dec 1875	Dec 30, 1875
SCHROEDER, William	17	Saturday	Aug 30, 1877
SCHROEHER, Elizabeth	18y 3m	5 Sep 1872	Sep 12, 1872
SCHROEHER, Margaret	43y 8m	10 Feb 1874	Feb 12, 1874
SCHULTZ, Mark	no age	no date	Apr 29, 1875
SCHUMAKER, (wife of John Henry)	no age	Mon	Jul 12, 1860
SCHUSTER, Martin	no age	4 Jul 1876	Jul 13, 1876
SCHWER, Sebastian	42	29 Jul 1865	Aug 3, 1865
SCOTT, (Mrs. Robert)	no age	18 Nov 1878	Nov 21, 1878
SCOTT, Elizabeth	78	21st inst	Aug 29, 1867
SCOTT, Frederick	no age	last Fri	Jun 10, 1858
SCOTT, Hannah	63rd y	30th ult	Sep 8, 1864
SCOTT, James	no age	4 Feb 1875	Feb 11, 1875
SCOTT, Otis	1y 9m 5d	2 Mar 1876	Mar 9, 1876
SCRUGHAM, William M.	no age	9th inst	Aug 15, 1867
SCULL, Elizabeth	76	no date	Dec 19, 1872
SCULLY, Mary	34	9 Sep 1871	Sep 14, 1871
SEABURY, Adam	83	16 Mar 1875	Mar 18, 1875
SEABURY, Adam Livingston	6m 28d	24 Mar 1865	Mar 30, 1865
SEABURY, Benjamin H.	no age	21 Aug 1875	Aug 26, 1875
SEABURY, Robert S.	b Mar 13, 09	Thursday	Mar 15, 1877
SEALEY, Margaret	36y 12d	18 Oct 1870	Oct 27, 1870
SEALEY, Richard	66	22 May 1862	May 29, 1862
SEAMAN, (Mrs.)	73	no date	Jan 4, 1872
SEAMAN, (child of John)	4	17 Oct 1864	Oct 20, 1864
SEAMAN, (dau. of John S.)	no age	21 Feb 1868	Feb 20, 1868
SEAMAN, (son of Charles P.)	8m	24 Mar 1873	Mar 27, 1873
SEAMAN, Ann Maria	56	22 Jan 1864	Jan 28, 1864
SEAMAN, Arden	79y 6m 27d	2 Apr 1875	Apr 22, 1875
SEAMAN, Benjamin	45	6 Feb 1861	Feb 14, 1861
SEAMAN, Benjamin	52	17 Oct 1874	Oct 29, 1874
SEAMAN, Carman D. Lane	3m 9d	18 Jul 1873	Jul 24, 1873
SEAMAN, Caroline A.	ca. 16	31st ult	Jan 24, 1861
SEAMAN, Charles	2y 1m	26 Feb 1868	Mar 5, 1868

Name	Age	Date of death	Date of newspaper
SEAMAN, Charles	2	24 Dec 1869	Dec 30, 1869
SEAMAN, Dorothy	73	12 Jun 1864	Jun 16, 1864
SEAMAN, Eleanor	50	29 Jul 1863	Jul 30, 1863
SEAMAN, Eliza	82	3 Feb 1875	Feb 11, 1875
SEAMAN, Elizabeth	40	no date	Aug 25, 1870
SEAMAN, Elizabeth F.	5y 7m 15d	23 Jun 1875	Jun 24, 1875
SEAMAN, Elma	8	1 Aug 1868	Aug 6, 1868
SEAMAN, Elvin	7m 1d	1 Oct 1875	Oct 7, 1875
SEAMAN, Emilie Louise	5y 8m 8d	4 Feb 1868	Feb 6, 1868
SEAMAN, Emma Jane	8m	24 Feb 1872	Feb 29, 1872
SEAMAN, George	no age	Thursday	Sep 6, 1877
SEAMAN, George B.	3m	24 Aug 1878	Aug 29, 1878
SEAMAN, Hannah	85	15 Feb 1875	Feb 18, 1875
SEAMAN, Helen Louisa	14y 10m 10d	13 Oct 1865	Oct 26, 1865
SEAMAN, James	5m	7 Aug 1874	Aug 13, 1874
SEAMAN, Jarvis	74	29 Jun 1858	Jul 1, 1858
SEAMAN, Joseph	55y 9m 5d	5 Oct 1873	Oct 9, 1873
SEAMAN, Lawrence	65	21 Sep 1861	Sep 26, 1861
SEAMAN, Lena	10m 24d	1 Jul 1874	Jul 2, 1874
SEAMAN, Maggie	11y 4m	6 Oct 1874	Oct 8, 1874
SEAMAN, Margaret	19y 9m	1 Aug 1873	Aug 7, 1873
SEAMAN, Margaret	78y 5m 20d	23 Aug 1877	Aug 30, 1877
SEAMAN, Maria	84y 5m	10 Mar 1877	Mar 15, 1877
SEAMAN, Martha	51	14 Jul 1873	Jul 31, 1873
SEAMAN, Mary	80y 6m 13d	30 Jul 1867	Aug 1, 1867
SEAMAN, Mary	81	2 May 1868	May 7, 1868
SEAMAN, Mary	89y 2m 3d	25 Sep 1875	Sep 30, 1875
SEAMAN, Mary A.	57y 3d	23 Nov 1873	Nov 27, 1873
SEAMAN, Mary Ann	no age	17 Oct 1874	Oct 22, 1874
SEAMAN, Mervin S.	6m 16d	16 Aug 1872	Aug 22, 1872
SEAMAN, Oliver	70y 11m	3 Aug 1873	Aug 7, 1873
SEAMAN, Richard	52	13th inst	Jan 23, 1868
SEAMAN, Ritla Amelia	8	11 Nov 1877	Nov 15, 1877
SEAMAN, Samuel	78y 6m	19 Sep 1875	Sep 23, 1875
SEAMAN, Sarah Jane	28	11 Apr 1864	Apr 14, 1864
SEAMAN, Smith	25y 5m 17d	27 Feb 1860	Mar 8, 1860
SEAMAN, Ward	24y 4m 21d	8 Jun 1875	Jun 10, 1875
SEAMAN, William	32y 7m 16d	15 Oct 1875	Oct 21, 1875
SEAMAN, William H.	32	18 Aug 1870	Aug 25, 1870
SEAMAN, William Henry	20y 3m	15 Jan 1876	Jan 20, 1876
SEAMAN, Zebulon	65	29 May 1859	Jun 2, 1859
SEARING, Adazetia R.	31y 7m	8 Jul 1872	Jul 18, 1872
SEARING, Ann E.	39y 9m 24d	5 Oct 1878	Oct 10, 1878
SEARING, Frederick Embree	15m 8d	23 Jan 1871	Jan 26, 1871
SEARING, James	60	16 May 1859	May 19, 1859
SEARING, James Stewart	6y 9m 10d	1 Nov 1867	Nov 7, 1867
SEARING, John A.	67	6 May 1876	May 4, 1876
SEARING, John A.	64	6 May 1876	May 11, 1876
SEARING, John A.	64th y	last Sat	May 11, 1876
SEARING, Lewis	62	20 Oct 1862	Oct 23, 1862
SEARING, Mary A.	28y 2m 22d	27 Sep 1870	Sep 29, 1870
SEARING, Rebecca	76	27 Jan 1871	Feb 9, 1871
SEARING, Susan E.	60y 8m 11d	27 May 1876	Jun 1, 1876
SEARING, Valentine F.	28y 7m 23d	10 Nov 1865	Nov 16, 1865
SEARING, Zebulon	no age	14 Nov 1865	Nov 16, 1865
SEAVEY, (Miss)	60	Thursday	Aug 28, 1873
SEDGWICK, Catherine Maria	78th y	31 Jul 1867	Aug 15, 1867
SELL, Jennie	75	28 Jul 1877	Aug 2, 1877
SERRELL, Minnie	3y 1m 1w	2 Apr 1865	Apr 6, 1865
SEUFERT, Margaret	72	26th ult	Dec 14, 1865

Name	Age	Date of death	Date of newspaper
SEXTON, John	no age	16 Jan 1861	Jan 17, 1861
SEZPANSKI, Frank	8	3 Apr 1877	Apr 5, 1877
SEZPANSKI, Maggie	6	3 Apr 1877	Apr 5, 1877
SHADRIC, Moses	60	8 Sep 1870	Sep 22, 1870
SHAFFER, (Mr.)	no age	16 Mar 1874	Mar 26, 1874
SHANAHAN, P. C.	no age	23 Apr 1869	Apr 29, 1869
SHANKEY, Robert	no age	Saturday	Feb 18, 1875
SHANKS, Sarah	no age	Friday	Dec 13, 1860
SHANNON, George W.	ca. 23	19th inst	Aug 29, 1867
SHANNON, Joanna C.	45	3 Nov 1861	Nov 7, 1861
SHANNON, Mary Amelia	21	22 Nov 1859	Nov 24, 1859
SHARKEY, Mary	101	last Sun	Feb 22, 1877
SHAROT, Emma Jane	6m	17 Sep 1862	Sep 25, 1862
SHARP, Ann	ca. 52	1 Dec 1863	Dec 3, 1863
SHARP, Jacob	52y 5m	28 Oct 1868	Oct 29, 1868
SHATTUCK, Warren	50	3 Nov 1874	Nov 12, 1874
SHAUGHNESSY, William	no age	Saturday	Aug 29, 1878
SHAW, Charles	2y 6m	4 Aug 1875	Aug 12, 1875
SHAW, Freddie	7y 28d	9 Aug 1876	Aug 10, 1876
SHAW, Harriet	54	14 Feb 1878	Feb 21, 1878
SHAW, Jacob	54	17 Oct 1860	Nov 1, 1860
SHAW, Rebecca	12y 8m 13d	13 May 1865	May 25, 1865
SHAW, Susan Maria	3y 10m 2d	1 May 1865	May 25, 1865
SHAY, George	no age	last Sun	Sep 14, 1876
SHEA, Isaac M.	25	30 Aug 1874	Sep 3, 1874
SHEEHAN, Daniel	no age	last Sat	Jul 25, 1878
SHELTON, Fanny Gardiner	21st y	6 Jun 1878	Jun 13, 1878
SHELTON, George A.	63	27 Dec 1863	Dec 31, 1863
SHELTON, John D.	no age	no date	Jan 22, 1863
SHEPARD, Jordon W.	35	23 Nov 1861	Nov 28, 1861
SHEPARD, M. (Mrs.)	no age	no date	Jul 8, 1858
SHERRY, (dau. of Samuel)	infant	19 Feb 1875	Feb 25, 1875
SHERRY, David	89	no date	Nov 21, 1861
SHERWOOD, Quintin	infant	18 Aug 1877	Aug 30, 1877
SHINE, George	no age	last Fri	Jan 13, 1870
SHIPERD, (son of Jacob R.)	young	Wednesday	Mar 8, 1877
SHOEMAKER, (Mrs Charles B.)	no age	Tuesday	Aug 2, 1877
SHORT, John	no age	no date	Jan 15, 1863
SHOTWELL, Joseph	47	14 Jun 1869	Jun 17, 1869
SHRADER, (female)	ca. 38	20 Jan 1871	Jan 26, 1871
SILLIMAN, Augustus G.	no age	24 Jan 1870	Feb 3, 1870
SILLIMAN, Gold	76	13 Mar 1865	Mar 23, 1865
SILVA, (male)	boy	4 Jul 1878	Jul 11, 1878
SIMMONS, (Mr.)	no age	Thur last w	Feb 3, 1876
SIMONS, Abby	74y 2m 6d	15 Jun 1872	Jun 20, 1872
SIMONS, Asa	105	18 Feb 1872	May 2, 1872
SIMONS, Charles	14m	11 Aug 1870	Aug 18, 1870
SIMONS, Emma	23	23 Aug 1870	Sep 1, 1870
SIMONS, John	67	2 Feb 1868	Feb 6, 1868
SIMONS, Nicholas	85y 11d	15 Mar 1870	Mar 17, 1870
SIMONSON, Ann	68	20th inst	Oct 26, 1865
SIMONSON, Cathryn	82	7 Sep 1871	Sep 21, 1871
SIMONSON, Charles	85	3 Jan 1861	Jan 10, 1861
SIMONSON, Charles	6	17 Jan 1864	Jan 21, 1864
SIMONSON, Cornwell	20	9 Nov 1862	Nov 20, 1862
SIMONSON, Daniel	47	last Sat	Aug 31, 1865
SIMONSON, David	59	22 Oct 1859	Oct 27, 1859
SIMONSON, Ella	2	7 Feb 1872	Feb 15, 1872
SIMONSON, Frederick	86	21 Aug 1858	Aug 26, 1858
SIMONSON, Isaac	31	2 Jun 1873	Jun 5, 1873

Name	Age	Date of death	Date of newspaper
SIMONSON, Jane	6	17 Dec 1865	Dec 21, 1865
SIMONSON, John	68	23 Mar 1859	Mar 31, 1859
SIMONSON, John	70	12 Nov 1863	Nov 26, 1863
SIMONSON, Mary	53y 8m 23d	1 Dec 1863	Dec 10, 1863
SIMONSON, Mary Ann	58	22nd inst	Jul 26, 1860
SIMONSON, Morris	66	13 Jan 1859	Jan 20, 1859
SIMONSON, Phebe	73	24 Jun 1873	Jun 26, 1873
SIMONSON, Richard	12	16 Jan 1864	Jan 21, 1864
SIMONSON, William	68	9 Nov 1876	Nov 16, 1876
SIMONSON, William H.	no age	12 Mar 1877	Mar 22, 1877
SINCLAIR, John	103	31 Jul 1859	Aug 18, 1859
SING, Charles B.	63rd y	28 Feb 1878	Mar 7, 1878
SING, William	97+	16 Jul 1858	Jul 29, 1858
SISSON, Benjamin H.	53	Friday	Jul 12, 1877
SKELLY, John	no age	10 May 1861	May 16, 1861
SKEPUNK, John	1y 6m	22 Jul 1876	Jul 27, 1876
SKIDMORE, Ada	infant	25 May 1861	May 30, 1861
SKIDMORE, Cornelia P.	21y 7m 27d	11th inst	Dec 21, 1865
SKIDMORE, David William	71	no date	Oct 24, 1878
SKIDMORE, F. (Dr.)	no age	15 May 1877	May 24, 1877
SKIDMORE, Henry C.	18	30 Jan 1864	Feb 11, 1864
SKIDMORE, Henry C.	no age	19 Nov 1874	Nov 26, 1874
SKIDMORE, Henry P. Seabury	1y 7m	9 Sep 1868	Sep 10, 1868
SKIDMORE, John	85th y	26 Nov 1863	Dec 3, 1863
SKIDMORE, Samuel	49y 17d	16 Apr 1864	Apr 21, 1864
SKIDMORE, Samuel R.	44y 4m 7d	21 Apr 1873	Apr 24, 1873
SKIDMORE, Stephen Tyson	12	26th ult	Mar 9, 1865
SKILLEN, Sarah Amelia	43	5th inst	Mar 8, 1860
SKILLIN, Elizabeth F.	no age	2 Dec 1868	Dec 10, 1868
SKILLIN, Simeon, Jr.	no age	no date	Apr 12, 1860
SKILLMAN, Caddie	19y 4m 23d	28 Sep 1867	Oct 10, 1867
SKILLMAN, John Henry	8y 1m 3d	5 Jan 1864	Jan 14, 1864
SKILMAN, (child of Joseph)	1	18th inst	Sep 30, 1858
SKINNER, Sarah	95	27 Feb 1876	Mar 16, 1876
SKIRM, Margaret	78y 5m 7d	23 Dec 1863	Dec 31, 1863
SLANE, Bernard	no age	20 Jun 1858	Jun 24, 1858
SLAUTERBACK, Frederick	45	26 Apr 1859	May 5, 1859
SLEIGHT, Cornelius	ca. 95	30 Oct 1869	Nov 11, 1869
SLEIGHT, Henry C.	85	7 Jan 1877	Jan 18, 1877
SMALLING, Mary	2	8 Mar 1876	Apr 13, 1876
SMALLING, Thomas	71	29 Aug 1865	Sep 21, 1865
SMALLING, William	21	16 Nov 1874	Nov 19, 1874
SMALLING, William	12d	9 May 1878	May 16, 1878
SMART, Elizabeth L.	no age	20 Dec 1873	Jan 1, 1874
SMART, Joseph	73y 4m 21d	10 Jul 1871	Jul 13, 1871
SMILH, Benjamin	ca. 60	14th inst	Apr 23, 1863
SMITH, (Mrs Nelson)	no age	20 Nov 1872	Nov 28, 1872
SMITH, (Mrs Stephen)	40	16 Nov 1867	Nov 21, 1867
SMITH, (Mrs. William)	no age	last Sat	Mar 28, 1872
SMITH, (Mrs.)	no age	Friday	Jun 30, 1864
SMITH, (ch. of Capt. Elias)	no age	4th inst	Jun 15, 1871
SMITH, (ch. of Henry)	no age	no date	Mar 11, 1869
SMITH, (child of Arrender)	ca. 5w	26 Jan 1864	Feb 4, 1864
SMITH, (child of Jacob)	10m	4 Jul 1859	Jul 7, 1859
SMITH, (child of Sidney)	15m	2 Jun 1865	Jun 8, 1865
SMITH, (dau. of Martin)	1y 10m	27 Mar 1876	Mar 30, 1876
SMITH, (son of Benjamin J.)	6m	3 Jul 1871	Jul 6, 1871
SMITH, (son of Charles H.)	1m	22 Jan 1877	Jan 25, 1877
SMITH, (son of Charles)	2m 7d	25 Apr 1876	Apr 27, 1876
SMITH, (son of Emery)	no age	no date	Oct 28, 1858

Name	Age	Date of death	Date of newspaper
SMITH, (son of George)	3m	13 Feb 1869	Feb 18, 1869
SMITH, (son of Henry)	3m	6 Jan 1873	Jan 9, 1873
SMITH, (son of Ira)	7d	5 Oct 1876	Oct 12, 1876
SMITH, (son of John & Emma)	2m	17 May 1865	Jun 15, 1865
SMITH, (son of Joseph)	11m	27 Aug 1867	Sep 12, 1867
SMITH, (son of Stephen)	2	26 Aug 1868	Sep 3, 1868
SMITH, (son of Willis)	2	28 Nov 1874	Dec 17, 1874
SMITH, (widow of Purcell)	32	29 Mar 1861	Apr 4, 1861
SMITH, (wife of Capt Elias)	no age	4th inst	Jun 15, 1871
SMITH, (wife of Mott)	no age	no date	Dec 8, 1859
SMITH, Addie R.	9y 10m	20 Aug 1876	Aug 24, 1876
SMITH, Albert	no age	last Thur	Oct 6, 1864
SMITH, Alice	24y 7m 10d	22 Mar 1864	Mar 24, 1864
SMITH, Alice	12	20 Jan 1876	Jan 20, 1876
SMITH, Alice F.	21y 8m 23d	26 Mar 1869	Apr 1, 1869
SMITH, Amelia	1y 6m 5d	13 Aug 1875	Aug 19, 1875
SMITH, Amos	80	25 Aug 1870	Sep 1, 1870
SMITH, Amy	91	17 Aug 1861	Aug 29, 1861
SMITH, Amy	81	5 Mar 1865	Mar 16, 1865
SMITH, Amy M.	27y 10m 14d	1 Aug 1868	Aug 6, 1868
SMITH, Anna	28	25 May 1871	Jun 1, 1871
SMITH, Anne	71	23 Feb 1859	Mar 3, 1859
SMITH, Annie	22	26 Feb 1865	Mar 2, 1865
SMITH, Annie M.	no age	21st ult	Mar 16, 1865
SMITH, April Telim	70	27 Apr 1877	May 10, 1877
SMITH, Benj.	no age	no date	Nov 1, 1860
SMITH, Benjamin	3	18th inst	Jul 29, 1869
SMITH, Benjamin B.	9m 2d	24 Jul 1878	Aug 1, 1878
SMITH, Benjamin E.	65	28 Jun 1859	Jul 7, 1859
SMITH, Benjamin T.	60y 3m 17d	?? Mar 1870	Mar 24, 1870
SMITH, Carl W.	20y 10m	23 Aug 1863	Sep 10, 1863
SMITH, Carman	76y 8m	9 Oct 1877	Oct 18, 1877
SMITH, Carman M.	31	30 Oct 1870	Nov 3, 1870
SMITH, Caroline Underhill	33	28 Nov 1875	Dec 2, 1875
SMITH, Catherine D.	57th y	7 Jul 1876	Jul 13, 1876
SMITH, Catherine G. Dale	no age	19 Feb 1876	Apr 20, 1876
SMITH, Charles	75	25 Mar 1859	Mar 31, 1859
SMITH, Charles	no age	last Wed	Oct 7, 1869
SMITH, Charles	8	26 Oct 1869	Oct 28, 1869
SMITH, Charles	19	25 Dec 1869	Dec 30, 1869
SMITH, Charles	36	28 Nov 1871	Dec 7, 1871
SMITH, Charles	14y 11d	21 Sep 1875	Sep 23, 1875
SMITH, Chauncey	9m 26d	12 Jul 1872	Jul 18, 1872
SMITH, Chauncey	11y 8m	3 Apr 1877	Apr 5, 1877
SMITH, Clarence D.	11m 22d	12 Feb 1874	Feb 19, 1874
SMITH, Cornelia	22y 1m 10d	29 Dec 1863	Jan 7, 1864
SMITH, Cyrus P.	77	Tuesday	Feb 15, 1877
SMITH, Daniel	74	no date	Oct 13, 1864
SMITH, Daniel	41y 10m 17d	20 Mar 1865	Mar 23, 1865
SMITH, Daniel	11y 10m	9 Sep 1870	Sep 15, 1870
SMITH, Daniel E.	no age	no date	Sep 1, 1870
SMITH, Daniel W.	45y 8m 14d	10 Jan 1875	Jan 14, 1875
SMITH, David	57	28 Mar 1875	Apr 1, 1875
SMITH, Edith	9m	7 Aug 1870	Aug 11, 1870
SMITH, Edmund	74	20 Feb 1874	Feb 26, 1874
SMITH, Edward	8m	21 Aug 1858	Sep 2, 1858
SMITH, Elbert	63	5 Jul 1873	Jul 10, 1873
SMITH, Elbert D.	24	23 Nov 1867	Nov 28, 1867
SMITH, Eliza	50	5 Jul 1858	Jul 8, 1858
SMITH, Eliza	57	18 Jul 1858	Jul 22, 1858

Name	Age	Date of death	Date of newspaper
SMITH, Eliza	16y 9m	1st inst	Mar 16, 1865
SMITH, Eliza	75	6 Aug 1867	Aug 8, 1867
SMITH, Elizabeth	78y 6m 2d	7 Sep 1867	Sep 12, 1867
SMITH, Elizabeth	88	7 Nov 1871	Nov 9, 1871
SMITH, Elizabeth	83y 3m 12d	12 Jun 1874	Jul 16, 1874
SMITH, Elizabeth Ann	17	29th inst	Dec 6, 1860
SMITH, Elizabeth Ann	25	17 Feb 1861	Feb 21, 1861
SMITH, Elizabeth Gardner	50	28 Feb 1865	Mar 2, 1865
SMITH, Ellen	34y 4m 9d	no date	May 8, 1873
SMITH, Elsie	3	14 Mar 1876	Mar 16, 1876
SMITH, Emeline A. Seabury	no age	no date	Jul 8, 1875
SMITH, Emily	6	3 Aug 1861	Aug 8, 1861
SMITH, Emma Lavinia	6y 9m	4 Jan 1864	Feb 4, 1864
SMITH, Ernest	ca. 10m	27 Jul 1867	Aug 8, 1867
SMITH, Ezra	no age	6 Nov 1861	Nov 21, 1861
SMITH, Floyd	80	23 Feb 1873	Feb 27, 1873
SMITH, Frank	8m	10 Sep 1875	Sep 16, 1875
SMITH, Fred Calvin	1	19 Jul 1878	Jul 25, 1878
SMITH, George	no age	Sat/Sun	Feb 19, 1863
SMITH, George D.	27y 7m 24d	23 Mar 1863	Mar 26, 1863
SMITH, George W.	40	2 Jun 1859	Jun 9, 1859
SMITH, George W.	28y 8m 17d	1 Sep 1873	Sep 4, 1873
SMITH, Georgianna	5	13 Mar 1876	Mar 16, 1876
SMITH, Gerritt	78	21 Dec 1874	Dec 31, 1874
SMITH, Gilbert H.	36y 29d	27 Aug 1876	Sep 7, 1876
SMITH, Grace C.	57	no date	Feb 20, 1862
SMITH, Gracie	8m	14 Aug 1875	Aug 19, 1875
SMITH, Hanna	82	20 May 1873	May 22, 1873
SMITH, Hannah	79y 3m 15d	15 Oct 1872	Oct 17, 1872
SMITH, Hannah J.	33y 7m 6d	19 Nov 1867	Nov 21, 1867
SMITH, Hannah J.	33y 7m 6d	19 Nov 1867	Nov 28, 1867
SMITH, Hannah Jane	44y 1m	3 Dec 1878	Dec 26, 1878
SMITH, Harriet	26	7 Apr 1859	Apr 21, 1859
SMITH, Hattie B.	2y 1m 13d	19 Aug 1868	Aug 27, 1868
SMITH, Havens	no age	no date	Nov 21, 1861
SMITH, Henrietta	19	6 Nov 1870	Nov 10, 1870
SMITH, Henry	43y 3m 14d	15 Jun 1869	Jun 17, 1869
SMITH, Henry	6m	10 Aug 1870	Aug 18, 1870
SMITH, Henry		last Tues	Jan 25, 1872
SMITH, Hewlett	63	22nd inst	Mar 30, 1865
SMITH, Hewlett	35	30 Aug 1870	Sep 1, 1870
SMITH, Hicks	34	1 Sep 1876	Sep 7, 1876
SMITH, I. Bryant	55y 8m 25d	6 Jul 1878	Jul 18, 1878
SMITH, Ida	17y 3m 23d	21 Jul 1876	Jul 27, 1876
SMITH, Ida	no age	recently	Jul 19, 1877
SMITH, Ida Augusta	6m 7d	21st inst	Aug 29, 1867
SMITH, Ida Belle	18y 5m	17 Sep 1877	Sep 20, 1877
SMITH, Ida F.	20y 1m	5 May 1876	May 18, 1876
SMITH, Jacob	57	11 Dec 1858	Dec 16, 1858
SMITH, Jacob	no age	11 Mar 1865	Mar 16, 1865
SMITH, James	75	20 Jul 1862	Jul 24, 1862
SMITH, Jarvis	20	18 Oct 1865	Oct 26, 1865
SMITH, Jeanie	5y 7m	20 Aug 1872	Aug 22, 1872
SMITH, Jemima	65	12 Oct 1858	Oct 21, 1858
SMITH, Jemima	83y 10m 17d	19 Mar 1877	Mar 22, 1877
SMITH, John	no age	no date	Aug 18, 1859
SMITH, John	40	30 Aug 1859	Sep 15, 1859
SMITH, John	65	Monday	Jun 27, 1867
SMITH, John	no age	recently	Aug 18, 1870
SMITH, John	15	7 May 1873	May 15, 1873

Name	Age	Date of death	Date of newspaper
SMITH, John	63	3 Sep 1878	Sep 26, 1878
SMITH, John B.	53y 4m 20d	6th inst	Mar 12, 1868
SMITH, John C.	60	23 Jul 1859	Jul 28, 1859
SMITH, John H.	22	19 Nov 1862	Dec 4, 1862
SMITH, John Nald	39	12 Mar 1872	Mar 14, 1872
SMITH, Jonathon	no age	no date	Jun 30, 1864
SMITH, Joseph	76	8 Jan 1870	Jan 13, 1870
SMITH, Joseph B.	23y 2m 10d	10 Apr 1875	Apr 15, 1875
SMITH, Joseph Nelson	17	3 Sep 1871	Sep 7, 1871
SMITH, Joshua B.	no age	17th inst	Jun 28, 1860
SMITH, Jotham	72y 8m 13d	22 Dec 1875	Dec 30, 1875
SMITH, Lavinia	16y 3m 26d	19 Jan 1877	Jan 25, 1877
SMITH, Letitia	70	20 Feb 1868	Mar 5, 1868
SMITH, Lizzie	8m 8d	29 Jan 1875	Feb 4, 1875
SMITH, Lott Carman	33y 2m 1d	25 Nov 1872	Nov 28, 1872
SMITH, Lottie L.	2	18 Jan 1864	Jan 21, 1864
SMITH, Lottie V.	5m 5d	19 Jul 1878	Jul 25, 1878
SMITH, Margaret	76	4 Sep 1877	Sep 6, 1877
SMITH, Margaretta (nee POWELL)	31y 8m 25d	8 Dec 1873	Dec 11, 1873
SMITH, Maria	48	17 Mar 1869	Mar 25, 1869
SMITH, Maria Ann	38	5 Aug 1859	Aug 11, 1859
SMITH, Marietta	8m	13 Sep 1874	Sep 17, 1874
SMITH, Marietta	29y 9m	21 Sep 1876	Oct 5, 1876
SMITH, Martha	21	1 Nov 1871	Nov 2, 1871
SMITH, Martin	26	12 Jan 1870	Jan 20, 1870
SMITH, Martin	27	14 Jan 1870	Jan 20, 1870
SMITH, Mary	55	27 Nov 1862	Dec 4, 1862
SMITH, Mary	65	9 Sep 1864	Sep 15, 1864
SMITH, Mary	78	4 Apr 1868	Apr 16, 1868
SMITH, Mary	68	11 Jan 1869	Jan 14, 1869
SMITH, Mary Ann	no age	23 Jun 1867	Jun 27, 1867
SMITH, Mary Ann	no age	9th inst	Aug 22, 1867
SMITH, Mary D.	9y 17d	6 Oct 1875	Oct 7, 1875
SMITH, Mary H. W.	20y 9m 10d	27 Sep 1874	Oct 1, 1874
SMITH, Mary J.	21y 7m 21d	2 Oct 1874	Oct 22, 1874
SMITH, Mary Jane	24y 6m	18 Feb 1873	Feb 20, 1873
SMITH, Minnie	17d	20 Jul 1867	Aug 8, 1867
SMITH, Mordecai A.	46	last Wed	Nov 9, 1865
SMITH, Nancy	73	19 Jan 1875	Jan 28, 1875
SMITH, Nathaniel	76	27th inst	May 3, 1860
SMITH, Oliver	70	6 May 1872	May 9, 1872
SMITH, Parmenus	no age	no date	Dec 19, 1861
SMITH, Percival	30	27th inst	Dec 6, 1860
SMITH, Phebe	45	4 May 1869	May 6, 1869
SMITH, Phebe	64y 1d	18 Jan 1872	Jan 25, 1872
SMITH, Phebe Ann	28	3 Mar 1865	Apr 27, 1865
SMITH, Phillis	ca. 85	1 Feb 1876	Feb 3, 1876
SMITH, Priscilla	55y 4m 21d	30th ult	Sep 8, 1864
SMITH, R. Annie (nee BAYLIS)	24	10 Feb 1877	Feb 22, 1877
SMITH, Raynor R.	84y 7m 6d	last Sun	Oct 7, 1869
SMITH, Raynor R.	84	3 Oct 1869	Oct 14, 1869
SMITH, Rhoda	69y 9m 27d	15 Oct 1875	Oct 21, 1875
SMITH, Richard Henry	10y 7m	21 Nov 1867	Nov 28, 1867
SMITH, Richard M.	ca. 50	16th inst	May 24, 1860
SMITH, Richard R.	82	22 Jun 1861	Jun 27, 1861
SMITH, Robert	no age	no date	Sep 1, 1870
SMITH, Rosalie	13y 9m 21d	13 Sep 1873	Sep 18, 1873
SMITH, Samuel	no age	29 Jan 1874	Feb 12, 1874
SMITH, Samuel C.	21y 8m 16d	27 Sep 1864	Oct 13, 1864

Name	Age	Date of death	Date of newspaper
SMITH, Sarah	94th y	15th inst	Mar 22, 1860
SMITH, Sarah	43	23 Aug 1861	Aug 29, 1861
SMITH, Sarah	86	17 Jan 1870	Jan 20, 1870
SMITH, Sarah	65	4 Nov 1871	Nov 9, 1871
SMITH, Sarah	23	8 Oct 1878	Oct 10, 1878
SMITH, Sarah C.	8m	13 Feb 1872	Feb 22, 1872
SMITH, Sarah E.	34y 7m	27 Jan 1878	Jan 31, 1878
SMITH, Sarah Eldert	50y 2m 15d	20th inst	May 26, 1864
SMITH, Sarah Jane	41y 3m	20 Jan 1876	Jan 27, 1876
SMITH, Silas	65	9 Mar 1875	Mar 18, 1875
SMITH, Silvanus	98y 6m 20d	3 Nov 1863	Nov 5, 1863
SMITH, Steward	18y 7m 21d	no date	Jan 10, 1878
SMITH, Stewart	no age	Tuesday	Nov 1, 1877
SMITH, Stewart	18y 7m 27d	31 Oct 1877	Nov 8, 1877
SMITH, Stratton V.	35	16 Nov 1864	Apr 27, 1865
SMITH, Susan	3y 3m	14 Nov 1864	Nov 17, 1864
SMITH, Susannah	81	22 Jan 1861	Jan 31, 1861
SMITH, Susannah	81y 6m 12d	30 Jan 1872	Feb 1, 1872
SMITH, Thomas	80	8 Sep 1868	Sep 10, 1868
SMITH, Thomas	6m	13 Nov 1875	Dec 2, 1875
SMITH, Thomas	65	24 Apr 1876	Apr 27, 1876
SMITH, Thomas Ralph	1y 5m 3d	2 Jun 1877	Jun 7, 1877
SMITH, Thomas, Sr.	90	15 Sep 1876	Sep 21, 1876
SMITH, Timothy	85	22 Aug 1868	Aug 27, 1868
SMITH, Timothy W.	60	16 Jan 1862	Jan 23, 1862
SMITH, Treadwell	40	last Fri	May 8, 1862
SMITH, Valentine	81y 8m 25d	23 Jun 1873	Jul 3, 1873
SMITH, W. H.	no age	no date	Dec 15, 1870
SMITH, Walter	72	13 Nov 1876	Nov 16, 1876
SMITH, Watson C.	46	5 Oct 1877	Oct 11, 1877
SMITH, Watson C.	46	no date	Jan 10, 1878
SMITH, Wessel S.	52	last Fri	Dec 6, 1860
SMITH, Willert F.	1y 8d	11 Mar 1869	Mar 18, 1869
SMITH, Willet	63y 3m 21d	16 Jun 1869	Jun 24, 1869
SMITH, Willet	9m	no date	Aug 11, 1870
SMITH, William	no age	26 Jun 1863	Jul 2, 1863
SMITH, William	28	5 Feb 1864	Feb 11, 1864
SMITH, William	no age	no date	Apr 1, 1875
SMITH, William	57y 7m	no date	Jul 29, 1875
SMITH, William Bruce	no age	last Fri	Feb 15, 1877
SMITH, William J.	72	12 Jan 1878	Jan 17, 1878
SMITH, William T.	no age	Saturday	Oct 31, 1867
SMITH, Zerah A.	72nd y	1 Jan 1872	Jan 11, 1872
SMITH, Zophar, Jr.	29y 1m 12d	14 May 1878	May 16, 1878
SNEDEKER, Abram S.	49y 10m	19 Feb 1863	Feb 26, 1863
SNEDEKER, Ann	90	12 Mar 1862	Mar 13, 1862
SNEDEKER, Dominicus	31	3 Sep 1876	Sep 7, 1876
SNEDEKER, Eliza J.	59y 11m 10d	23 Jul 1864	Jul 28, 1864
SNEDEKER, Elizabeth	65y 2m 14d	20 Nov 1867	Nov 21, 1867
SNEDEKER, Elizabeth A.	no age	23 Jan 1870	Jan 27, 1870
SNEDEKER, Hannah	88th y	7 Jan 1872	Jan 11, 1872
SNEDEKER, Harry Livingston	8m	27 Jul 1868	Aug 6, 1868
SNEDEKER, Jane	70	22nd inst	Dec 29, 1864
SNEDEKER, Mary	75	3 Dec 1878	Dec 12, 1878
SNEDEKER, Mary Ann	51y 10m 16d	31 Jul 1864	Aug 4, 1864
SNEDEKER, Mary E.	ca. 18	16th inst	Nov 20, 1862
SNEDEKER, Samuel C.	22y 10m 25d	1 Oct 1870	Oct 6, 1870
SNEDEKER, Spencer	20y 1m 13d	25 Nov 1876	Nov 30, 1876
SNEDEKER, Stephen C.	61	last Tues	Nov 1, 1860
SNEDIKER, Annie	67th y	22nd inst	Aug 29, 1867

Name	Age	Date of death	Date of newspaper
SNEDIKER, Martin Duryea	9m 5d	1st inst	Aug 8, 1867
SNIPKINK, Henry	32	no date	Jul 15, 1858
SNYDER, William	no age	15 Aug 1875	Aug 19, 1875
SOLMON, William	no age	19 Jul 1874	Jul 30, 1874
SOMERINDYKE, (son of Jacob)	no age	17 Nov 1859	Nov 24, 1859
SOMERS, Elizabeth	22	29 Jun 1861	Jul 4, 1861
SOMERS, Sarah J.	45y 4m	1 Feb 1878	Feb 7, 1878
SOPER, Abraham	74y 4m 18d	6 Mar 1873	Mar 13, 1873
SOPER, Ada Frances	no age	no date	Aug 12, 1858
SOPER, George	67y 10m 11d	27 Feb 1873	Mar 13, 1873
SOPER, Joseph	51y 6m	22 Apr 1865	Apr 27, 1865
SOPER, Lewis	50	6 Apr 1874	Apr 9, 1874
SOPER, William	87y 2m	2 Mar 1875	Mar 11, 1875
SOPER, William	no age	10 Mar 1875	Apr 15, 1875
SOUTHARD, Annie Elizabeth	ca. 4m	26 Jul 1867	Aug 8, 1867
SOUTHARD, Augusta	33	2 Jun 1858	Jun 3, 1858
SOUTHARD, Eliza	17	27 May 1871	Jun 1, 1871
SOUTHARD, Henry	82	last Fri	Apr 26, 1860
SOUTHARD, Henry	no age	1 Jun 1874	Jun 4, 1874
SOUTHARD, James	78	6 Apr 1878	Apr 11, 1878
SOUTHARD, Jane A.	10y 7m 6d	14 Jul 1873	Jul 17, 1873
SOUTHARD, John	53	2 Feb 1862	Feb 20, 1862
SOUTHARD, Mary	57y 7m 19d	17 Feb 1878	Feb 21, 1878
SOUTHARD, Mary Emma	17y 7m 4d	20 Sep 1876	Sep 21, 1876
SOUTHARD, Minnie	6m 18d	5 Sep 1872	Sep 19, 1872
SOUTHARD, Thomas	33y 7m	30 Nov 1867	Dec 12, 1867
SOUTHARD, Wallace E.	1y 10m	18th inst	Nov 9, 1865
SPADER, John	71	no date	Dec 20, 1860
SPALDING, Byron	ca. 3	9th inst	May 26, 1864
SPALDING, Johnny	7y 10m	18th inst	May 26, 1864
SPILLET, Eliza	71y 21d	10 Oct 1874	Oct 22, 1874
SPILLETT, Mary	no age	10th inst	Sep 17, 1874
SPONNER, Frank G.	33	14 Apr 1876	Apr 20, 1876
SPOONER, Alden Grenville	5y 4m	27 Nov 1876	Nov 30, 1876
SPOONER, Mary Ann Wetmore	84	18 Dec 1877	Dec 27, 1877
SPRAGUE, Chas.	25	6 Jun 1859	Jun 9, 1859
SPRAGUE, Elbert Percy	1y 10m	7 Feb 1876	Feb 10, 1876
SPRAGUE, Eliza Morton	64	11 Dec 1877	Dec 13, 1877
SPRAGUE, Elizabeth	82	18 Nov 1875	Dec 2, 1875
SPRAGUE, Elizabeth	88	2 Jan 1877	Jan 4, 1877
SPRAGUE, Elwood	53y 7m 26d	13 Nov 1867	Nov 21, 1867
SPRAGUE, Henry	25y 2m 16d	24 Dec 1863	Dec 31, 1863
SPRAGUE, Henry	66y 9m 22d	16 Jan 1864	Jan 21, 1864
SPRAGUE, Jane Ann	57y 8m 19d	17 May 1874	May 21, 1874
SPRAGUE, Jeremiah	15	5 Feb 1861	Feb 7, 1861
SPRAGUE, John H.	37	11 Dec 1861	Jan 16, 1862
SPRAGUE, Lorenzo	40	24 May 1863	May 28, 1863
SPRAGUE, Mary Emma	14y 3m 18d	29 Jan 1870	Feb 3, 1870
SPRAGUE, Newbury	60y 1m 4d	4 Apr 1870	Apr 28, 1870
SPRAGUE, Oliver	no age	2 Jul 1864	Jul 21, 1864
SPRAGUE, Phebe Ann	3y 6m	22 Oct 1865	Oct 26, 1865
SPRAGUE, Sylvanna	79y 4m	18 Feb 1878	Feb 21, 1878
SPRAGUE, Townsend	27	28 Apr 1873	May 1, 1873
SPRAGUE, William Edward	15	last Wed	Mar 17, 1864
SPRINGSTEAD, Samuel	no age	last Fri	May 22, 1862
SQUIRES, John	no age	12 May 1874	May 14, 1874
STACK, (dau. of John)	7	29 Jun 1873	Jul 3, 1873
STACK, Fanny	4y 7m	12 Jul 1873	Jul 17, 1873
STACK, Mary	2y 2m	5 Jul 1873	Jul 10, 1873
STADLER, Charles	2	Wednesday	Dec 27, 1877

Name	Age	Date of death	Date of newspaper
STAGG, Anna	no age	30 Apr 1861	May 9, 1861
STAHL, Ernest	8	26 Apr 1875	Apr 29, 1875
STANCHELL, Lena	14m	8 Aug 1870	Aug 11, 1870
STANDSIL, Frances R.	2-3	Tuesday	Aug 29, 1878
STANTON, John	no age	2 Nov 1870	Nov 10, 1870
STATTLEL, Valentine	no age	no date	Nov 11, 1869
STEADMAN, Margaret	40	no date	Jul 22, 1858
STEELE, Robert T.	21	12 Oct 1861	Oct 24, 1861
STELGER, (6 ch. of Michael)	various	various	May 10, 1877
STELGER, (ch. of Lewis)	9	29 Apr 1877	May 10, 1877
STEPHENS, Isabella Jane	8y 6m 15d	Saturday	Feb 23, 1860
STEPHENS, James	no age	last Fri	Feb 9, 1860
STEVENS, Mahlon	81	no date	May 9, 1872
STEVENS, Mary A.	60	14 Jan 1872	Jan 18, 1872
STEVENS, Thomas H.	32	8 Mar 1861	Mar 14, 1861
STEVENSON, Elizabeth	43y 1m 17d	27 Sep 1861	Oct 3, 1861
STEWART, David	60	2 Feb 1861	Feb 7, 1861
STEWART, Virginia	25	23 Jul 1859	Jul 28, 1859
STEWART, Virginia	no age	no date	May 17, 1860
STEWART, Willie Moffett	7m 17d	8 Aug 1874	Aug 13, 1874
STILLMAN, (Mr)	no age	no date	Dec 27, 1877
STILLMAN, (Mrs)	no age	no date	Dec 27, 1877
STILLRECHT, Gotlieb	no age	Friday	Jan 11, 1877
STILLWAGGON, Elmer	ca. 7	last Thurs	Nov 21, 1867
STILLWELL, Amelia	88y 4m 12d	30 Sep 1865	Oct 19, 1865
STILLWELL, Daniel	30	1 Aug 1871	Aug 24, 1871
STILLWELL, Eliza	83y 9m 2d	18 Oct 1875	Nov 4, 1875
STILLWELL, Jas. M.	45y 6m 28d	29 Dec 1862	Jan 8, 1863
STILWELL, Sarah Ann	60	21st inst	Sep 27, 1860
STINER, Frederic J.	9m 20d	25 Aug 1878	Aug 29, 1878
STOCKBINE, Florent[?]	84	Thurs(?)	Nov 7, 1872
STONE, (wife of Henry)	no age	24 Feb 1859	May 5, 1859
STONEBANK, John	no age	Wed	Jul 7, 1864
STOOTHOFF, Catharine	84th y	13 Feb 1876	Feb 17, 1876
STOOTHOFF, Catharine Jane	24y 4m 29d	23rd inst	Aug 27, 1868
STOOTHOFF, Jane	79	12th inst	Sep 22, 1864
STOOTHOFF, John C.	70y 7m 23d	7th inst	Jul 13, 1865
STORMS, John	73	20 Feb 1859	Mar 3, 1859
STORY, Hannah	27y 4m 23d	1 May 1875	May 6, 1875
STORY, James	ca. 31	19 Nov 1863	Nov 26, 1863
STORY, Joanna	16y 8m	no date	Jan 10, 1878
STOUVENAL, Marguerite	58th y	14 Nov 1867	Nov 21, 1867
STRASBAUGH, Frederick William	8	8 Feb 1865	Feb 16, 1865
STRATTON, William	47	23 Aug 1858	Sep 2, 1858
STRAWINSKI, Thaddeus S.	18	26 Jan 1861	Feb 7, 1861
STREATER, Bridget	28	17 Mar 1876	Mar 23, 1876
STREETER, George	9m	11 Oct 1877	Oct 18, 1877
STRINGHAM, (dau. of Thomas)	no age	5 Nov 1877	Nov 8, 1877
STRINGHAM, Alonzo W.	1y 10m	3 Apr 1874	Apr 9, 1874
STRINGHAM, John	50	12 May 1876	May 25, 1876
STRINGHAM, Katie	9	22 Sep 1873	Sep 25, 1873
STRINGHAM, Sarah Jane	1	no date	Jan 10, 1878
STRINGHAM, William	12	12 Sep 1873	Sep 18, 1873
STRONG, Ellis	ca. 80	8 Apr 1872	Apr 18, 1872
STRONG, Henry Nichol	1y 2m	4 Jul 1873	Jul 10, 1873
STYMUS, Epenetus S.	6y 2m 1d	25 Jan 1870	Feb 3, 1870
SUBTERLY, Alexander	24	5 Nov 1873	Nov 13, 1873
SULLIVAN, Jeremiah	50	12 Nov 1874	Nov 19, 1874
SULLIVAN, Peter	16	20 Jul 1876	Dec 27, 1877
SULLIVAN, Timothy	no age	Friday	Jul 19, 1877

Name	Age	Date of death	Date of newspaper
SUMNER, Grace	6	11 Apr 1875	Apr 15, 1875
SUTPHIN, Margaret	73y 24d	13th inst	Aug 22, 1867
SUTTON, Martha	90	16 Oct 1867	Oct 24, 1867
SUTTON, Persy	56y 11m	12 Aug 1858	Sep 2, 1858
SUYDAM, John	ca. 90	no date	May 26, 1870
SWEENEY, Lizzie	14	Tuesday	Jul 25, 1878
SWEENEY, Lizzie	16	23 Jul 1878	Oct 10, 1878
SWEEZY, --?--	infant	last week	Dec 22, 1870
SWEZEY, Van Rensallaer	69th y	22 Jul 1878	Jul 25, 1878
SWITZER, Jacob	no age	9 Mar 1874	Mar 12, 1874
SYLVESTER, James	no age	last Thur	Mar 26, 1874
TABER, Samuel T.	47	4 Jan 1871	Feb 9, 1871
TABOR, James M.	no age	13 Aug 1864	Aug 25, 1864
TAFT, Christina	40	16 Sep 1871	Sep 21, 1871
TALBOT, Thomas	no age	28 Aug 1870	Sep 8, 1870
TANNER, --?--	80	no date	May 16, 1872
TAPPEN, John	no age	16 Jan 1871	Jan 26, 1871
TARLETON, Robert H.	84	no date	Sep 23, 1858
TATTERSON, John	no age	28 Feb 1859	Mar 10, 1859
TATTERSON, Rachel	no age	12 Feb 1859	Feb 17, 1859
TAYLOR, (dau. of Fred.)	8	3 Jul 1874	Aug 6, 1874
TAYLOR, (dau. of Lloyd)	child	16 Oct 1874	Oct 22, 1874
TAYLOR, (wife of Joseph)	no age	no date	Mar 14, 1872
TAYLOR, (wife of Thomas)	50	no date	Jan 10, 1861
TAYLOR, Bayard	54	19 Dec 1878	Dec 26, 1878
TAYLOR, Eliza M.	24y 2m	13 Sep 1886	Sep 21, 1876
TAYLOR, James	ca. 30	7 Jan 1860	Jan 12, 1860
TAYLOR, Matilda	no age	no date	Aug 26, 1858
TEEPLE, Orphany	103	1 Jul 1875	Jul 22, 1875
TERHUNE, George	no age	22 Jun 1872	Jul 4, 1872
TERRELL, Jonathan	85	no date	Apr 30, 1868
TERREY, Abbey Eliza	2	1 May 1860	May 3, 1860
TERRILL, (son of A. T.)	4	15 Jul 1872	Jul 25, 1872
TERRY, (Mrs Daniel)	no age	23 Jun 1877	Jul 12, 1877
TERRY, (child of Noah)	no age	no date	Sep 1, 1859
TERRY, Adaline	38y 6m 15d	25 Apr 1870	Apr 28, 1870
TERRY, Adaline	4m	no date	Aug 11, 1870
TERRY, Daniel	79y 11m	28 May 1871	Jun 1, 1871
TERRY, David	19	10 Aug 1858	Aug 19, 1858
TERRY, David	80	9 Sep 1858	Sep 23, 1858
TERRY, Elizabeth Ann	11m	9th inst	Nov 9, 1865
TERRY, Frederick	3m	25 Aug 1869	Sep 2, 1869
TERRY, Margaret	19	18 Apr 1862	Apr 24, 1862
TERRY, Mathias	ca. 50	yesterday	Sep 20, 1860
TERRY, Sidney	34y 9m 18d	4 Aug 1867	Aug 8, 1867
TERRY, Thomas	22	22 Nov 1861	Nov 28, 1861
TERRY, Tuthill	no age	11 Jul 1878	Jul 18, 1878
TERRY, William	no age	8 Dec 1876	Jan 4, 1877
TEXIDO, Elizabeth	78y 3m 8d	30 Oct 1867	Nov 7, 1867
TEYEW, Jane E.	41	5 Feb 1864	Feb 11, 1864
THALER, Joseph	no age	last Sat	Dec 16, 1869
THAYER, Alexandre Decio	4m 14d	5 Aug 1870	Aug 11, 1870
THAYER, Georgie Wheeler	1y 2m 26d	18 Dec 1867	Dec 26, 1867
THEAL, Samuel	7	8 Jun 1874	Jun 11, 1874
THIELMAN, Charles	45	4 Jul 1872	Jul 11, 1872
THISCALL, Frank	2	7 Sep 1875	Sep 9, 1875
THOMAS, Charles	no age	Sunday	Sep 15, 1859
THOMAS, George H.	no age	29 Mar 1870	Apr 7, 1870

Name	Age	Date of death	Date of newspaper
THOMAS, Henry	no age	no date	Feb 9, 1871
THOMAS, Henry Alfred	infant	3 Jun 1865	Jun 15, 1865
THOMAS, Lydia Ann	no age	no date	Jun 17, 1858
THOMAS, Mary A.	44y 11m	14 Apr 1870	Apr 21, 1870
THOMAS, Noble Ware	80y 4m 18d	12th inst	May 17, 1860
THOMAS, Sarah Ann	24	1 Feb 1863	Feb 5, 1863
THOMPKINS, John H.	2y 4m 15d	1 Mar 1876	Mar 9, 1876
THOMPSON, (dau. of Oliver)	16m	9 Mar 1873	Mar 20, 1873
THOMPSON, George E.	11m	29 Jan 1878	Jan 31, 1878
THOMPSON, George H.	3m	29 Jul 1870	Aug 11, 1870
THOMPSON, Harriet	63	16 Jul 1874	Jul 30, 1874
THOMPSON, James	no age	recently	Apr 12, 1877
THOMPSON, John M.	35	27 Nov 1858	Dec 2, 1858
THOMPSON, Maria Louisa	2y 1m	17 Mar 1876	Mar 23, 1876
THOMPSON, Mary H.	74	24 Oct 1868	Oct 29, 1868
THOMPSON, Samuel Ludlow	65y 11m 1d	6 Feb 1865	Feb 23, 1865
THOMPSON, Sophier Sands	55	26 Jan 1865	Feb 2, 1865
THOMSON, Anna	2	23 Aug 1858	Sep 2, 1858
THOMSON, William	4	18 Jan 1861	Jan 24, 1861
THORBORN, Grant	90	last Wed	Jan 29, 1863
THORNE, Hannah	67	25 Oct 1877	Nov 8, 1877
THORNE, Nathaniel	ca. 80	18th inst	Dec 1, 1864
THORNE, Samuel	7	19 Feb 1872	Feb 22, 1872
THORNTON, (ch. of Charles B.)	no age	Tues last w	Jan 27, 1870
THORNTON, (ch. of Charles B.)	no age	last Mon	Jan 27, 1870
THORPE, Eli	no age	4 Feb 1875	Feb 11, 1875
THRAHEN, Elizabeth	2y 8m	13 Dec 1872	Dec 19, 1872
THURMUR, Bruno	35	5 Jul 1875	Jul 8, 1875
THURSTON, Margaret	75y 10m	25 Feb 1864	Mar 17, 1864
THURSTON, Peter	7	25 Apr 1865	May 4, 1865
TICE, Phoebe	55	23 Nov 1874	Nov 26, 1874
TICTREK, Caroline	75	12 Jan 1875	Jan 21, 1875
TIEDERMAN, Frederic	39	3 Aug 1874	Aug 6, 1874
TIEMANN, Caroline Breath	no age	10 Jan 1875	Jan 14, 1875
TIERS, Francis H.	56th y	25th inst	Aug 29, 1867
TILLEY, Edwin A.	no age	no date	Sep 1, 1870
TILTON, Ann Amelia	43	28 Mar 1859	Mar 31, 1859
TIMMINS, John P.	41	3 Nov 1871	Nov 9, 1871
TITUS, (Mr.)	no age	4th inst	Jul 11, 1872
TITUS, Annie	9m 23d	23 Jun 1867	Jun 27, 1867
TITUS, Elizabeth	40	6 Mar 1859	Mar 10, 1859
TITUS, Emily	14	1 Mar 1860	Mar 8, 1860
TITUS, George	no age	a month ago	Dec 27, 1877
TITUS, Henry	92	31 Jan 1861	Feb 7, 1861
TITUS, Henry	61	15 Jan 1865	Jan 19, 1865
TITUS, Jane	ca. 70	6 Sep 1864	Sep 15, 1864
TITUS, Jane E.	40	last Fri/Sa	Nov 29, 1860
TITUS, Mary	78y 10m	10 Jun 1865	Jun 15, 1865
TITUS, Phebe	79th y	12th inst	Jul 20, 1865
TITUS, Platt	50y 2m 9d	25 Nov 1878	Dec 5, 1878
TITUS, Robert	7m 10d	25 Aug 1873	Aug 28, 1873
TITUS, Robert W.	50	9 Sep 1873	Sep 11, 1873
TITUS, Sarah P.	31	2 Sep 1859	Sep 8, 1859
TITUS, Zipporah	85th y	10 Jan 1875	Jan 21, 1875
TODD, Ellen A.	30y 8m 17d	18 Aug 1865	Aug 24, 1865
TOMLINSON, Joseph	84	4 Jan 1859	Jan 20, 1859
TOMPKINS, Abby B.	83	3 Dec 1877	Dec 6, 1877
TOMPKINS, Edward	76y 20d	26 Jun 1864	Jun 30, 1864
TOMPKINS, Hannah W.	no age	13 Dec 1874	Dec 17, 1874
TOPPEN, Joseph	36	4 Aug 1861	Aug 15, 1861

Name	Age	Date of death	Date of newspaper
TOTTEN, Anna Rachael	90	10 Apr 1869	Apr 15, 1869
TOUMEY, John	8	no date	Mar 8, 1877
TOUSLEY, Orson William	3rd y	24th ult	Apr 5, 1860
TOWN, Eliza	no age	7 Jun 1864	Jun 9, 1864
TOWNSEND, --ard	92y 1m 16d	14th	Mar 22, 1877
TOWNSEND, Annanias Hunter	10	1 Oct 1872	Oct 3, 1872
TOWNSEND, Eleanor C.	65y 3m 25d	16 Nov 1876	Nov 23, 1876
TOWNSEND, Ephraim	80	16 Oct 1871	Oct 19, 1871
TOWNSEND, George	no age	no date	Sep 12, 1872
TOWNSEND, Harriet Wright	95y 11m 4d	4 Oct 1873	Oct 9, 1873
TOWNSEND, James	no age	3 Jul 1861	Jul 11, 1861
TOWNSEND, John K.	84	4 Dec 1861	Dec 12, 1861
TOWNSEND, Sarah	74	7 Nov 1874	Nov 12, 1874
TOWNSEND, Susan	35y 5m	3 Sep 1876	Sep 7, 1876
TRACEY, Mary Ann	11	Monday	Jul 19, 1877
TRAVIS, (Mr.)	no age	12 May 1875	May 20, 1875
TREADWELL, (colored man)	no age	13 Mar 1864	Mar 24, 1864
TREADWELL, (son of George)	15m	21 Oct 1867	Oct 24, 1867
TREADWELL, Abigail	70	6 Dec 1859	Dec 8, 1859
TREADWELL, Charity	46	13 Jan 1868	Jan 23, 1868
TREADWELL, Edward L., Jr.	23	11 May 1861	May 16, 1861
TREADWELL, Elbert	68	3 Apr 1876	Apr 6, 1876
TREADWELL, Elizabeth	64y 2m 25d	21 Aug 1873	Aug 28, 1873
TREADWELL, Elizabeth Ann	42y 2m 10d	20 Feb 1869	Feb 25, 1869
TREADWELL, Samuel	68	25 Sep 1873	Oct 2, 1873
TREADWELL, Stephen	47	25 Jul 1872	Aug 1, 1872
TREADWELL, Susan A.	2y 9m 23d	no date	May 25, 1865
TREADWELL, Thomas	90	20 Dec 1875	Dec 23, 1875
TREADWELL, William	62	2 Sep 1870	Sep 8, 1870
TREADWELL, Willie H.	4y 25d	24 Mar 1875	Apr 1, 1875
TREDWELL, Daniel	80	14 Aug 1865	Aug 17, 1865
TREDWELL, Lydia	79	5th inst	May 7, 1863
TREDWELL, Samuel	no age	no date	Jun 18, 1874
TREDWELL, Samuel	infant	3 Sep 1875	Sep 9, 1875
TREMBLY, Willie	13m	19 Jul 1872	Aug 1, 1872
TREUBIG, Anna Mary	20	1st inst	Sep 14, 1865
TROWARD, Charles	ca. 72	19 May 1870	May 26, 1870
TROWARD, Eliza	74	12 Jan 1871	Jan 19, 1871
TROWARD, Mary Ann	76	23 Nov 1872	Nov 28, 1872
TUM, William	6	16 May 1871	Jun 15, 1871
TUOLCY, Mary	no age	no date	Apr 5, 1860
TURNER, (3 children)	no age	last week	Nov 10, 1864
TURNER, Columbus P. C.	16y 9m 8d	25 Sep 1864	Sep 29, 1864
TURNER, Grace Lydia	2y 10m	2 Sep 1864	Sep 8, 1864
TURNER, Timothy	78	13 Mar 1877	Mar 22, 1877
TURNER, William	no age	26 Dec 1876	Jan 4, 1877
TURNEY, Florence Irene	13y 2m 6d	7 Jun 1878	Jun 20, 1878
TUTHILL, Salem C.	70y 9m 2d	12 Dec 1875	Dec 23, 1875
TYRELL, Lucy	74th y	8th inst	Apr 23, 1863
TYSON, Samuel	no age	14 Oct 1861	Oct 24, 1861
TYSON, Steven	86y 2m 14d	28 Dec 1875	Dec 30, 1875
UDALL, Joseph	no age	Monday	May 26, 1870
UNDERHILL, Benjamin T.	82	9 Nov 1870	Nov 10, 1870
UNDERHILL, Benjamin T.	81	9 Nov 1870	Nov 24, 1870
UNDERHILL, Clara L.	19	6th inst	Sep 21, 1865
UNDERHILL, Elizabeth	73	16 Aug 1858	Aug 19, 1858
UNDERHILL, Jacob	82	26 Aug 1869	Sep 2, 1869
UNDERHILL, Mary	59y 9m	25 May 1877	May 31, 1877

Name	Age	Date of death	Date of newspaper
UNDERHILL, Mary	77th y	10 Feb 1878	Feb 14, 1878
UNDERHILL, Richard C.	47	20 Dec 1871	Jan 4, 1872
UNDERHILL, Townsend B.	21st y	17 Mar 1874	Mar 19, 1874
UNDERHILL, William Oscar	10m	no date	Sep 1, 1864
URIAR, (Mr.)	no age	1 Sep 1875	Sep 16, 1875
VAIL, Joseph B.	no age	4th inst	Jul 27, 1871
VAIL, Julia O.	no age	8 Sep 1872	Sep 12, 1872
VAIL, Sally Fleet	87	27 Jul 1875	Nov 4, 1875
VALENTINE, (child of W. B.)	no age	no date	Jan 10, 1878
VALENTINE, (widow of Richard)	84	3 Sep 1865	Sep 7, 1865
VALENTINE, Abbie Jane	45	28 Oct 1875	Nov 4, 1875
VALENTINE, Ann E.	57	28 Jan 1871	Feb 9, 1871
VALENTINE, Caroline	54y 24d	27 May 1865	Jun 1, 1865
VALENTINE, Charles	78	13th inst	Jan 23, 1868
VALENTINE, Eliza	35	17 Jan 1865	Jan 26, 1865
VALENTINE, Elizabeth	76	7 Sep 1875	Sep 9, 1875
VALENTINE, Elizabeth	no age	22 Jan 1877	Jan 25, 1877
VALENTINE, Ephraim	69	13 Feb 1873	Feb 20, 1873
VALENTINE, Ettie	11	last Sun	Sep 15, 1864
VALENTINE, George	2	last Mon	Sep 15, 1864
VALENTINE, George	71	2 May 1870	May 5, 1870
VALENTINE, Horatio	2m	16 Jul 1861	Jul 25, 1861
VALENTINE, John	4	last Thur	Sep 15, 1864
VALENTINE, John	45	1 Mar 1872	Mar 7, 1872
VALENTINE, Marion	no age	1 Aug 1876	Aug 3, 1876
VALENTINE, Mary	55	no date	Nov 6, 1862
VALENTINE, Mary	67th y	10 Oct 1869	Oct 14, 1869
VALENTINE, Oliver	20y 9m 3d	3 Jul 1863	Aug 6, 1863
VALENTINE, Phebe	63	no date	May 5, 1859
VALENTINE, Phebe	68	29th inst	Dec 6, 1860
VALENTINE, Phebe	77	12 Aug 1873	Aug 21, 1873
VALENTINE, Richard T.	14y 5m 8d	8 Sep 1873	Sep 11, 1873
VALENTINE, Ruth	87	5 Dec 1877	Dec 13, 1877
VALENTINE, Smith	10	12 Sep 1864	Sep 15, 1864
VALENTINE, Stephen	82nd y	27 Apr 1878	May 2, 1878
VALENTINE, William	85th y	24 Nov 1863	Dec 3, 1863
VALENTINE, William	74	4 Mar 1868	Mar 12, 1868
VALENTINE, William Edgar	27	22 Jul 1862	Jul 24, 1862
VAN ALST, Elizabeth	82	28 Sep 1865	Oct 5, 1865
VAN CLEFF, Ester Louisa	no age	1 Sep 1858	Sep 9, 1858
VAN COTT, Abby	13	2 Sep 1865	Sep 7, 1865
VAN COTT, Catharine A.	2y 5m	20 Oct 1867	Oct 24, 1867
VAN COTT, Elizabeth	67y 7m 23d	11 Oct 1877	Oct 18, 1877
VAN COTT, John	no age	10 Apr 1861	Apr 18, 1861
VAN COTT, Mary	43	23 Aug 1865	Sep 7, 1865
VANDENBURGH, George W.	20y 6m 4d	30 Oct 1872	Oct 31, 1872
VANDERBILT, Cornelius	56	26 Jun 1858	Jul 1, 1858
VANDERBILT, Sarah	53	4 Jan 1859	Jan 13, 1859
VANDERGRAW, Catherine L.	34	1 Aug 1867	Aug 8, 1867
VANDERHOOF, Harriet Satterlee	46th y	1 Nov 1864	Nov 3, 1864
VANDERVEG, George	68	6th inst	Jul 12, 1860
VANDERVERE, John	70	1 Aug 1875	Aug 5, 1875
VANDERVERG, (4 ch. of Jane)	no age	no date	Mar 14, 1872
VANDERVERG, John	75y 5m 12d	22 Mar 1872	Apr 4, 1872
VANDERVOORT, Phebe	91	26 Oct 1877	Nov 1, 1877
VANDERWATER, Freelove	78th y	16 Sep 1867	Sep 19, 1867
VANDERWATER, John P.	no age	9 May 1874	May 14, 1874
VAN DE WATER, Andrew	1y 8d	29 Jul 1873	Jul 31, 1873

Name	Age	Date of death	Date of newspaper
VAN DE WATER, Ann	50y 8m	no date	Jan 10, 1878
VANDEWATER, Ann	84y 8m 16d	29 Jan 1865	Feb 2, 1865
VANDEWATER, Anne	34y 8m	25 Oct 1877	Nov 1, 1877
VAN DEWATER, Cornelia King (nee KELLY)	27	8 Mar 1877	Mar 15, 1877
VANDEWATER, G. Conklin	59y 2m	22 1871	Dec 7, 1871
VAN DE WATER, James P.	54	6 Jul 1873	Jul 10, 1873
VANDEWATER, Jessie	52y 3m 9d	28 May 1874	Jun 4, 1874
VANDEWATER, John	50	31 Jan 1874	Feb 26, 1874
VANDEWATER, John	19	6 Sep 1875	Sep 9, 1875
VANDEWATER, Livingston	47y 9m	3 Dec 1871	Dec 14, 1871
VANDEWATER, Margaret	no age	4 of 2nd mo	Feb 11, 1864
VANDEWATER, Maria	70y 10m	22 Mar 1873	Apr 10, 1873
VANDEWATER, Martha	59	8 Oct 1864	Oct 13, 1864
VAN DE WATER, Martha Travis	85th y	5 Jul 1877	Jul 19, 1877
VAN DE WATER, Oakley	16y 6m 16d	7th inst	Mar 12, 1863
VAN DEWATER, Oliver	55y 3m 8d	7 Apr 1877	Apr 12, 1877
VANDEWATER, Phebe	70y 2m 20d	13 Jun 1863	Jun 18, 1863
VAN DINE, Ann	74y 4d	1 Aug 1867	Aug 8, 1867
VAN DINE, Mary	66	13 Oct 1868	Oct 22, 1868
VAN DUYNO, Nicholas	41	Saturday	Oct 6, 1859
VAN LAW, Catharine	67y 10m 26d	20 Jul 1873	Jul 24, 1873
VAN NOSTRAND, Aaron	32	25th ult	Mar 12, 1863
VAN NOSTRAND, Adeline	63	19 Nov 1876	Nov 23, 1876
VAN NOSTRAND, Benjamin	88y 3m	9 Nov 1877	Nov 15, 1877
VAN NOSTRAND, Donald	59y 1m	1 May 1874	May 7, 1874
VAN NOSTRAND, Fanny	73y 3m 11d	9 Mar 1868	Mar 19, 1868
VAN NOSTRAND, George	no age	23 Apr 1869	Apr 29, 1869
VAN NOSTRAND, George	76	9 Aug 1873	Aug 21, 1873
VAN NOSTRAND, Isaac	63rd y	11 Dec 1867	Dec 19, 1867
VAN NOSTRAND, John	15	11 Jul 1871	Jul 20, 1871
VAN NOSTRAND, Mary	45	11 Nov 1862	Nov 20, 1862
VAN NOSTRAND, Mary	17y 16d	7 Sep 1868	Sep 10, 1868
VAN NOSTRAND, Seaman	42	23 May 1876	May 25, 1876
VAN NOSTRAND, William	8m	10 Feb 1870	Feb 17, 1870
VAN NOSTRAND, Willie W.	2y 8m 20d	17 Dec 1871	Dec 21, 1871
VAN SCHUYLENBORGH, Jacob G.	50	no date	Mar 14, 1872
VAN SICKLEN, Maria R.	18y 1m 21d	5 Apr 1864	Apr 14, 1864
VAN SICLEN, Ditmars	41y 4m 5d	6 May 1878	May 16, 1878
VANSICLEN, Ida K.	87	21 Nov 1878	Nov 28, 1878
VANSISE, Evart	no age	Thursday	May 17, 1877
VAN SIZE, Jeremiah	ca. 73	23 Feb 1864	Mar 17, 1864
VANTASSEL, Elizabeth	81y 11m	12 Feb 1874	Feb 19, 1874
VAN VELSOR, Elizabeth	80y 9m	11 May 1878	May 16, 1878
VAN VOAST, Eben A.	25	25 Mar 1862	Apr 3, 1862
VAN WICKEL, Sarah E.	31	6 Apr 1878	Apr 11, 1878
VAN WICKLE, Letitia	56y 6m	3 Aug 1871	Aug 10, 1871
VAN WICKLEN, Cornelius	88	24 Nov 1877	Nov 29, 1877
VAN WICKLEN, Garret	48	18th inst	Jan 23, 1868
VAN WICKLEN, Hendrick	80	5th inst	Feb 8, 1872
VAN WYACK, Stephen	86	17th inst	Nov 22, 1860
VAN WYCK, Charles	23	5 Sep 1868	Sep 10, 1868
VAN WYCK, Jane Sands	14y 8m 24d	17 Mar 1878	Mar 21, 1878
VAN WYCK, Mary	78	31 Aug 1876	Sep 7, 1876
VAN WYCK, Sarah	87y 2m 15d	12 Mar 1878	Mar 14, 1878
VAN WYCK, Smith	80	18 Apr 1874	Apr 30, 1874
VAN WYCK, Zernah	5th y	12 Mar 1863	Mar 19, 1863
VAN ZANDT, Rem	no age	3rd inst	Nov 7, 1867
VASSER, Anna L.	3y 11m 28d	28 Dec 1863	Dec 31, 1863
VELSOR, Josiah	65	no date	Sep 30, 1858

Name	Age	Date of death	Date of newspaper
VELSOR, Sarah	3m 15d	23 Aug 1872	Aug 29, 1872
VERITY, Ada Florence	1m 10d	11 Aug 1870	Aug 18, 1870
VERITY, Amy	74	14 Oct 1870	Oct 20, 1870
VERITY, Emma Louise	3y 7m	2 Feb 1874	Feb 5, 1874
VERITY, Fannie Haff	5m	8 Jan 1874	Jan 15, 1874
VERITY, George Nelson	5m 10d	3 Jul 1872	Jul 11, 1872
VERITY, James	52	7 Oct 1867	Oct 10, 1867
VERITY, Richard	58	9 Oct 1859	Oct 13, 1859
VERITY, Richard	no age	6th inst	May 10, 1860
VERITY, Stephen S.	23y 10m 2d	5 Jun 1863	Jun 25, 1863
VERITY, William	no age	18 Nov 1859	Nov 24, 1859
VERITY, William	19	4 Nov 1863	Nov 26, 1863
VERITY, William	no age	Thursday	May 27, 1875
VERNON, Carman	40	26 Aug 1858	Sep 2, 1858
VERNON, James, Jr.	no age	9 Jun 1863	Jun 25, 1863
VICKERS, Edwin F.	26y 11m	28 Jul 1865	Aug 31, 1865
VICKERS, Eliza	72y 8m 12d	1 May 1873	May 8, 1873
VINCENT, Mary	80y 10m	5 Sep 1873	Sep 11, 1873
VOCE, Johanna	no age	Tuesday	Apr 12, 1877
VOGEL, (Mrs.)	ca. 80	last Thurs	Dec 17, 1874
VOGOL, (Mrs. Jackson)	80	10 Dec 1874	Dec 17, 1874
VON NOSTRAND, Elizabeth	85	17 Jun 1878	Jun 20, 1878
VOORHIES, Elizabeth	80y 3m 8d	22 Mar 1876	Mar 30, 1876
VOORIES, Susie	19m	25 Apr 1870	May 5, 1870
VOORIS, Amy V.	88y 1m 14d	5 Jun 1876	Jun 15, 1876
VOORIS, Susan E.	no age	16 Apr 1878	Apr 18, 1878
WADDELL, John	no age	23 Nov 1859	Dec 1, 1859
WADDEN, Elizabeth	80	14 Jan 1875	Jan 21, 1875
WADE, John	no age	12th inst	Aug 15, 1867
WADE, Katie	4y 3m	19 Jan 1874	Jan 22, 1874
WAGNER, (Mrs. William)	no age	no date	Sep 3, 1874
WAGNER, Stephen	2y 10m	24 Mar 1872	Mar 28, 1872
WAGSTAFF, Alfred	75th y	26 Apr 1878	May 2, 1878
WAHLE, Caroline	5m	1 Sep 1868	Sep 3, 1868
WAKE, Richard	78y 10m	19 Oct 1874	Oct 22, 1874
WAKEMAN, Harwood	no age	last Thurs	Aug 22, 1878
WALDO, Mary	no age	18 Sep 1859	Sep 29, 1859
WALDO, Mills Elizabeth	9m	2 Aug 1863	Aug 6, 1863
WALDRON, Gertrude	60	21 Aug 1863	Aug 27, 1863
WALEY, Jane	33	19 Dec 1876	Dec 21, 1876
WALKER, Alpheus	6m	18 Aug 1870	Aug 25, 1870
WALKER, Charles	2m	22 Sep 1874	Sep 24, 1874
WALKER, Samuel	15m 15d	24 Sep 1872	Sep 26, 1872
WALKER, William C.	49y 8m 15d	3 Oct 1873	Oct 9, 1873
WALKER, William F.	41y 9m 8d	27 Feb 1874	Mar 5, 1874
WALKER, William F.	1y 4m 14d	no date	Jun 17, 1875
WALL, (female)	no age	last Sat	Aug 22, 1878
WALL, (male)	infant	30 Aug 1873	Sep 11, 1873
WALL, John	no age	23 Sep 1878	Sep 26, 1878
WALLABER, George	30m	29 Oct 1865	Nov 2, 1865
WALLABER, Harriet P.	28	29 Oct 1865	Nov 2, 1865
WALLACE, George Lee	5y 3m 4d	26 Jan 1864	Feb 4, 1864
WALLACE, William	72	18 Aug 1863	Aug 27, 1863
WALLER, Arthur	no age	3 Jan 1874	Jan 8, 1874
WALSH, Richard	ca. 60	Tuesday	Jan 18, 1877
WALSH, Willie J. H.	3y 8m	21 Apr 1872	Apr 25, 1872
WALTERS, (ch. of Joseph & Bridget)	no age	25 Jul 1873	Jul 31, 1873

Name	Age	Date of death	Date of newspaper
WALTERS, Birch	ca. 6	23 Feb 1864	Mar 3, 1864
WALTERS, Charles	20y 1m 25d	10 Sep 1864	Sep 22, 1864
WALTERS, Cornelius B.	30y 8m 29d	14 Dec 1868	Dec 17, 1868
WALTERS, Deborah	81y 8m 21d	28 Mar 1869	Apr 1, 1869
WALTERS, Edith	6wks	20 Oct 1873	Oct 30, 1873
WALTERS, Edna	7wks	26 Oct 1873	Oct 30, 1873
WALTERS, Frank Godfrey	2	21 Feb 1868	Feb 20, 1868
WALTERS, George	21y 1m 20d	20 Apr 1863	Apr 23, 1863
WALTERS, George W.	37th y	13 Mar 1877	Mar 15, 1877
WALTERS, Henry	71y 4m 8d	29 Sep 1873	Oct 2, 1873
WALTERS, Isaac	no age	last Tue	Jan 9, 1862
WALTERS, Isabel	infant	18 Mar 1861	Mar 21, 1861
WALTERS, John	no age	Friday	Jun 3, 1858
WALTERS, Joseph	2y 6m	16 Sep 1874	Sep 24, 1874
WALTERS, Letty	80y 9m 5d	8 Oct 1876	Oct 12, 1876
WALTERS, Mary Ann	26	3 Jan 1873	Jan 9, 1873
WALTERS, Oliver	27	14 Oct 1862	Oct 30, 1862
WALTERS, Samuel	33y 1m	30 Sep 1864	Oct 6, 1864
WALTON, John	no age	last Sat	Jul 5, 1860
WANKE, August	no age	3rd inst	Dec 16, 1875
WANSER, Abby	66	22 Aug 1868	Aug 27, 1868
WANSER, Daniel	83	21 Apr 1878	Apr 25, 1878
WANSER, Hannah	39	23rd inst	Sep 27, 1860
WANSER, Mary A.	40	15 Mar 1874	Mar 19, 1874
WANSOR, Avery	no age	30 Jul 1873	Aug 7, 1873
WANSOR, Daniel	no age	23 Aug 1861	Aug 29, 1861
WANTOR, Anna	83	29 Aug 1858	Sep 9, 1858
WANZOR, Sophia	82	25 Aug 1858	Sep 2, 1858
WARD, Hannah	22	23 Mar 1870	Mar 24, 1870
WARE, Francis H.	no age	no date	Jan 10, 1878
WARE, Francis Hutchinson	4m 12d	1 Aug 1868	Aug 13, 1868
WARING, Anthony	78	21 Feb 1868	Feb 20, 1868
WARMUTH, Andrew	17y 6m 17d	9 Dec 1878	Dec 12, 1878
WARNER, Fidella	32	15 Dec 1864	Jan 5, 1865
WASHBURN, Clinton	2y 11m	25 Jun 1877	Jul 5, 1877
WASHBURN, Grace	5y 11m	23 Jun 1877	Jul 5, 1877
WASHBURN, Stephen O.	30y 7m	no date	Oct 1, 1874
WATERS, Cornelius	70	21 Aug 1865	Aug 24, 1865
WATERS, Daniel S.	51y 7m 24d	10th inst	Aug 18, 1864
WATERS, George G.	56	27 Jun 1875	Jul 8, 1875
WATERS, Thomas Hallet	53	26 Dec 1867	Jan 2, 1868
WATROUS, Charles S.	75	22 Mar 1877	Mar 29, 1877
WATROUS, Mary C.	46	28 Jan 1861	Jan 31, 1861
WATTS, (son of Elbert)	infant	10 Sep 1877	Sep 13, 1877
WATTS, Elbert Francis	10m 10d	8 Aug 1870	Aug 11, 1870
WATTS, James	8y 8m	23 Nov 1873	Nov 27, 1873
WATTS, John	65	27 Sep 1859	Sep 29, 1859
WATTS, Madora	2y 1m 6d	5 Aug 1874	Aug 13, 1874
WATTS, Oliver	no age	Wednesday	Mar 29, 1860
WATTS, Rachel V.	8m	17 Aug 1868	Aug 27, 1868
WATTS, Smith (?)	no age	Wednesday	Mar 29, 1860
WATTS, Susan	no age	no date	May 1, 1873
WATTS, William	ca. 50	last Thur	Nov 29, 1860
WAY, Magdalen	64	27 Oct 1877	Nov 1, 1877
WAY, Thomas	no age	6 Oct 1875	Oct 28, 1875
WAYRICH, Philipine	28y 10m	8 Sep 1878	Sep 12, 1878
WEAKER, George W.	no age	7th inst	Jul 13, 1876
WEAVER, I. L.	no age	12 Sep 1878	Nov 7, 1878
WEAVER, Isaiah L.	no age	12 Sep 1878	Sep 19, 1878
WEAVER, John P.	2y 3m	27 Nov 1863	Dec 3, 1863

Name	Age	Date of death	Date of newspaper
WEAVER, Mary C.	18y 10m 17d	no date	Mar 20, 1873
WEAVER, Nathan Bell	11	26 Jun 1875	Jul 1, 1875
WEAVER, Rachael	58	22 Nov 1863	Dec 3, 1863
WEBB, Edwin, Jr.	20y 11m 22d	31 Jul 1860	Aug 2, 1860
WEBB, Elizabeth	no age	5th ult	Aug 15, 1867
WEBB, George	58y 7m 15d	9 Apr 1868	Apr 16, 1868
WEBB, Jane E.	no age	15th inst	Jan 26, 1865
WEBB, John Stagg	22y 3m 5d	5 Mar 1872	Mar 7, 1872
WEBB, Samuel	60y 5m 3d	2 Dec 1863	Dec 10, 1863
WEBSTER, Erastus	no age	15 Jun 1864	Jul 7, 1864
WECKMAN, Adam	79	9 Jun 1876	Jun 15, 1876
WEED, Eliza M. G.	78	Thursday	Aug 22, 1878
WEEDEN, Hester G.	68th y	4 Feb 1870	Feb 10, 1870
WEEDEN, James	no age	7th inst	Jul 21, 1864
WEEDEN, James T.	67	9 Jul 1864	Jul 14, 1864
WEEDEN, Janes Hubbard	3y 9m 10d	12 Dec 1868	Dec 19, 1867
WEEK, Richard	no age	20 Apr 1877	Apr 26, 1877
WEEKES, Caroline S.	38	30 Aug 1868	Sep 3, 1868
WEEKES, Clarence Van deWater	23	26 Jul 1867	Aug 1, 1867
WEEKES, Elizabeth	76y 7m	3 Nov 1873	Nov 6, 1873
WEEKES, Mary Ann	83	19 Mar 1876	Mar 23, 1876
WEEKES, Nettie	6y 7m 10d	28 May 1873	Jun 5, 1873
WEEKES, Phebe Ann	51	19 Jun 1876	Jun 22, 1876
WEEKES, Rachel M.	66y 5m 18d	19 Jul 1878	Jul 25, 1878
WEEKES, Richard	1y 9m	20 Mar 1874	Mar 26, 1874
WEEKES, Silas M.	55	last Fri	Aug 23, 1860
WEEKES, Van de Water	46	22 Dec 1865	Dec 28, 1865
WEEKS, (son of Charles C.)	infant	28 May 1859	Jun 2, 1859
WEEKS, Ada Anna	1y 9m	6 Nov 1873	Nov 13, 1873
WEEKS, Albert	no age	19 Mar 1875	Mar 25, 1875
WEEKS, Alfred Stuart	23	19 Feb 1877	Feb 22, 1877
WEEKS, Carrie E.	6y 6m 19d	3 Jul 1876	Jul 6, 1876
WEEKS, Clarence Luther	1y 9m 2d	19 May 1872	May 23, 1872
WEEKS, David	no age	1st inst	Oct 13, 1864
WEEKS, George	ca. 70	last Thur	Mar 24, 1864
WEEKS, Gilbert	ca. 72	27 Feb 1864	Mar 3, 1864
WEEKS, Ida May	3m 10d	11 Aug 1858	Aug 12, 1858
WEEKS, Jacob M.	44	22 Apr 1876	Apr 27, 1876
WEEKS, Jedidiah	88	30 Dec 1864	Jan 12, 1865
WEEKS, John	no age	25 Apr 1877	May 17, 1877
WEEKS, Julia	no age	26 Aug 1859	Sep 1, 1859
WEEKS, Lizzie	16	25 Aug 1876	Aug 31, 1876
WEEKS, Margaret M. (nee RAPELYES)	24th y	15 May 1876	May 18, 1876
WEEKS, Martha Emma	8m	14 Oct 1862	Oct 23, 1862
WEEKS, Mary	no age	Sat 24th	Apr 12, 1877
WEEKS, Nellie M.	6m	9 Oct 1877	Oct 11, 1877
WEEKS, Nellie N.	6m	no date	Jan 10, 1878
WEEKS, Phebe	22	9 May 1862	May 15, 1862
WEEKS, Phebe A.	40	1 Jun 1862	Jun 5, 1862
WEEKS, Rebecca	76	no date	Aug 26, 1858
WEEKS, Sarah	65y 5m	last Fri	Apr 26, 1860
WEEKS, Sarah Anna	22y 5m 24d	23 Mar 1872	Mar 28, 1872
WEEKS, Thomas W.	63	2 Jul 1859	Jul 7, 1859
WEEKS, Warren W.	38	18 Oct 1858	Oct 21, 1858
WEEKS, William W.	37	17 Apr 1861	Apr 25, 1861
WEIR, George	32	Mon. (?)	Dec 20, 1860
WELCH, (male)	no age	last Wed	Aug 8, 1878
WELCH, Thomas, Sr.	75y 6m	27 Feb 1860	Mar 1, 1860
WELDEN, John	40	no date	Aug 12, 1858

Name	Age	Date of death	Date of newspaper
WELLES, John A.	56	18th inst	Aug 31, 1865
WELLING, Eliza	70	28 May 1865	Jun 15, 1865
WELLING, John T.	69th y	27 Mar 1863	Apr 2, 1863
WELLINGHAUSER, John C.	50	20 Oct 1865	Oct 26, 1865
WELLS, George	no age	31 May 1864	Jun 23, 1864
WELLS, Jeremiah	85	18 Sep 1877	Sep 27, 1877
WELLS, Wait	83	23 Oct 1865	Oct 26, 1865
WELLS, William G.	29	no date	Aug 26, 1858
WELLS, Wm. G.	29	8th inst	Aug 19, 1858
WEST, Elianna	no age	24 Jun 1867	Jun 27, 1867
WEST, Nathan	no age	10 Jun 1874	Jun 25, 1874
WESTFIELD, Christina	no age	10 Nov 1878	Nov 14, 1878
WESTLAKE, Julia	no age	10 Oct 1865	Oct 19, 1865
WHAL, John	15m	25 Jun 1878	Jul 4, 1878
WHALEY, (wife of Cornelius)	60	17 Mar 1861	Mar 21, 1861
WHALEY, Albert L.	17y 3m 24d	13 Feb 1869	Feb 18, 1869
WHALEY, Catharine	48	4 Mar 1868	Mar 12, 1868
WHALEY, Edgar	4	7 Jun 1859	Jun 9, 1859
WHALEY, Edward	8m 17d	23 Jan 1874	Feb 5, 1874
WHALEY, Franklyn	1m	18 May 1875	May 27, 1875
WHALEY, Jennie Augusta	24y 8d	20 May 1878	May 23, 1878
WHALEY, Jesse	ca. 48	7 Mar 1864	Mar 10, 1864
WHALEY, John	28	31 Mar 1865	Apr 13, 1865
WHALEY, Josiah	64y 10m	7 Nov 1877	Nov 15, 1877
WHALEY, Josiah	64y 10m	no date	Jan 10, 1878
WHALEY, Mary	23	22 Jun 1873	Jul 3, 1873
WHALEY, Mary	93	18 May 1877	May 24, 1877
WHALEY, Sarah	67	6 Oct 1865	Oct 19, 1865
WHALEY, Stephen	8m	4 Feb 1874	Feb 12, 1874
WHALEY, William P.	no age	21 Jun 1872	Jun 27, 1872
WHEELER, Mary	58	14th inst	Jan 19, 1860
WHEELER, William	72y 7m 1d	3 Feb 1872	Feb 8, 1872
WHITAKER, Hiram A.	59th y	10 Oct 1869	Oct 14, 1869
WHITE, Clarissa	74	21 Oct 1876	Oct 26, 1876
WHITE, Esta R.	55y 24d	15 Aug 1864	Aug 25, 1864
WHITE, Ida	6m	20 Feb 1876	Mar 2, 1876
WHITE, John	72	4 Dec 1877	Dec 6, 1877
WHITE, John	72	no date	Jan 10, 1878
WHITE, Margaret	67	20 May 1875	May 27, 1875
WHITE, Mary	66	1 Jul 1861	Jul 4, 1861
WHITE, Mary Catherine	28	no date	Apr 16, 1863
WHITE, Stephen	61	6 Jul 1858	Jul 15, 1858
WHITE, Stephen	no age	2 Jan 1875	Jan 14, 1875
WHITMORE	22	11 Nov 1864	Nov 17, 1864
WHITMORE, Guly A.	76	16 Jan 1865	Jan 19, 1865
WHITMORE, John	46y 9d	19 Apr 1875	Apr 29, 1875
WHITSON, (widow of Abraham)	no age	15th inst	Aug 24, 1865
WHITSON, Andrew	no age	Sunday	May 17, 1877
WHITSON, Ann	91st y	10 Oct 1869	Oct 14, 1869
WHITSON, Marianna	2y 10m 15d	11th inst	Sep 19, 1867
WHITSON, Sarah	71st y	16 of 2nd m	Feb 25, 1864
WHITTING, Frances M.	no age	27 Mar 1874	Apr 9, 1874
WHITTINGTON, Ann	69y 11m 13d	27 Jan 1872	Feb 1, 1872
WICH, Eliza H. B.	7	22 Sep 1873	Sep 25, 1873
WICK, Catherine	45y 6m 5d	6 Sep 1873	Sep 11, 1873
WICKS, Carman	no age	Tue last wk	Jul 21, 1864
WICKS, Charles	ca. 27	3 Nov 1871	Nov 9, 1871
WICKS, Edward Gerard	1y 21d	no date	Mar 15, 1877
WICKS, F. M. A.	56	8th inst	Nov 21, 1867
WICKS, Henry	66	last Tues	Aug 29, 1878

Name	Age	Date of death	Date of newspaper
WICKS, Robert H.	no age	Friday	May 24, 1877
WIGGINS, Brinson	85y 18m 17d	1st inst	Mar 19, 1874
WIGGINS, Nathaniel	no age	27 Mar 1859	May 26, 1859
WIGGINS, Stephen R.	70	10 Aug 1863	Aug 20, 1863
WIGGINS, Walter N.	49	1 Aug 1865	Aug 10, 1865
WIGHT, Elizabeth	no age	12 Jul 1875	Jul 29, 1875
WIGHT, Harry	4m 12d	last Sun	Sep 21, 1865
WILCOX, (son of Caroline)	13d	3 Jun 1871	Jun 8, 1871
WILCOX, Caroline (nee PETTY)	27y 4m	3 Jun 1871	Jun 8, 1871
WILCOX, Mary	79y 10m 28d	the 21st	May 24, 1860
WILCOX, Paulina	60y 6m 29d	4 Nov 1878	Nov 7, 1878
WILDER, John	77	29th ult	Dec 21, 1865
WILKINS, Sarah Ann	29y 11m	14 Sep 1865	Sep 21, 1865
WILKINS, William	14	20th inst	Oct 31, 1867
WILKINSON, Henry	18	no date	Apr 12, 1877
WILLETS, Amos	72	last Mon	Oct 27, 1864
WILLETS, Andrew J.	36y 6m	23rd inst	May 26, 1870
WILLETS, Carrie Beech	2	15 Mar 1862	Mar 20, 1862
WILLETS, Charles W.	no age	10 Mar 1873	Mar 13, 1873
WILLETS, Deborah B.	20y 4m 1d	3 Dec 1865	Dec 21, 1865
WILLETS, Ester G.	37	20 Aug 1871	Aug 24, 1871
WILLETS, Franklin F.	3	16th inst	Aug 22, 1867
WILLETS, Frederick Nichols	4y 7m 12d	23 Jul 1872	Jul 25, 1872
WILLETS, Jane P.	no age	last Tues	Oct 27, 1864
WILLETS, John Henry Seaman	2	9 Mar 1862	Mar 13, 1862
WILLETS, Maria	50	2 May 1877	May 10, 1877
WILLETS, Mary	87th y	11 Mo, 1st	Nov 11, 1869
WILLETS, Rebecca	76y 4m 22d	20 Feb 1868	Feb 20, 1868
WILLETS, Richard	86	17 Sep 1858	Sep 30, 1858
WILLETS, Sarah	94	3 Dec 1878	Dec 12, 1878
WILLETS, Smith T.	42y 6m 20d	31 Jul 1867	Aug 1, 1867
WILLETS, William P.	54	18 Aug 1877	Aug 23, 1877
WILLETS, William V.	32	16th inst	May 26, 1864
WILLETTS, Amy	90	3 Jan 1862	Jan 9, 1862
WILLETTS, Ann	33	6 Jan 1862	Jan 9, 1862
WILLIAMS, (Miss)	no age	Friday	Aug 15, 1867
WILLIAMS, (Mrs)	no age	Tuesday	Jul 11, 1878
WILLIAMS, (child of Mr.)	3m	6 Aug 1867	Aug 8, 1867
WILLIAMS, (wife of Henry)	no age	17 Oct 1862	Oct 23, 1862
WILLIAMS, Amos	78	16 Aug 1872	Aug 22, 1872
WILLIAMS, Ann	74	28 Aug 1858	Sep 2, 1858
WILLIAMS, Austin	77	4 May 1877	May 10, 1877
WILLIAMS, Charity	74	29 Oct 1863	Nov 5, 1863
WILLIAMS, David S.	no age	25th inst	Aug 29, 1867
WILLIAMS, George	61y 6m	9 Apr 1875	Apr 29, 1875
WILLIAMS, George	64	11 Feb 1878	Feb 14, 1878
WILLIAMS, George Gibbons	64	24 Sep 1875	Oct 7, 1875
WILLIAMS, Henrietta	12	18 Aug 1861	Aug 22, 1861
WILLIAMS, Henry R.	54	29 Apr 1878	May 2, 1878
WILLIAMS, Isaac	34y 3m 14d	23 Oct 1875	Nov 4, 1875
WILLIAMS, Isaac	80y 18d	14 May 1877	May 17, 1877
WILLIAMS, Jacob	ca. 70	15 Jul 1858	Jul 29, 1858
WILLIAMS, Jacob	77	4 Jan 1874	Jan 8, 1874
WILLIAMS, John R.	80th y	28 Feb 1864	Mar 17, 1864
WILLIAMS, Katie	101st y	15 Apr 1877	Apr 26, 1877
WILLIAMS, Margaret	no age	no date	Sep 1, 1870
WILLIAMS, Mary	ca. 90	24 Oct 1863	Oct 29, 1863
WILLIAMS, Mary	no age	20th ult	Oct 13, 1864
WILLIAMS, Miriam F.	52y 14m	24 Aug 1873	Aug 28, 1873
WILLIAMS, Nathaniel	73	23 Nov 1872	Nov 28, 1872

Name	Age	Date of death	Date of newspaper
WILLIAMS, Phebe	82nd y	2 May 1878	May 9, 1878
WILLIAMS, Richard	57	23rd ult	Mar 9, 1865
WILLIAMS, S. D.	24y 3m	5 Oct 1868	Oct 15, 1868
WILLIAMSON, Cynthia	77y 1m 19d	19 Dec 1859	Dec 22, 1859
WILLIAMSON, Darius	no age	last Fri	Jul 18, 1872
WILLIAMSON, Lydia	83	last Mon	Feb 10, 1870
WILLIAMSON, Rachel A.	1y 2m 20d	2 Aug 1864	Aug 4, 1864
WILLIAMSON, Rachel A.	1y 2m 20d	2 Aug 1864	Aug 11, 1864
WILLIAMSON, Stephen	1y 2m 22d	4 Aug 1864	Aug 11, 1864
WILLIAMSON, William R.	55	last Sun	Apr 3, 1862
WILLIS, (Mr)	no age	Monday	Jan 11, 1877
WILLIS, (widow of Samuel)	70	no date	Oct 7, 1858
WILLIS, Benjamin	ca. 60	no date	Apr 12, 1860
WILLIS, John T.	17y 9m	19 Jun 1875	Jun 24, 1875
WILLIS, Mary J.	63	30 Apr 1877	May 10, 1877
WILLIS, Mary W.	82	28 Jun 1873	Jul 3, 1873
WILLIS, Phebe	90y 7m	1 Aug 1877	Aug 2, 1877
WILLIS, Thomas	93	14 Sep 1864	Sep 22, 1864
WILLIS, William	no age	last Tues	Sep 8, 1864
WILLIS, William	58y 5m 18d	19 Oct 1867	Oct 24, 1867
WILLIS, William T.	07th y	?8 Aug 1864	Sep 1, 1864
WILMARTH, Charles E.	18th y	22 Mar 1878	Mar 28, 1878
WILSON, (Dr.)	no age	1 Nov 1859	Nov 3, 1859
WILSON, (Mrs.)	ca. 75	no date	Jan 14, 1864
WILSON, (son of George G.)	15m	26 Aug 1864	Sep 1, 1864
WILSON, George W.	28y 7m 6d	20 Apr 1874	Apr 23, 1874
WILSON, Henry	no age	Wednesday	Aug 16, 1877
WILSON, John Henry	17	5 Nov 1865	Nov 16, 1865
WINANT, Cornelius W.	37	25 Feb 1872	Feb 29, 1872
WINNER, Margaret	35	25 May 1864	Jun 2, 1864
WINTER, Jane	no age	19 Apr 1862	Apr 24, 1862
WINTERN, (daughter of Jane)	2	14 Jul 1859	Jul 21, 1859
WINTERN, Jane	21	14 Jul 1859	Jul 21, 1859
WINTERS, Clarissa	66	30 Jul 1858	Aug 12, 1858
WISE, Willie R.	9y 9m 6d	18 Aug 1871	Aug 24, 1871
WITT, Margaretta	48	4 Sep 1867	Sep 12, 1867
WITTY, Eleanor Maude	5y 3m 5d	14 Jun 1876	Jun 22, 1876
WOLLABER, (child of Harriet?)	4m	29 Oct 1865	Nov 2, 1865
WOLLEY, Phebe	no age	5 Mar 1865	Mar 16, 1865
WOOD, (wife of Silas)	no age	17 Dec 1859	Dec 29, 1859
WOOD, Agnes	no age	last Sat	Aug 22, 1867
WOOD, Benjamin B.	no age	25 Dec 1877	Jan 10, 1878
WOOD, Charles	no age	last Sun	Jan 16, 1862
WOOD, Cornelius	no age	Friday	Feb 1, 1872
WOOD, Elizabeth	57y 7m 4d	last Thur	Mar 26, 1863
WOOD, Elizabeth	ca. 60	10 Jun 1864	Jun 23, 1864
WOOD, Elkanah	88	8 Aug 1870	Aug 11, 1870
WOOD, Epenetus, Jr.	58 (38?)	15 Apr 1863	Apr 23, 1863
WOOD, Esther P.	47y 3m	27 Mar 1873	Apr 3, 1073
WOOD, George	no age	last week	Mar 22, 1860
WOOD, Harriet	71	31 Aug 1871	Sep 7, 1871
WOOD, Henry C.	41	5 Feb 1878	Feb 7, 1878
WOOD, Huldah	100y 3m	9 Jan 1864	Jan 14, 1864
WOOD, John Henry	5	24 Sep 1861	Sep 26, 1861
WOOD, Joseph, Sr.	73y 2m 28d	18 Jan 1877	Jan 25, 1877
WOOD, Julia	12y 2m 4d	9 Aug 1874	Aug 13, 1874
WOOD, Mary	8y 9m 4d	4 Jun 1875	Jun 10, 1875
WOOD, Robert	61y 4m	10 Nov 1869	Nov 25, 1869
WOOD, Samuel	ca. 40	no date	Jul 14, 1864
WOOD, Samuel	83	20 Mar 1878	Mar 28, 1878

Name	Age	Date of death	Date of newspaper
WOOD, Sarah Ann	61	28 Aug 1876	Sep 7, 1876
WOOD, Sarah E.	21	6 Apr 1869	Apr 8, 1869
WOOD, Simon	no age	15 Jun 1874	Jun 18, 1874
WOOD, Steven	74y 10m 13d	22 Jan 1873	Jan 30, 1873
WOOD, Thomas	79	11 May 1865	May 18, 1865
WOOD, Thomas W.	27y 10m 14d	18 Jan 1872	Jan 25, 1872
WOOD, Walter	ca. 17	last Fri	Jun 18, 1863
WOOD, William	no age	9 Apr 1878	Apr 11, 1878
WOOD, William W.	23y 11d	29th ult	Jul 11, 1867
WOOD, William W.	no age	1 Mar 1870	Mar 3, 1870
WOODBRIDGE, James	50y 9m	3 Apr 1874	Apr 9, 1874
WOODBRIDGE, Joseph	89y 9m	3 Apr 1874	Apr 16, 1874
WOODBRIDGE, Mary Lavenia	ca. 30	30 Dec 1859	Feb 2, 1860
WOODBRIDGE, Silvester, Jr.	no age	3 Nov 1871	Dec 7, 1871
WOODHULL, Josiah	ca. 50	29 Jun 1863	Jul 9, 1863
WOODHULL, Mary Anna	20	16th inst	Nov 29, 1860
WOODHULL, Nancy	81y 9m 10d	no date	Aug 26, 1875
WOODHULL, Nathan	ca. 80	11th inst	May 24, 1860
WOODHULL, Robert	81y 9m 26d	no date	Aug 26, 1875
WOODMAN, O. O. (Mr.)	no age	30 Aug 1859	Sep 15, 1859
WOODWARD, Rosanna	54	21 Jun 1858	Jul 22, 1858
WOODWORTH, Volney	10	23 Dec 1859	Dec 29, 1859
WOOLEY, John	83	19 Jan 1871	Jan 26, 1871
WOOLEY, William Henry	38y 9m 16d	21 Aug 1863	Aug 27, 1863
WOOLLEY, (Mrs. Robt S.)	28	3 May 1874	May 7, 1874
WORDEN, Nancy	ca. 51	7th inst	Apr 12, 1860
WORTH, Evelyn	17y 11m 7d	19 Apr 1878	Apr 25, 1878
WORTMAN, August	16y 12d	7 Jul 1873	Jul 10, 1873
WOTHERSPOON, James	ca. 70	6 Aug 1864	Aug 11, 1864
WRIGHT, (child of W.)	ca. 1	4 Oct 1858	Oct 7, 1858
WRIGHT, (dau. of Anthony)	22	18 Jul 1865	Jul 20, 1865
WRIGHT, (son of Charles)	10	30 Aug 1865	Sep 7, 1865
WRIGHT, (widow of Isaac)	60	27 Jun 1858	Jul 1, 1858
WRIGHT, Alexander	6	30th ult	Sep 14, 1865
WRIGHT, Alexander	6th y	30 Aug 1865	Sep 21, 1865
WRIGHT, Cassius M.	6y 2d	16 Dec 1870	Dec 22, 1870
WRIGHT, Elizabeth	78th y	24 Feb 1864	Mar 3, 1864
WRIGHT, Elizabeth	50	6 Mar 1875	Mar 11, 1875
WRIGHT, Elmira	23	4 Mar 1861	Mar 7, 1861
WRIGHT, Fannie M.	26y 9m	20 Jul 1872	Jul 25, 1872
WRIGHT, Florence G.	2y 1m 7d	22nd inst	Aug 29, 1867
WRIGHT, G. Mott	57	9 Nov 1869	Nov 18, 1869
WRIGHT, Isreal	65	25 Feb 1869	Mar 18, 1869
WRIGHT, James	75	18 Oct 1863	Oct 22, 1863
WRIGHT, Jane	60	no date	Mar 14, 1872
WRIGHT, Jeremiah Skidmore	1y 1m 18d	30 Jul 1864	Aug 4, 1864
WRIGHT, Mary Ann	83	30 Mar 1874	Mar 26, 1874
WRIGHT, Myron	10m 23d	17 Aug 1868	Aug 27, 1868
WRIGHT, Robert	57	3 Sep 1875	Sep 9, 1875
WRIGHT, Sarah	82	1 Mar 1878	Mar 14, 1878
WRIGHT, Thomas F.	44y 1m 11d	26th ult	Jul 11, 1867
WRIGHT, William	27	29 Aug 1858	Sep 9, 1858
WRIGHT, William	ca. 80	22nd inst	Dec 1, 1864
WRIGHT, William	77	4 Jun 1875	Jun 24, 1875
WRIGHT, William Clarence	12	8 Aug 1870	Aug 11, 1870
WRIGHT, William H.	43	25 Mar 1873	Mar 27, 1873
WYCKOFF, Abraham H.	28	15 Jun 1859	Jul 21, 1859
WYCKOFF, Ferdinand Lott	no age	24 Jan 1859	Jan 27, 1859
WYCKOFF, John	30	11 Jun 1858	Jun 17, 1858

Name	Age	Date of death	Date of newspaper
YOUNG, (son of Mitchell)	8	last Thurs	Jul 25, 1872
YOUNG, Alfred	no age	last Sat	Apr 12, 1877
YOUNG, Daniel H.	no age	25th ult	Jul 4, 1872
YOUNG, John	no age	Monday	Aug 25, 1870
YOUNG, John C.	56	21 Jun 1858	Jun 24, 1858
YOUNG, Keturah	ca. 75	last Sat	Mar 20, 1862
YOUNG, Mary	6m 1d	30 Jul 1875	Aug 5, 1875
YOUNG, Oliver	99	last Sat	Dec 16, 1875
YOUNG, Oliver C.	25	21 Jun 1858	Jul 29, 1858
YOUNG, Sydney	no age	31 Jul 1873	Aug 7, 1873
YOUNG, Walter J.	54	12 Feb 1871	Feb 23, 1871
YOUNGS, Ann	70	28 Mar 1870	Apr 7, 1870
YOUNGS, Marie	69	last Tues	Sep 15, 1864
ZANDIGO, William	14	30 Jul 1875	Aug 5, 1875
ZENNER, Frederick	61	8 May 1862	May 15, 1862
ZEUNER, Robert August F.	18m 12d	21 Aug 1872	Aug 29, 1872

Made in the USA
Monee, IL
07 July 2026

56550371R00069